# Evil Next Door

*Berkley titles by Amanda Lamb*

DEADLY DOSE:
THE UNTOLD STORY OF A HOMICIDE INVESTIGATOR'S
CRUSADE FOR TRUTH AND JUSTICE

EVIL NEXT DOOR:
THE UNTOLD STORY OF A KILLER UNDONE BY DNA

# EVIL
# NEXT DOOR

The Untold Story
of a Killer
Undone by DNA

**AMANDA LAMB**

BERKLEY BOOKS, NEW YORK

**THE BERKLEY PUBLISHING GROUP**
**Published by the Penguin Group**
**Penguin Group (USA) Inc.**
**375 Hudson Street, New York, New York 10014, USA**

Penguin Group (Canada), 90 Eglinton Avenue East, Suite 700, Toronto, Ontario M4P 2Y3, Canada
(a division of Pearson Penguin Canada Inc.)
Penguin Books Ltd., 80 Strand, London WC2R 0RL, England
Penguin Group Ireland, 25 St. Stephen's Green, Dublin 2, Ireland (a division of Penguin Books Ltd.)
Penguin Group (Australia), 250 Camberwell Road, Camberwell, Victoria 3124, Australia
(a division of Pearson Australia Group Pty. Ltd.)
Penguin Books India Pvt. Ltd., 11 Community Centre, Panchsheel Park, New Delhi—110 017, India
Penguin Group (NZ), 67 Apollo Drive, Rosedale, North Shore 0632, New Zealand
(a division of Pearson New Zealand Ltd.)
Penguin Books (South Africa) (Pty.) Ltd., 24 Sturdee Avenue, Rosebank, Johannesburg 2196,
South Africa

Penguin Books Ltd., Registered Offices: 80 Strand, London WC2R 0RL, England

The publisher does not have any control over and does not assume any responsibility for author or
third-party websites or their content.

EVIL NEXT DOOR

A Berkley Book / published by arrangement with the author

PRINTING HISTORY
Berkley mass-market edition / April 2010

Copyright © 2010 by Amanda Lamb.
Cover photos: *Grunge Background* © Merkusher Vasiliy; *Guarded Window* © Jonathan Lewis;
*Glove/Test Tube* © Miguel Pinheiro; *North Carolina Map* © Stasys Eidiejus.
Cover design by Diana Kolsky.
Interior text design by Kristin del Rosario.

ISBN: 978-0-425-23334-4

BERKLEY®
Berkley Books are published by The Berkley Publishing Group,
a division of Penguin Group (USA) Inc.,
375 Hudson Street, New York, New York 10014.
BERKLEY® is a registered trademark of Penguin Group (USA) Inc.
The "B" design is a trademark of Penguin Group (USA) Inc.

PRINTED IN THE UNITED STATES OF AMERICA

10  9  8  7  6  5  4  3  2  1

Most Berkley Books are available at special quantity discounts for bulk purchases for sales, promotions, premiums, fund-raising, or educational use. Special books, or book excerpts, can also be
created to fit specific needs.

For details, write: Special Markets, The Berkley Publishing Group, 375 Hudson Street, New York,
New York 10014.

# Acknowledgments

I would first like to thank profusely all of the people who helped facilitate and who did interviews with me for this project. This includes current members of the Raleigh Police Department—Jim Sughrue, Lieutenant Clem Perry, Sergeant Jackie Taylor, and Detective Ken Copeland—as well as retired members—investigator Chris Morgan and psychologist Michael Teague. I'd also like to thank prosecutor Susan Spurlin, SBI Agent Mark Boodee, Lansing Detective Joey Dionise, Joanne Reilly, Dr. Gordon LeGrand, and former WRAL reporters Len Besthoff and Melissa Buscher. A special thanks goes to Glenna Huismann for her candid and touching words about her daughter. Without all of your generous contributions of time, information, and insight, I would not have been able to write such an accurate and comprehensive version of this story.

I thank Chad Flowers for his feedback and excellent photographs and Kelly Gardner for his expertise in helping me create usable photographs from WRAL's archive. As always, I thank WRAL for giving me their blessing and the resources to pursue my "other" career while also allowing me to stay involved with my first passion, television reporting.

I want to thank my mother, Madeline Lamb, for her stellar editing job, and my real editor, Shannon Jamieson Vazquez, for patiently partnering with me to complete another true crime book we can both be proud of.

As always, I thank my agent, Sharlene Martin, for believing in me and working hard with my best interest at heart and, of course, my family for their continued and unwavering support.

Finally, I want to thank Carmon Bennett and Mollie Hodges for always being so gracious and kind to me over the years as I covered their tragedy and for sharing their memories of their beloved daughter Stephanie with me. I will never forget her.

# Prologue

## October 19, 2005

*In justice is all virtues found in sum.*
—ARISTOTLE

"We've made an arrest in the Stephanie Bennett murder case," my confidential source said to me as I stood in my kitchen on a Wednesday evening making dinner. The words rolled off of his tongue slowly, and he spoke with the unnatural cadence of a man who was trying to be painfully thorough in his delivery. Looking back on that moment, I have no doubt that he was trying to make sure he had my full attention. Still, I pressed the receiver closer to my ear to make sure I had heard him correctly. My brain was having trouble focusing on what he was saying because it was so unexpected and remarkable. Despite my excellent sources, I hadn't had any inkling that an arrest was imminent.

At first, I was so stunned by the news I almost dropped the phone into the boiling pot on the stove in front of me. The steam scalded my face as I leaned in to turn off the burner so I could think about what I had just heard. I had never been good at multitasking when it came to balancing work and even the most minor of domestic tasks. Work always won out. I had burned many a meal while answering an e-mail or a phone call.

These words—that the police had finally made an arrest—were what I had been waiting to hear for more than three years. As a local television reporter for WRAL-TV, I had covered the Stephanie Bennett case from nearly the beginning, but tonight wasn't just about getting a big scoop. Like so many other murder cases I had immersed myself in, this one had become *personal*. My first thoughts went immediately to the victim's family and friends. My emotions surrounding the arrest had more to do with me wanting to see justice done for a young, innocent murder victim than with wanting to have the lead story on the 11:00 news.

"He's at the police station now being questioned," my source said.

"I need to go now, don't I?" I said to him as I cradled the cordless phone in the crook of my neck against my shoulder. My hands were on autopilot as I poured the pasta into the strainer in the sink; my mind was racing three steps ahead of my body as I plotted all of the people I would need to call to make it on the air by 11:00. In order to do my job, I had to get in the zone—a place where emotions and distractions were prohibited. The news was on at the same time every night whether you were ready to present your story or not.

"Yes, you need to go," he said with almost boyish enthusiasm. Looking back on the conversation now, I appreciate the delicate way he shared the news. I was in a fog, and I needed someone to lead the way. My source knew the news would overwhelm me on so many levels that he was careful to make sure his message was clear and direct. At the same time, he wanted to make sure I got my butt in gear and made it down to the police station in time to get the whole story.

The Raleigh Police Department had worked for three

and a half years to solve this case. Many people thought there would never be an arrest. On darker days, I was one of those people who felt like there would never be a conclusion to one of Raleigh's most horrific crimes. Now there was an arrest, an ending, an answer to all of the questions the media had relentlessly posed throughout the long investigation. It was surreal and, admittedly, slightly thrilling to see a high-profile cold case cleared after so many doubted it would ever be solved.

I mumbled something to my two young daughters about having to go back to the office. My older daughter groaned, and my little one whined. She repeatedly asked me why, tugging on the edge of my untucked, wrinkled blouse that was about to be retucked for a second round of television that evening. They had seen me come home only to turn around and go out the door again too many nights. Being a television news reporter wasn't a good gig for a mother. They reminded me of that on a daily basis.

My husband, Grif, knew I had to go. He had seen my wide eyes and overheard bits and pieces of the conversation, enough to know something major was going on. "They arrested someone in the Stephanie Bennett murder," I told him, still not believing the words even as they tumbled out of my mouth. Grif nodded. He knew enough about me and my passion for the cases I covered to realize that I would go. Instinctively, he had already picked up my car keys from the kitchen counter and grabbed my jacket from the back of a chair and handed them to me.

As it did my daughters, my leaving annoyed him, but he wisely kept quiet. We had been here on more than one occasion in our eleven-year relationship. He understood, as he had so many times before, that news is almost never planned and is rarely convenient. It wasn't that he liked it, but he had learned to tolerate it for the most part. It was the price he had paid for marrying someone in the news business.

As a veteran crime reporter for the local CBS television station, I had had some exciting moments over the years when big cases finally came to a head. Sometimes these moments were in the form of an arrest; other times they occurred when a jury returned a guilty verdict after many hours of grueling deliberations. Still, there are few things that matched the exhilaration I felt upon hearing that someone had been arrested for the murder of Stephanie Bennett.

Maybe it was because Stephanie was a young girl who had graduated from college and moved away from her home and family to start her life as an independent young woman. I had done the same thing in 1989 when I left my comfortable small town in Pennsylvania and moved to Myrtle Beach, South Carolina, in order to take my first job in television news. I remembered what a hopeful time that was, my life full of possibilities stretching out in front of me like an endless highway disappearing into the horizon. I was sure Stephanie had felt the same way.

But through no fault of her own, Stephanie became the victim of one of the most vicious rapes and homicides the city of Raleigh had ever seen. Stephanie was a truly innocent victim who had done nothing to contribute to her own death. She didn't engage in any risky behavior that would have put her in a dangerous situation; she was just a regular girl minding her own business. Her murder exemplified the kind of random violence we as a society pray doesn't really exist. It creates a feeling of hopelessness when we realize how little we can do to truly prevent it.

I was stopped at my third red light before I remembered that I hadn't eaten. I pictured the pot of steaming hot pasta on the counter in the kitchen at home. My stomach was rumbling. I pushed the thought out of my mind and tried to concentrate. I had been talking on my cell phone with the newsroom making sure everything was in place—the photographer, the live truck, and the reams of file tape we would need to give the audience background and context for the story that would air in less than an hour. I was thinking about everything I needed to do to make it happen as seamlessly as possible. Most important, I needed to call Stephanie Bennett's father, Carmon Bennett, in Virginia and get his reaction to the arrest. I knew this wasn't going to be an easy call. I had interviewed Carmon many times over the years throughout the investigation. This arrest, while it was something he had desperately hoped for, would also put a name and a face to the evil that had been done to his daughter. I couldn't possibly imagine how that was going to make him feel. Knowing Carmon the way that I did, I figured he was likely to have a variety of emotions, ranging from relief to disgust. Carmon had taken on the mantle as the family spokesperson. Over the years, I had also spoken to Stephanie's mother, Mollie Hodges, on several occasions, but Carmon was the one who always had the strength to talk to the media when Mollie's emotions overwhelmed her.

I drove as fast as possible without being reckless, my thoughts jumping from Carmon and Mollie, to the newscast, to the suspect. I was consumed with curiosity about this man in police custody. What did he look like? Where had he been for the past three years? How had he evaded investigators for so long? How had they finally caught him? I hoped my questions would be answered, if not that night, then very soon.

The first hour after I arrived at the police station was a blur. I immediately phoned Stephanie's father, and despite my reservations about making the call, I was instantly comforted by Carmon's tone of palpable relief. I could practically see him smiling over the phone. Yet we both knew, even in that moment of shared relief, that there would be no closure for him, not then, not ever. His daughter was dead, and no arrest would bring her back. But in my heart, I hoped it might bring him a small slice of peace, something he and his family had been lacking for so many years.

Carmon told me he had been briefed by the investigators earlier that day and was told the suspect was a loner, an oddball, someone with whom his daughter surely hadn't associated. It was clear his quest for answers was not over; in fact, it was a quest he had been on every single day since May 21, 2002, the day his daughter had been found raped and murdered in her North Raleigh apartment, the day his life changed forever.

But on the night of the arrest, Carmon changed a little from the broken man I had gotten to know over the years. His sorrow was now tempered by a measure of hopefulness. He shared with me that night that he prayed he might now learn *why* Stephanie had died. It was a question he had wrestled with since the day her life was so tragically taken.

"Tonight is a night of relief," he said, his voice cracking under the weight of his emotions. I could tell that his normally stoic demeanor was being tested by this new development in the case. It was impossible for Carmon to hide his strong feelings now that someone was being held responsible for the death of his precious daughter. "We're just happy to know this animal is off of the streets and this can't happen to another young lady."

After I hung up with Carmon, I began to rummage through the boxes of file tapes in the news van. The boxes contained everything I had amassed on the case over the past three years, from videos of cops and yellow crime scene tape, to smiling pictures of Stephanie, to tearful interviews with her family and friends. I knew that at any moment the suspect would be escorted from the police station to a waiting blue and white patrol car which would then whisk him off to the Wake County Jail, so I kept one eye on the front door of the building, and the other on the video screen in front of me as I rapidly shuttled through the boxes of tape.

At the same time, I had a growing anxiety about getting this major story just right. I wanted it to convey everything—the immense loss of a beautiful person, the hard work and dedication of the police, and the thrill of an arrest in what was thought to be a cold case—all in a minute and a half. This was always my quandary in television news, one I had wrestled with incessantly throughout my career: to touch the viewer and be thorough in a very short segment of time. On this night, I was not only under my usual pressure to do a good job, but I had the additional intense feeling that I owed it to Stephanie and her family to make the story everything it was meant to be.

I had seen Stephanie's pictures and home videos a thousand times before—Stephanie with her shoulder-length brown hair, her big brown eyes, and her infectious smile looking directly into the camera lens. There was Stephanie in home video graduating from college, putting her arm around her proud father, who looked teary-eyed. There she was again on Christmas morning surrounded by her family, turning away from the video camera and making jokes about the photographer. There was Stephanie in still photos, embracing her college sweetheart, Walter Robinson, with their heads tilted in toward one another. They were shining examples of young, blushing, uncomplicated love. But tonight, as I scrolled through the home videos and looked at Stephanie's pictures again, it was as if I were seeing her for the first time. Even with the deadline pressure looming over me, I slowed down the video and really looked at her, her movements, her expressions, and the light in her eyes as they darted playfully away from the camera. Suddenly, the normal sadness I felt when I viewed Stephanie's image was slowly being replaced by a sense of peacefulness. I felt as if she were telling me that her spirit was finally free from the limbo it had been suspended in since her death.

But I had little time to ponder my own emotions about

whether Stephanie was looking down from heaven at the events unfolding on earth. Out of the corner of my eye I saw photographers taking their spots around the front door of the police station, snapping on the bright lights on top of their television cameras, jockeying for the best position. Without missing a beat, I jumped out of the van and made a beeline for my photographers, Robert Meikle and Tom Normanly. One of them handed me a wireless microphone to be used for the proverbial shout-out to the defendant: "Did you kill her?" We only have twenty seconds or less to get questions in as the suspect is walked from the door of the police station to the waiting patrol car.

People in police custody rarely, if ever, respond to these questions, but there's always a chance they might, so we keep on asking. But unlike the way these ambushes are dramatized on television—a gaggle of reporters acting like wild animals, pushing and shoving to get a better spot and screaming to be heard over the din of the crowd—in Raleigh, North Carolina, at least, the scene is actually a lot tamer, and we journalists are much more polite than you would think.

I didn't know what to expect that night when the glass front doors of the Raleigh Police Department were flung open, but the man I saw being led out by two detectives was unlike anything I could have imagined. He was just over six feet tall and looked to weigh around 140 pounds, making him appear emaciated. He had long, scraggly, light brown hair that hung in his face, obscuring his eyes. His hands were cuffed behind his back. I don't know what I would've said a monster looks like, but this wasn't it. This man looked weak, frail, and not physically capable of the heinous crimes he was accused of.

Sergeant Clem Perry led the parade. He pushed open the doors and bore the first brunt of the blinding television camera lights and flashes from the still photographers.

Perry moved directly through the crowd toward the waiting patrol car without acknowledging the chaos around him. Behind Perry, Detectives Jackie Taylor and Ken Copeland were on either side of the suspect, clasping his elbows tightly as they walked him to the police car. They too ignored the action around them, and looked determinedly straight ahead.

The suspect's body seemed almost spineless, as if he might just slink to the ground at any moment if the officers weren't holding him up. He hung his head and closed his eyes; maybe to keep the lights off his face, or more likely, to keep our cameras from getting a good shot of his face. In either case, he was successful in preventing us from getting any real look at the man behind the mop of tangled hair hanging limply in front of his features, which only added to the horror-show quality of the moment. *Who was this guy? Where did he come from?* I couldn't stop the questions bouncing around inside of my head.

My pulse was racing as I gingerly elbowed through the gaggle of photographers to get as close as I could to the strange-looking man. I knew this would likely be my only shot at him. By the next day he would have a lawyer and wouldn't speak until he was on trial in a courtroom, maybe not even then. Most people accused of serious crimes rarely talked to the press. I knew a good defense attorney would keep his client quiet.

"Did you murder Stephanie Bennett?" a male reporter yelled from somewhere behind me in the crowd, beating me to the punch. As predicted, there was no answer. The prisoner was off the curb now, his elbows being swiftly guided by the two detectives to the car which was just about fifteen feet away. Our precious time for questions was running out.

"Can you tell me how you knew Stephanie Bennett?" I yelled this time. Nothing. He was now just a few steps from the car. I had maybe five to eight seconds left. My gut told me this man was not going to say anything, but I knew there was no harm in trying. The payoff if he did crack and say something was too big to ignore.

"Do you have anything to say?" I said even louder this time, hoping to rattle him into saying something, *anything*. Detective Copeland was now easing the suspect into the backseat of the patrol car, holding the man's head down gently with his free hand so it would not hit the door frame as he entered. It was obvious, despite how he pretended not to see us, that Copeland was painfully aware that his every move was being videotaped and would be re-examined many times in the days to come.

Copeland shut the door to the police car and moved around to the other side. He slid into the backseat next to the suspect, who was leaning back onto the headrest. The prisoner's entire body had collapsed into the seat, and the gray leather seemed to envelop him as he sunk even deeper out of the view of our cameras. He looked like a balloon with a slow leak, deflating before our eyes.

As the car pulled away, Detective Copeland stared directly at the man beneath the glare of our lights as if he were still trying to figure out the same thing we all were—*why?* It would be years before I would know what went through Ken Copeland's mind that night as he escorted the man he believed killed Stephanie Bennett to the Wake County Jail. This is both Detective Ken Copeland's story, and the story of everyone who helped find justice for Stephanie. It's a story I believe was well worth waiting for.

# CHAPTER ONE

# Death of an Angel

## May 21, 2002

*He who does not punish evil, commands it be done.*
—LEONARDO DA VINCI

Stephanie Bennett wasn't thrilled about spending time alone in her Raleigh apartment, but her roommates were out of town and she had little choice. She had to go to work that week at IBM and figured she would be alone in the apartment for only a couple of nights.

It was a very rare occasion for Stephanie to ever be alone. She'd moved to the Bridgeport Apartments in Raleigh, North Carolina, a year earlier, shortly after graduating from Roanoke College in Salem, Virginia. While it was her first time away from Virginia, Stephanie was ready to be more or less on her own in North Carolina. She'd made the move with her stepsister, Deanna Powell, and her close friend from college, Emily Metro. It always seemed like at least two of the girls were at the apartment together. But during this particular week in May 2002, Dee, as Stephanie referred to her stepsister, had returned to their hometown of Rocky Mount, Virginia, to attend a funeral, and

Emily was also back in Virginia, taking some additional classes at Roanoke College.

While Stephanie was a very independent young woman, she was particularly uneasy about spending time alone at the apartment because she'd heard that some bad things had been going on lately near her complex. For example, she was told that a woman had recently been raped while on a jogging trail at Lake Lynn, which bordered the property. Stephanie also learned that her neighbor had had her car stolen from the apartment complex parking lot. And the most personally upsetting news—there had been a Peeping Tom spotted peeking into a window; not just any window either, but Stephanie's *own* window.

Stephanie had just returned from a weekend in Greenville, South Carolina, where she was visiting her longtime boyfriend, Walter Robinson. Walter was in graduate school studying engineering at the University of South Carolina. Stephanie and Walter had met at Roanoke College, and after being together for four years, a long-distance relationship was not something either of them wanted. They wanted to be together and had mutually decided it was time to make that happen. So, Stephanie was getting ready to move to South Carolina in July. The couple had already looked at apartments and houses in preparation for the move. The young couple had the enthusiastic support of their parents, who also envisioned that the two would eventually get married.

Stephanie was moving to be close to Walter, the man with whom she wanted to spend the rest of her life, but she also wanted to get away from the Bridgeport Apartments. She was literally counting down the days until she could leave what had become a fearful environment for her, and to feel safe again in South Carolina with the man she loved.

"She had mentioned to me a couple of times that it was a bad neighborhood and that she didn't like being home alone," Walter said in a 2002 interview with WRAL-TV. "And I knew that because when I went there for the weekends to see her I heard the stories."

The one story that Stephanie couldn't get out of her head was the one about the Peeping Tom at her window. Less than a month before this night, a neighbor had seen a man dressed in black, his head obscured by a hooded sweatshirt, crouching in the bushes outside Stephanie's ground-floor bedroom. The neighbor said the mysterious man appeared to be looking into the window. Because the bushes surrounding the window were high, and the lighting on the outside of the apartment building was dim, the neighbor couldn't give a good description of the man's face. Still, she reported the incident to the management of the apartment complex, who in turn reported it to the Raleigh Police Department.

Walter had been visiting Stephanie from Greenville, celebrating her twenty-third birthday, the same April weekend that the Peeping Tom was spotted near her window. Walter remembered a neighbor calling and warning Stephanie to make sure her blinds were turned in such a way that no one could see into her apartment. Walter was a chivalrous southern man who was highly protective of his girlfriend, but at the time, he didn't think anything of it. Later, he would remember with anger just what this incident foreshadowed and wished out loud that he could turn back time.

That same day the Peeping Tom was spotted, April 27, 2002, Stephanie wrote an e-mail to her aunt, Kaye, who lived in California telling her about the incident and how it made her want to move out of her apartment complex immediately:

Yesterday our neighbors told us all this bad stuff. The lady caught a peeping tom on Saturday night. She said she had seen him a couple of times, but just thought he was walking through the yard, but she said he was dressed in all black and had a black hood on and was just standing beside the bushes looking in the window. So they called the cops and the cops are now on the lookout for him, but the place where he stands and looks is right outside my window. Needless to say I didn't sleep well last night. I shut my windows and woke up drenched in sweat so I had to turn the air on. Pretty scary. . . . We obviously aren't in a safe place. I am so ready to get out of here.

## No Sweet Dreams

Just a little more than a month, that's what Stephanie kept saying. Hang in there. She would be out of this apartment soon. But whenever she returned from visiting her boyfriend, Walter, in South Carolina, Stephanie told him she had a lingering sadness that only seemed to worsen every time she left him. It was a combination of her love for him and her fear of returning to the apartment where she no longer felt safe.

Their most recent visit had been on the weekend of May 18 and 19, 2002. Stephanie returned home that night of Sunday, May 19, to an empty apartment. But she tried to put her concerns out of her mind, and instead prepare for the busy week ahead of her.

"When she went home that Sunday I remember thinking, *only one month left in that apartment*," Walter said. "Every time that we left each other, she always cried."

On Monday, May 20, Stephanie went to work as usual at IBM in Research Triangle Park, Raleigh's business park, which housed major technology and pharmaceutical companies. That night, by all accounts, was also routine for Stephanie. As usual, she talked to Walter on the phone around 8:00 P.M. He was trying to figure out a way to get an application for an apartment to her. She told him the fax machine in her office was broken, but that in the morning she would try to find another fax machine in the building and call him or e-mail him with the number. It was an ordinary conversation about ordinary things. Neither knew it would be their last.

Stephanie also talked to one of her roommates, Emily Metro, on the phone that evening. Emily clicked in on the call waiting while Stephanie was on the line with Walter. Emily was planning to permanently move back to Salem, Virginia, where she was attending classes at Roanoke College, their alma mater. Emily was switching career paths from business to psychology and was back in school taking courses in her newly chosen field.

Stephanie's other roommate, her stepsister, Dee Powell, was also planning a move of her own to Richmond, Virginia. The girls were collectively excited about their independent futures, but at the same time they were sad about splitting up. They didn't know what they were going to do without being entwined in each other's daily lives.

## Morning Comes

The next morning, on Tuesday, May 21, Walter Robinson waited for Stephanie to contact him regarding the apartment application he was trying to fax to her from Greenville. He sent her an e-mail at her office at IBM in Research Triangle Park around 11:00 A.M. When he didn't hear back from her immediately, Walter assumed she must have gotten busy at work or had taken an early lunch. So he decided to go to lunch and try to reach her later. In the afternoon, he sent Stephanie another e-mail and called her cell phone. Still, he got no answer. That's when he really started to worry. It wasn't like Stephanie not to be reachable. She was one of the most reliable people Walter knew. His gut started to churn as he tried to figure out what could possibly be going on. He thought about jumping in the car and heading to North Carolina, but he was four hours away.

Walter then decided to call Stephanie's roommate and stepsister, Deanna Powell. Dee agreed it wasn't like Stephanie not to answer her phone or e-mails. She was a responsible girl, the kind of girl who was always where she was supposed to be and always did what she was supposed to do. Even throughout her workday, Stephanie maintained close contact with her family and friends. So when Dee, who was still out of town, couldn't reach her stepsister either, she too became extremely worried.

Through a series of phone calls, Dee ultimately discovered that Stephanie had not shown up for work at IBM Tuesday morning. This was totally out of character. Stephanie was thrilled at the opportunity to be working as a subcontractor for IBM and would never have done anything to jeopardize her employment. Dee immediately knew something was wrong, *very* wrong.

"She didn't show up for work, and of course work had called, and so I had tried to get in touch with her a couple different ways, and I sent a friend to go see if she was at home to check on her," Dee said.

She called a male friend and asked him to go by the apartment. Stephanie's car was parked outside the apartment, but the friend got no answer when he knocked on the door. When he relayed this information to Dee, she then did the only thing she could think of—she called the office at the Bridgeport Apartments and asked them to check up on Stephanie. She gave the management permission to go into their apartment with a pass key.

At the request of the female apartment manager, a maintenance employee unlocked the door to the apartment the girls shared. The manager entered tentatively. At first, she called out to see if anyone was home, even though she had already knocked loudly on the door. When no one answered, she walked slowly down the hallway toward the bedrooms. She peeked into the open doorway of Emily Metro's bedroom and made a gruesome discovery. Twenty-three-year-old Stephanie Bennett was dead on the floor of the bedroom. And that wasn't all. Stephanie was nude, and it looked like she had been tied up and raped. A deep purple mark on her neck was evidence Stephanie had been strangled. In her mouth was a pair of blue underwear.

The manager ran out of the apartment and quickly called 911. The time was 3:33 P.M. on Tuesday afternoon, May 21, 2002. Murders like this were uncommon, and the Raleigh Police Department responded immediately with every available officer to the Bridgeport Apartments.

"Dee returned my phone call around 5:00 P.M. and told me [Stephanie] had been murdered," Walter said, fighting back tears as he recalled the day to WRAL reporter Len Besthoff. "I remember exactly where I was. It seemed like everything stood still. My legs and everything went weak, *numb.*"

Other than the disturbing image of Stephanie's tortured body, the rest of the scene was the opposite of chaos. Her body lay on the floor next to Emily's bed, which was neatly made with a patchwork quilt and a blanket folded at the foot of the mattress. Almost everything else looked to be in order in the room, except for some leaves inside the room, beneath the window where it appeared the killer had entered. Only a few items had been moved. They had been placed carefully out of the way in the closet—a phone, some stuffed animals from the bed, and a few knickknacks from the windowsill.

In Stephanie's bedroom, across the hallway from where she lay dead, her covers were pulled back and neatly piled on the floor at the foot of the bed. Her three pillows were in a U-shape as if she had snuggled them around her like a cocoon while she slept. There were multiple reminders that the young woman was in many ways still a girl: two teddy bears sat prominently on a dresser on either side of a jewelry box, and a Harry Potter novel with a bookmark in it lay on the night stand alongside a glass half full of iced tea, and a cordless telephone. It looked like Stephanie had been just settling in for a quiet evening in bed when someone brutally attacked her.

The killer had left an important calling card, one that would eventually identify him beyond any reasonable doubt—DNA. His semen had been left in multiple orifices of the young woman's body. It was if he were saying to the investigators, "Catch me if you can."

## Body of Evidence

For Lieutenant Chris Morgan, the head of the Major Crimes Task Force in Raleigh, the afternoon had started out mundane. He was in the Information Technology Department having someone work on his computer when his cell phone rang. He hated computers almost as much as he hated cell phones. Morgan was an old-school cop who had forced himself to get used to the way the world was operating in the twenty-first century. But that didn't mean he had to like it. It was one of the many reasons he was considering retirement. Police work had changed. It wasn't what it used to be. Morgan missed the good old days when police work meant pounding the pavement and knocking on doors, not "Googling." With his stockpiled sick time and vacation time, he was getting close to thirty years on the force and thus was eligible to take his retirement money and move on. At forty-nine, he was still young enough to do something else, although he still wasn't sure what that something would be.

When Lieutenant Morgan answered his phone, the watch commander told him that a girl had been found dead at an apartment complex in North Raleigh, and it might be a good idea for Morgan to head over that way. It wasn't the kind of neighborhood where murders usually happened. The watch commander knew the lieutenant well enough to realize that Morgan would want to be involved in the case from the beginning, especially if the crime was out of the ordinary. The watch commander was right. Morgan jumped in his car and headed in the direction of the Bridgeport Apartments.

Ultimately, Morgan was the first detective on the scene, primarily because everyone else had gotten lost. Luck had always been Morgan's calling card. He spent a lot of his career on the police force stumbling into cases that then became his main obsessions.

Morgan, a veteran cop who truly lived and breathed his work, took murder cases personally. A big, imposing man with an even bigger personality, he was also known for wearing a white fedora. The first one he owned had been a present to himself when he solved his first murder case, and from there the tradition continued until he had a closetful of hats. Now he was known to the public as "the guy in the white hat." But with the hat came a lot of responsibility. Sometimes, he thought, people imagined it had magic powers to steer him in the right direction. He hoped they were right.

The first uniformed officer who'd arrived had secured the scene in preparation for the detectives' arrival. He walked Morgan into the apartment and pointed him down the hallway in the direction of Stephanie's body. The patrol officer's job was to keep the perimeter of the crime scene surrounded with yellow tape so that people could not come in and out and contaminate evidence.

Morgan had witnessed a lot of murder victims during his decades on the force, but seeing Stephanie Bennett was an image he will never forget. There was something so innocent and vulnerable about the young girl who had been raped, tortured, and discarded like trash on the floor of Emily Metro's bedroom, that it made him sick to his stomach.

"Never saw anything like it, never want to see anything like it again as long as I live," Morgan said definitively. "I could show you pictures of guts, gore, things that would turn your stomach and make you lose your lunch, but nothing, absolutely nothing that I've ever seen even came close to this."

Stephanie's nude body had been simply left lying on her back almost as if the killer meant to humiliate her in death. According to witnesses at the scene, her head was tilted to the side, her eyes swollen and closed, her arms and legs outstretched. It appeared that her hands had been tied at one time behind her back, and her ankles had been tied together. The restraints around her ankles and wrists were gone, but the red marks remained. The deepest and most obvious mark was a deep purple line around her neck where it looked like she had been strangled to death.

"It was just such a cold, detached crime scene, I started feeling cold myself even though it was a warm day in May," Morgan said, shuddering as his mind transported him back to that moment. "It rocked my world," he added after a long silence.

Morgan said he could literally see the dried semen around the victim's body when he first entered the apartment, and while it made him sick to his stomach, it also made him hopeful this was a crime he would be able to solve. After spinning his wheels on several other high-profile unsolved cases, he was ready to put someone behind bars, especially someone who had taken the life of an innocent young woman not much older than his own twin daughters.

"This is a slam dunk," Morgan recalled thinking, compared to other cases he had handled. "I knew from the very beginning that we were going to have the evidence needed to get a conviction."

Lieutenant Morgan had to wait for the crime scene investigators to collect the forensic evidence, but he got down on his hands and knees and observed Stephanie's injuries without touching anything. He couldn't believe how pronounced the strangulation mark on her neck was. "I had never seen one that deep," Morgan said, exhaling loudly.

While he was not a doctor, Morgan knew from his experience investigating homicides that it wasn't necessary to make such a deep mark in someone's neck in order to kill her, especially someone as petite as Stephanie. He immediately realized he was dealing with more than just a killer. He was dealing with a *monster*.

He speculated that the killer had not only taken with him when he left the restraints from Stephanie's ankles and wrists, but also whatever he'd used to strangle her. Morgan assumed this was because the killer was smart enough to know these things could be traced back to him. In the world of sexual deviants, a set of devices used to restrain and kill someone was known as "a kit." Morgan assumed Stephanie's killer had brought his kit to the apartment with him, and then had in turn taken it with him when he made his getaway.

It looked like the killer had entered through a window in Emily's bedroom. He may even have hidden in the closet in Emily's bedroom and waited for Stephanie to go to sleep so that he could attack her when she was most vulnerable.

Morgan noticed items from the windowsill—a small box, a plate, and a beer glass—had been placed in the closet. This made sense if the killer had in fact come in the window and intended to go out the same way. The knick-knacks would have been in his way. It also made sense if he was lying in wait in the closet waiting for just the right moment to attack Stephanie.

Items that had been on Emily's bed, including several stuffed animals, were also placed on the floor of the closet. A framed photograph that Emily later said had been laying on the bed when she left the apartment was now propped up on the floor at the edge of the closet facing the wall. This also made sense to Morgan if the killer had used Emily's bed as a location to assault Stephanie at some point during the crime. He had removed everything in the room that could've possibly gotten in his way in preparation for the crime he was about to commit.

Morgan surmised that the killer had surprised Stephanie in her own bedroom and then had taken her into her roommate's room because he wanted to be able to leave quickly through the same window he'd come in if someone happened to come back to the apartment. However, if he had been watching the apartment, the killer would have also known that Emily had rarely been there in recent months, and therefore it was unlikely she would come home and interrupt the crime in progress.

One thing didn't make sense to Morgan. A phone from beneath the nightstand next to Emily's bed was disconnected and had also been moved into the closet. This puzzled Morgan because it was a cordless phone, and removing the handset would have disabled the phone just as easily. There was no need to move the entire unit. It was one of the tedious details that didn't seem to bother any of the other investigators, but Morgan simply couldn't get it out of his head. It may have meant absolutely nothing, or it may have meant everything.

"That's one of the jillions of questions that I had," Morgan remembered, taking it all in that first night.

But his number one question was, "What kind of monster could do this to a young woman?" Morgan could see his retirement on the horizon just over the next hill. The last thing he needed was to get emotionally tied up in a new case that would churn in his gut day and night. He already had a few of those on his plate. Nevertheless, he made a promise to himself he would do everything he could to catch the killer, if it were the last thing he ever did as a cop.

## Lights, Camera, Action

"I remember everything about that night, honest to God I do," said photographer Chad Flowers. "I don't know why I remember that day so well, but I do."

At the time, the eager television photographer was thirty years old and had just six years in the field under his belt. He was an aggressive photojournalist who had not yet been damaged by the cynicism most longtime employees in broadcasting usually suffer from.

On the evening of May 21, 2002, Flowers was working the night shift with WRAL's crime reporter at the time, Len Besthoff. Besthoff was an equally eager journalist who had an affinity for the crime beat. It had taken time for the good ol' boys in the Raleigh Police Department to get used to Len's Boston brogue and Yankee ways, but he had developed a good relationship with the men and women in uniform, especially with Lieutenant Chris Morgan.

Flowers and Besthoff were taking a dinner break around 6:15 P.M. at an Italian buffet in the nearby city of Durham when the newsroom called to tell them there had been a murder in Raleigh. They shoveled a few more bites of food into their mouths, and then hustled outside to the news car to make the twenty-minute drive to the crime scene at the Bridgeport Apartments.

Both men had covered dozens of murders, and there was no expectation that this one would be anything out of the ordinary. After a while, even murders seemed somewhat mundane to journalists who covered crime on a daily basis. But they also knew that time mattered. They had to get over to the scene and get a story in time for the 10:00 P.M.

newscast. So their urgency was driven more by deadline pressure than excitement about the story.

When they arrived at the scene, they were greeted by chaos—a crowd of police officers moving in every possible direction. Flowers staked out a position with his camera and tripod at the edge of the yellow crime scene tape, while Besthoff circulated through the crowd of officers trying to get information. Two things were immediately clear: This was no routine case, and it was going to be a very long night.

Besthoff remembered how unusually tight-lipped all the cops at the apartment complex were that night. No one was giving him anything. Usually, someone would at least throw him a bone off-the-record, knowing that he would keep the information close to the vest until it was confirmed through the proper channels. Not tonight. Besthoff was getting nothing, and that meant something.

Even his good buddy Lieutenant Morgan was staying almost entirely mum. "He told me without going into details, 'This is a bad one,' a remark he would make on the really horrific crimes he investigated," Besthoff recalled his conversation with Morgan.

"And we didn't even know the gravity of the situation yet," Flowers added.

## Calling in the Troops

Lieutenant Morgan called in every available detective. Investigators descended on the apartment complex and fanned out in an effort to talk to potential witnesses while their memories were fresh. Crimes like this didn't happen in Raleigh, North Carolina. Morgan knew the case was going to get a lot of attention from the cops and from the media.

Yellow tape was strung up like Christmas lights around

every possible perimeter of the crime scene to keep people out. A sea of cops in blue periodically gathered in clumps to debrief and then scattered again looking for evidence and more people to interview.

Investigators with the City County Bureau of Identification, known as CCBI, the forensic crime scene investigators for the city of Raleigh, concentrated on a narrow wooded area about fifty yards from the apartment. The thin swatch of woods separated the Bridgeport Apartments from the adjacent Dominion on Lake Lynn Apartments. Police talked to neighbors and passed out fliers telling everyone to be cautious, to lock their doors and windows, and to be on the lookout for anyone suspicious.

One thing suspicious had been found not far from Stephanie's apartment. No one knew what it meant yet, but it was on Morgan's radar screen. Investigators had found a bush not far from Stephanie's bedroom window covered with about a dozen pairs of women's cotton thong underwear. It looked like someone had quite literally thrown the underwear up in the air, and a few pairs had landed on the bush, some on a utility meter attached to the building, and others on the ground beneath the bush. Also on the ground was a red duffel bag with a hotel logo written on it in white bold letters. Because Stephanie's murder was clearly a sex crime, this bizarre scene could not be simply written off by investigators as a mere coincidence. It was just one of the many strange pieces of evidence that would be filed away only to be sorted out later. At the moment, the investigators' primary job was to speak to as many people in the area as possible.

Sergeant Clem Perry had been one of the first officers on the scene, after Lieutenant Morgan. He was part of the police department's robbery squad, but everyone was on deck for this case, even if they did not work in homicide. Thirty-three-year-old Perry had been with the Raleigh Police Department since 1991. He had a boyish face that made him look more like a paperboy than a police officer. But Perry was every ounce a cop. He couldn't remember a time when he wanted to be anything other than a cop. It had been in his blood since childhood, when he'd spent days hanging out with his father, a firefighter, at the fire station, which was frequented by local police officers.

On the night of Stephanie's murder, Sergeant Perry brought several of his detectives from the Robbery Unit with him. They joined the other investigators in canvassing the neighborhood. All of the detectives knew that the more time that passed after the murder, the more likely witnesses would disappear or forget details that might be important to solving the case. They had to get to as many people in the apartment complex as they could, as fast as possible.

## Family Ties

A few hours after police secured the crime scene, Carmon Bennett, Stephanie's father, and her stepmother, Jennifer, arrived at the apartment complex. Jennifer's daughter, Dee, Stephanie's roommate, had told them how neither she nor Walter had been able to get in touch with Stephanie. Walter had also called the Bennetts during the day and shared his concerns. When Dee finally heard back from the manager after authorizing her to go into the apartment that the body of a woman had been found inside, she broke the news to her mother and stepfather. Carmon and Jennifer jumped into their car immediately upon hearing this and headed straight for Raleigh to see for themselves exactly what was going on.

When they got to the apartment complex, they frantically hopped out of their car and took a spot right at the edge of the crime scene tape waiting for officers to come by so they could flag them down for information. Photographer Chad Flowers remembers seeing the agitated middle-aged couple with pained expressions on their faces. With one look he knew, he just *knew,* that they had to be the victim's parents. His heart went out to the couple.

After a few minutes of leaning across the yellow crime scene tape and waving his hands, Carmon was finally able to get an officer's attention. The officer then in turn relayed the message to Morgan that the victim's family had arrived from Virginia and wanted to know what was going on. Lieutenant Morgan was tied up in the evidence-gathering phase of the case, and the last thing he needed to complicate things was a grieving father. So, Morgan asked Sergeant Perry to deal with the daunting task of handling Stephanie's loved ones. He asked Perry to talk to Stephanie's father and try to keep him calm, despite what was turning out to be a very bad night for him and his family.

From the bottom of the hill where Stephanie's apartment was, Perry could see the Bennetts standing at the edge of the tape near the apartment complex clubhouse. Perry was told the couple had come to the scene from their home in Rocky Mount, Virginia, as soon as they heard something might have happened to their daughter. Perry was terrified to walk up the hill and speak to the man whose daughter was lying dead just a few yards away, but he knew it was something that had to be done.

"When Carmon first got there, he was frantic to go down there and go in the apartment," Morgan recalled. Not only would that have contaminated the crime scene, Morgan was not about to let a father see his daughter that way. Morgan knew Carmon would never be able to get the gruesome image out of his mind. Morgan vowed not to permit him to see his daughter until she was delivered to the funeral home after an autopsy was performed by the medical examiner.

Officers had found Stephanie's purse on a table near the

door in the front hallway of the apartment. They compared the driver's license photograph to the victim's face and were able to make a preliminary positive identification. It wasn't as scientific as an autopsy, which is the official way bodies are identified, but until they could get the final word from the medical examiner, it would have to do.

As soon as Morgan saw the name and picture of the smiling, attractive brunette on the North Carolina driver's license, "I knew it was his daughter," he said.

Besides an army of detectives, Morgan had also called his colleague and old friend, Michael Teague, the Raleigh Police Department's forensic psychologist, to come to the scene and help figure out what kind of monster might have done this. Teague, whom many of the cops referred to as "Doc," had worked closely with Morgan on many homicide cases and often assisted in creating a possible profile of a killer, as well as lending a hand when he could in dealing with victims' families.

Almost as soon as Teague arrived on scene, Morgan motioned to where Sergeant Clem Perry was standing with Stephanie's father and asked Teague to go and assist Perry in handling the delicate situation. As the gray-haired, affable-looking psychologist walked over, Carmon Bennett turned his attention to Teague, who looked to Carmon like someone who might be more in the know than the fresh-faced young cop in front of him.

"Who is in that room?" Carmon asked Teague.

"Sir, we don't know for sure yet," Teague responded somewhat nervously.

"Listen to me," Carmon said with an escalating level of angst in his voice. "Two of the girls who stay in that apartment are in my house right now in Virginia. The only one missing is *my daughter*."

Teague tried to soft-pedal the situation at first, telling Carmon that police wouldn't be able to confirm identity of the victim until an autopsy was completed. It wasn't his place, after all, to notify the next of kin. He was just trying to keep the family calm until Morgan could break away and come talk to them himself. But Carmon continued to wear Teague down until he felt like he had to give the man *something*.

"Sir, it doesn't look good for your daughter," Teague finally admitted, not wanting to add to the man's growing frustration by appearing to be trying to withhold information from him.

"As soon as I said that, the extreme anger he had immediately melted into the grieving mode," Teague recalled.

"He was not a man to wear emotions on his sleeve," Sergeant Perry said of Carmon Bennett. "But he was visibly shaken. It was a very, very tough thing to do."

As the father of a then five-year-old girl himself, Perry felt that telling any parents that their child was dead was the most gut-wrenching part of his job. It was something he had done a handful of times in his career, but it never got any easier. Thinking about his own daughter made him sick to his stomach as he spoke with Carmon that night.

"It always makes it harder," Perry said. "You can't help but think, that could be *my* daughter."

And that was what was going through everyone's minds that night—Perry's, Teague's, Morgan's—Stephanie Bennett represented everyone's daughter. She was proof that no one was immune to violence, not any one of their loved ones.

"The family was the quintessential all-American family, and as a result, everyone could relate to their tragedy," photographer Chad Flowers said as he remembered the clean-cut, well-dressed, middle-aged couple grieving off-camera.

Morgan finally trudged up the hill to where Carmon and his wife stood supporting one another at the edge of the crime scene tape. He felt he'd made Perry and Teague do his dirty work for long enough, and it was time for him to step in and give the grieving father some straight answers. He couldn't make these people wait any longer for the inevitable bad news.

"I've looked at her driver's license. I've looked at the girl who's dead in there, and I think it's your daughter," Morgan told the Bennetts, never one to sugarcoat the truth. "There's absolutely nothing you can do by staying here. Go home, just *go home*."

Morgan pulled Carmon's wife, Jennifer, aside and encouraged her to take her husband back to Virginia where he could be surrounded by loving family and friends. He told her there was nothing good that was going to come out of Carmon staying at his daughter's murder scene into the wee hours of the morning. Morgan bluntly added that there was absolutely nothing Carmon could do to help the investigation at this point, and Morgan definitely did *not* want him there when the medical examiner rolled Stephanie out of the apartment on a gurney in a black body bag.

"I told her to get his ass in the truck and get him back to Rocky Mount," Morgan said with the typical unapologetic bravado of a man who always knew best, or at least thought he did.

Morgan gave Jennifer his cell phone number and told her he would keep them updated on any developments in the case. He fully expected to hear from Carmon Bennett before the sun rose.


## Going Public

Lieutenant Chris Morgan held an impromptu press conference just outside the perimeter of the crime scene tape to bring the media up to speed. He had removed his signature white fedora as the oppressive North Carolina humidity had pasted it quite uncomfortably to his forehead. His voice was solemn, and his face was purposely expressionless as he fielded questions from hungry reporters. Even though Morgan considered most journalists in the Raleigh area his friends, he also knew they had a job to do. They loved it when cops got emotional; it made for a better story. He refused to give in on this night.

"We just got a report that a body had been found here," Morgan said as reporters followed up with questions about specifics that the detective was clearly not going to answer. "We're doing a thorough search for any evidence that might be available," Morgan said with a measured tone, saying something while really saying nothing at all—a technique he had perfected from years of dealing with journalists. He had already learned from the officers' preliminary interviews that a Peeping Tom had been seen in the area just a few weeks earlier, but that wasn't something he was about to let the media in on just yet. He needed to know if there was a possible connection between the peeper and the murder before he started running his mouth.

Even though investigators were releasing few details about the murder, there was nothing the police could do to quell the growing fear that was quickly developing in this quiet southern city. While Morgan didn't specifically say it was a random act of violence, the look in his eyes said it all. The police obviously weren't treating this as a case of domestic violence. They were throwing all of their resources into scouring the area, looking for a killer, looking for a *stranger*. It appeared that Raleigh had its first random murder in as long as anyone could remember, and suddenly no one felt safe.

One reporter shouted out a question to Morgan about whether there was a dangerous person roaming around that the community needed to worry about. For the first time since the press conference started, Morgan's expression changed. His mouth tightened, and his eyes widened. Morgan mechanically turned his head toward the camera lens with a flabbergasted look on his face and paused. For a minute it looked like he might simply ignore the reporter's inane question. But that wasn't Morgan's style. His inner pit bull was scratching to get out.

"We've got a homicide," he replied with razor-edge sharpness in his voice. "Obviously there is somebody dangerous somewhere."

## The Perfect Victim

Morgan finally left the Bridgeport Apartment complex at about 4:00 A.M. on Wednesday, May 22. He instructed his detectives to go home and get a couple hours of rest before returning to continue their work at 9:00 A.M. He commanded several uniformed officers to guard Stephanie's apartment and not to let anyone in until the detectives came back. Morgan basically "froze" the crime scene until the detectives could get back to work with a few hours of sleep under their belts.

The first thing Morgan himself did upon getting home was open the door to his twin sixteen-year-old daughters' room to make sure they were okay. Seeing what had happened to Stephanie Bennett had reinforced his lifelong fear that something could happen to his own precious children. He tried not to let his family know that, because of what he did for a living, he had constant fears for their safety. Morgan didn't want to transfer his lifelong paranoia to his wife and kids. But he couldn't help feeling the way he did; it was something that unfortunately came with the job.

"I don't think I can face this night," Morgan recalled thinking. "I'm going to need something to drink."

Earlier in the evening, Morgan had realized he had no beer in his house and would not get off work in time to buy any. He had instructed his buddy, police department psychologist Michael Teague, to run to a nearby convenience store and get him a six-pack so it would be waiting for him

when he got home. Another friend might not have acquiesced to such a mission, especially someone with multiple
degrees like Teague, but Doc was only too happy to help
Morgan deal with his demons the old-fashioned way—by
drowning them.

After checking on his peacefully sleeping family, Morgan sat down at the kitchen table and popped open the
first of the long-awaited cold beers. As he gulped down
the foamy liquid, trying to placate his brain into a quick
and easy buzz, the events of the day continued to trickle
back into his consciousness even as he tried with all of
his might to push them away. The past thirteen hours had
been some of the hardest hours of Morgan's life, and at this
point, he didn't see things getting any better in the immediate future.

"I was thinking, how could a man do this to another
human being?" Morgan said. "I was almost ashamed that
I was part of the male gender. It was obviously a totally
sexually motivated crime. There was no rage. There was
no revenge. This was nothing but a sexual sadist."

From what Morgan had already learned about Stephanie, he had begun to form an image in his mind of a young,
sweet, shy southern girl whose gentility made her what he
referred to as "the perfect victim." Morgan believed her kind
and gentle nature had probably made her more vulnerable
because the killer assumed he would have a more passive
victim, someone who would not as readily fight back. Morgan knew from experience that rapists often chose women
whom they thought they could easily subdue instead of
women who seemed like they might heartily resist.

Morgan imagined that the killer had probably spent a
lot of time before the murder watching Stephanie, studying
her, following her, learning about who she was and what
her daily patterns were like. Based on the methodical way
in which the crime scene was laid out, Morgan assumed
the killer did not just randomly pick this particular apart-

ment and this particular girl on this particular night. Given this hunch, the Peeping Tom who had been spotted at the apartment complex a few weeks earlier was quickly flying to the top of the list of possible suspects. If only they knew who he was.

"I think he knew as much about Stephanie as you could ever know about someone without actually meeting them," said Morgan.

It was about 4:45 A.M. when Morgan's cell phone rang. At that time, he was still sitting at his kitchen table pondering things and rounding the corner on cold beer number three. He was working on a pretty strong buzz, which had momentarily numbed his visceral reaction to the tragedy. But he was violently jarred right back into reality when he heard the voice on the other end of the phone. Morgan was not at all surprised that Carmon Bennett would be calling him at such an ungodly hour. He had given the man his cell phone number because he had expected him to call. The victims' family members always called Morgan, eventually. It was never a question of *if* they would call him, but just *when*. Never a man to mince words, Carmon got right to the point.

"Are you going to find out who did this to my daughter?" Carmon asked Morgan.

"I can't guarantee anything but I'll promise you this, I'll keep trying until I can't try anymore," Morgan replied honestly.

Morgan meant every word he said to Carmon and if nothing else, Morgan was a man of his word. He sensed he and Carmon had that in common.

Morgan could tell by the scratchiness in Carmon's voice he had probably been up crying most of the night. He couldn't blame the man. Morgan started to get a lump in his throat just listening to the broken father. He hung up the phone wondering just how he was going to deliver on his promise.

## Hail to the Chief

A few hours later, Lieutenant Morgan got wind that Raleigh's police chief, Jane Perlov, was raising hell because he and his detectives had left the crime scene in the hands of patrol officers and had gone home for a few hours to get some sleep. Major Don Weingarten, one of Morgan's superiors, called Morgan on his cell phone that morning to tell him Chief Perlov was on the warpath and was looking for him. Weingarten, an affable company man, wasn't about to get in the middle of a dispute between the lieutenant and the chief. He simply relayed the message, and let Morgan take it from there.

Morgan explained to Weingarten his detectives were exhausted and had needed a little break in order to come back and process the crime scene with fresh eyes. Weingarten told Morgan that Perlov was currently at Stephanie's apartment and wanted to see Morgan there *immediately.* So Morgan brushed his teeth, washed his face, threw on a clean shirt, and jumped in the car heading for the Bridgeport Apartments, all the while cursing under his breath.

Since coming to lead the Raleigh Police Department in the fall of 2001, Chief Perlov, a petite blond New Yorker with a fiery personality, had knocked heads with Morgan on more than one occasion. It was no secret that many of the officers didn't accept Perlov because she was a woman and a Yankee, but that wasn't why Morgan didn't get along with her. Despite her diminutive stature, Perlov had a big personality and a desire to take charge of situations in the same way that Morgan did. On the surface they couldn't have been more different, but at the core, they had more in common than either of them would ever own up to.

Morgan pulled up to the scene, put on his fedora, got out of the car, and ducked gingerly under the yellow tape. Like someone climbing into a yard expecting to be attacked by a guard dog, Morgan turned quickly in either direction. He spotted with his peripheral vision Perlov advancing on him, ready for a confrontation.

Chief Perlov told Morgan she needed to show him something in the parking lot in front of Stephanie's apartment. She brought him to a set of keys, lying on the ground right in the center of the black asphalt parking area just outside the yellow crime scene tape. Perlov pointed to the keys and asked Morgan how he and his team could have missed what could be a *crucial* piece of evidence.

"Man, Chief, I was all over this parking lot for thirteen hours, I don't think those keys were there last night when I left," Morgan told the chief without hesitation.

Again, Perlov asserted that Morgan might have missed what could be a critical piece of evidence. In addition, she said, Morgan had been irresponsible to let all of the detectives just go home and take a break in the middle of a high-profile murder investigation. Perlov asked him why he hadn't had detectives out there in the parking lot searching on their hands and knees all night long. Morgan said Perlov told him she wanted to see the detectives growing beards right in front her eyes as they worked on the case around the clock.

"I told her that tired detectives make poor decisions, and they miss things," Morgan said as he recalled trying to keep his growing anger at the chief's inquisition in check.

Morgan explained the crime scene had essentially been frozen, and that nothing had been touched during the few hours they were gone. The uniformed officers had guarded the scene since the detectives had left at 4:00 and no one had been permitted to go back inside the yellow tape until Perlov had arrived.

About that time, a blue and white Raleigh Police Department patrol car pulled up, and a young officer climbed out of the passenger seat. He yelled over to Morgan, who was still deep in conversation with Perlov. He apologized for interrupting, but wondered if they had found a set of car keys because his were missing, and he suspected they had fallen out of his jacket pocket in the parking lot shortly before he got off of his shift at 7:00 A.M.

"[Chief Perlov] looked at me with another stare of disgust," Morgan recalled as he smugly reached down, picked up the keys, and tossed them to the grateful young officer.

The chief then asked Morgan to take her into the apartment. He cautioned Perlov that the crime scene had not been fully processed yet, and she should be careful not to touch anything. Somehow, Morgan knew his stern admonition would likely goad her into touching something, and he was right. The first thing the chief went for, he said, was the base of a cordless phone in the den. The receiver had been found on Stephanie's bedside table. There was a red light indicating that at least one message had been left on the machine. Perlov wanted to know if the investigators had checked the messages. Morgan told her they had not checked the messages yet because they still needed to dust for fingerprints on the base of the phone before anyone else touched it.

"Well, the key to this case might be right here on this answering machine," the chief theorized. Morgan said Perlov then took her hand out of her pocket and started reaching down toward the phone.

"Chief, that hasn't been processed yet," Morgan recalled saying anxiously. She kept reaching. "Chief, please don't touch that. It hasn't been processed yet." The chief moved closer to the phone, as did Morgan, to block her.

Morgan felt like the chances of fingerprint evidence on the phone being relevant to the case were pretty minimal. Still, he had a dead girl at the medical examiner's office that he was obligated to find justice for. He wasn't going to take any chances that potential evidence might be contaminated, not even by the chief of police.

He said Perlov looked at him and must have seen the

rage in the eyes of a "tired old fat man" and decided touching the phone wasn't worth setting off the firestorm that would surely follow. Whatever the reason, ultimately she backed away, and so did he. They both had bigger fish to fry. Their petty differences would not derail their common goal of *catching a killer.*

## Stranger Than Fiction

In the early stages of an investigation *everything* is considered evidence. Nothing is ignored because until a working theory of the case is developed, anything might ultimately have something to do with the crime.

Investigators kept circling back to their puzzling discovery of the underpants on the bush not far from Stephanie's apartment. It looked like someone had been running by and had tossed a bagful of underwear in the air. The empty red duffel bag lay in the dirt near the bush. What were the chances that women's underwear just happened to end up on shrubbery the same night a woman is raped and murdered in a nearby apartment?

"That caused us all kinds of concern. What does this have to do with anything?" Morgan recalled his thoughts at the time.

Investigators discovered that the local hotel chain had given out as many as six thousand of those particular duffel bags to guests as a promotion in the past year. They also discovered that a flood at one of the hotels had soiled about a thousand of the bags. The damaged bags had in turn been offered to any employee who wanted them; the rest were thrown away. With the sheer number of bags given out, it was simply impossible for investigators to track where this particular one had come from.

Officers quickly determined that an adolescent boy who lived in the apartment right next to Stephanie's was responsible for leaving the underwear on the bush. Initially, the thirteen-year-old boy told investigators he found the underwear in a Dumpster in the apartment complex parking lot. But after more questioning, the boy admitted to having stolen the underwear from the apartment complex laundry room. In a strange twist, the boy's bedroom was found to share a wall with Stephanie's, but there was no indication that any of the underwear had belonged to Stephanie Bennett or either of her roommates. The boy swore in multiple interviews he had nothing to do with the murder. While Morgan thought the boy was a "budding pervert," he believed him. He didn't think the kid was capable of committing such a serious crime. But this left the never-ending question in Morgan's mind—who *was?*

## CHAPTER TWO

# False Leads

### Summer 2002

The function of wisdom is to discriminate between good and evil.

—CICERO

On May 27, 2002, the Raleigh Police Department released to the public a sketch of a man seen in the vicinity of Stephanie Bennett's apartment. They didn't refer to him as a suspect in the murder, but simply as a man whom they "wanted to talk to." The person pictured in the composite was thin with short brown hair, narrow features, and glasses. The sketch, like most composites, was so nondescript it was almost comical. It could have been any young white man.

To be fair, the first composite in a case often looks a little cartoonish, because people have tenuous memories at best when it comes to recalling someone's exact features. Ten people could see the same person and describe him in ten slightly different ways, depending on their vantage point, how long they had observed the person, and what built-in biases they brought to the table.

This picture of a man, drawn in charcoal on a stark

white background, looked more like the guy who might mow your lawn or change the oil in your car than a cold-blooded killer. But there is almost always some minute detail, some key feature witnesses subliminally pick up on, that makes its way into a composite sketch, something that seems to inevitably ring true about the initial image. Years later, if that rudimentary drawing were to be put next to the person police ultimately arrested, there would arguably be some minor resemblance.

As a rule, Sergeant Clem Perry didn't like composites. He worried they might be too restrictive and keep the public from considering other possibilities. But in this case, as in many others in which the suspect was elusive, he felt that it was a necessary evil.

"It was the right thing to do. It's all we had," Perry said, outstretching his arms and opening his palms to the ceiling. He recalled how detectives were already fresh out of leads and going nowhere fast. They needed something, *anything,* to give them some traction in the case.

Investigators had interviewed dozens of people who lived in Stephanie's apartment complex or in nearby apartment complexes. They had gotten a description from a neighbor of the Peeping Tom seen near Stephanie's apartment on April 27, just a few weeks before her murder. This was the man on whom they based the composite. But despite the fact that he seemed like the most obvious suspect, not everyone was on board with the theory that the Peeping Tom was the killer.

"There were a lot of discussions about the Peeping Tom as a suspect, some rather heated discussions," Perry recalled.

Perry said investigators spent countless hours just talking to people in the area, hoping someone would give them a shred of information, a tidbit, anything that might lead them in the right direction. They knocked on hundreds of doors and spoke to anyone who answered while they canvassed the majority of the apartments encircling Lake Lynn.

Detectives were specifically looking for people with criminal records, people who had been seen walking around late at night, people with what Lieutenant Morgan called "obvious red flags." What Morgan couldn't have known at the time was that one of those people wasn't waving any red flags, but still had something very big to hide.

## Weird Science

It was clear from the beginning, based on the amount of semen the killer had left at the scene, that the case would ultimately hinge on DNA. The technology of DNA had recently gone from somewhat unreliable to undeniably accurate in just a decade.

Assistant Special Agent Mark Boodee with the North Carolina State Bureau of Investigation (SBI) was on the cutting edge of this breakthrough science. After graduating from the University of Virginia, he started working for a private company in Maryland in 1989 called Selmark Diagnostics doing forensic DNA analysis.

"I was doing DNA analysis even before the FBI had DNA analysis," Boodee said proudly.

Not long after his stint in Maryland, Boodee was recruited by the North Carolina SBI to help them set up their DNA analysis program. He was excited to be given almost free rein in creating the brand-new laboratory that would turn out to be a model for DNA analysis across the country.

On May 24, Boodee agreed to work over Memorial Day weekend to analyze vaginal, rectal, and oral swabs from Stephanie Bennett. Boodee was a dedicated scientist who believed passionately in DNA analysis, and he welcomed the opportunity to use the process to solve a major crime.

"The victim's DNA is mixed up with the suspect's DNA and your job is to try to get out as much of the victim's DNA in order to be left with the suspect's profile so you can use that for comparison purposes," Boodee explained.

Boodee was able to create a solid profile of the killer's DNA. Any suspect's DNA brought to him by police would then be analyzed against this profile throughout the investigation to see if it matched.

He then compared the killer's DNA profile to four DNA samples that the detectives had already submitted in the initial stages of the investigation. Several of the samples came from Stephanie's family members, whom police needed to eliminate as suspects before they could begin looking at people outside of her inner circle. Another sample, according to Morgan, came from a rape suspect in a separate case in Alabama in which the attacker had tied up his victim with her own underwear. Because of the use of the underwear and restraints, investigators felt there might be the chance of a connection between the Alabama case and Stephanie's murder.

Morgan got a call from Boodee at about 10:00 that Saturday night, telling him that the Alabama suspect was not their guy. He was disappointed but, at the same time, was impressed with Boodee's work ethic and glad he was the SBI agent assigned to the case.

"I was just flabbergasted because I never knew anyone at the SBI worked on weekends," Morgan said with a chuckle.

Investigators continued to send DNA samples to Boodee from practically everyone they interviewed. Morgan kept the swabs used for collecting DNA—long sticks with cotton on the tips—in a jar on the corner of his desk, and told his detectives to take a handful every time they went back out to the Lake Lynn area. They were the same kind of swabs doctors used to test patients for strep throat. It was a simple, quick, and painless process for the officers to take a quick sample of saliva from the inside of someone's cheeks.

"I'd say, 'You got your swabs? Don't come back here with less than five swabs,'" Morgan recalled his perpetual command to his officers.

On one occasion, detectives were having a hard time getting three young men who lived in an apartment above Stephanie to give DNA samples. Several different detectives had approached them, and each time, they had refused to cooperate. Morgan decided to put his most tenacious detective, Mary Blalock, on the mission.

"Mary Blalock is a woman who knows how to *get things done*," Morgan said slapping his open hand on his desk. "If I had a difficult job I needed to have done, I knew I could go to Mary."

Morgan told Blalock she had to get samples from these three men. They were the only holdouts in Stephanie's building. They had told the other detectives who had tried and failed that "they didn't believe in giving DNA samples," to which Morgan naturally responded with a stream of obscenities.

Two hours later, Blalock returned to the police station and threw three envelopes on Morgan's desk. Each one contained a swab from one of the three men who lived above Stephanie. Blalock's young, eager partner, Amy Russo, related to Morgan how Blalock got the samples.

"She walked right up to [one] boy and told him to open his goddamn mouth. She stuck the stick in his mouth and told him to spit on it. She put the stick in the bag and went to the next one," Russo told Morgan as she recalled Blalock's heroic efforts.

The samples Blalock took, like all of the other samples, were sent to Boodee to analyze. Like all of the samples before them, they didn't match the killer's DNA.

"Initially they came in groups of five, and then they started coming in groups of twenty or thirty," Boodee said with a weary smile, remembering the massive amount of work he did on the case.

"A lot of them would just sit on the shelf because we wouldn't analyze them right away because we had a lot of other active cases," Boodee pointed out as he remembered the juggling act required to keep up with all of his work at the time. "They would pile up; *months'* worth of these suspects would pile up."

Eventually, Boodee asked investigators to submit the DNA samples in groups of ten to make it easier to test them and record the data without overwhelming the laboratory. The state lab had never before had a case with so many DNA samples that needed to be tested. It was a learning experience for everyone involved, including Boodee who until then thought he had seen it all.

Boodee wasn't cavalier about his job; quite the opposite. But he was quite sure that anyone who willingly gave a DNA sample was probably innocent, and so running the samples at times seemed like a futile and tedious process. "You're never going to get people who volunteer to give their sample and think they're going to fool the system," said Boodee.

Yet he knew for legal reasons it had to be done. Investigators could not definitely rule people out unless they had been tested and eliminated as a match to the killer's DNA. So Boodee kept eliminating suspects and kept hoping one day investigators would come to him and say, *this is the one.* He was sure it would eventually happen; he just had no idea how long it would take.

## If the DNA Doesn't Fit

Investigators determined that Walter Robinson, Stephanie's boyfriend, had been the last person to talk to her before she died. They'd spoken on the telephone at around 8:00 on the evening of Monday, May 20. At the time, Walter was in Greenville, South Carolina, about 270 miles southwest of Raleigh. Investigators quickly determined he was too far away to have come to Raleigh and committed the murder. Nevertheless, like Stephanie's other friends and relatives, Walter willingly submitted to a DNA test. As a result, he was quickly eliminated as a potential suspect in the case. Walter's eager cooperation fit in with Agent Mark Boodee's theory that innocent people had nothing to hide and were more than willing to provide DNA samples.

After eliminating people in Stephanie's family and tight-knit circle of friends, investigators started looking more closely at the bigger pool of suspects in and around the Lake Lynn apartment complexes. Dozens of Raleigh police detectives in plain clothes were sent out to troll the area undercover at various hours of the day and night to see if they ran into anyone who looked suspicious. The goal was for the officers to be able to observe people when they didn't think they were being watched, to catch them off guard.

On June 3, 2002, an officer at the Governor's Point Apartment complex, which was just across the lake from the Bridgeport Apartments, saw a man peeking into a window. The officer kept his distance and observed the man to see if he might try to break into the apartment. A few minutes passed, and the man then moved to another window. That's when the officer noticed that the man had pulled down his pants and was masturbating. Within a few minutes, a group of Raleigh police officers surrounded the Peeping Tom, took him to the ground, and arrested him.

Investigators interviewed the three women who lived in the apartment where the man had been peeping and discovered at least two of them had been getting in or out of the shower during the time the suspect was looking into their bathroom window.

The man police arrested was thirty-four-year-old Christopher Lee Campen. He was charged with "secret peeping," a misdemeanor crime that police often considered a gateway crime to more serious sex crimes like rape. The arrest seemed to be the first promising lead in the Bennett case. Campen had a long criminal record for minor charges including peeping and stalking. He was convicted of misdemeanor stalking in 1998. Everything seemed to fit the working profile of the killer in Stephanie Bennett's case.

"There was a moment of *this could be the guy*," Sergeant Clem Perry said, recalling his hopefulness at the time Campen was arrested.

"We looked at him hard," Morgan agreed.

But unlike Perry, Morgan had a gut feeling that this was not going to be their guy. He didn't think Campen had the wherewithal to commit such a heinous and highly organized crime; it just didn't fit with his track record of being charged with minor crimes for so many years, crimes that never escalated into more violent acts.

It turned out that Morgan's gut feeling was right. Within days, DNA tests cleared Campen of any involvement in Stephanie's murder. The investigators' promising lead had vanished almost as quickly as it had surfaced. But this first squashed lead didn't deter them from aggressively exploring other potential connections to the Bennett case.

Investigators thought they had another possible lead when a man in Florida, who was wanted in connection with the kidnapping and rape of a girl in Columbia, South Carolina, committed suicide. He had also been a primary suspect in the murders of three girls near Fredericksburg, Virginia. But once again, the magic of science eliminated this lead when the man's DNA failed to match that of Stephanie Bennett's killer.

DNA from the Bennett murder scene was also continually run through the state's DNA database, which contained roughly sixty-five thousand samples at the time, and through the national database called VICAP (for Violent Criminal Apprehension Program). But no matter how many times they ran it, the answer was the same every time—*no match*.

It was as if the killer were invisible, a ghost, someone who didn't really exist. In a sense he was taunting the investigators. Their strongest piece of evidence, DNA, was ruling out almost everyone and pointing to no one.

## Trophies

Initially, investigators discovered Stephanie Bennett's murderer took eight dollars from her wallet, a boom box, and a laundry basket from her bedroom. At least that's what they *knew* he took. It was possible other items were missing that had not been identified.

Police learned, with the help of Stephanie's roommates, that a small portable stereo was missing from a console in her room. It had been a gift from one of her mother's boyfriends. Police described it as a 1995 compact JVC MXC-220 stereo system with both dual cassette decks and a three-compact disc changer. The stereo had sat in a small open cabinet against the wall beneath a portable television set near Stephanie's bed. Investigators circulated pictures of the stereo with a detailed description to the media and the public hoping it would generate some new leads in the case.

Investigators knew the five-year-old laundry basket was taken from Stephanie's apartment because the killer had dumped out her clothing onto the floor in the very spot her roommates confirmed the basket always sat. Detectives spent weeks trying to figure this one out.

"Why take a damn laundry basket you can buy at any Wal-Mart?" Morgan said.

Ultimately, the supposition was that the killer used the laundry basket to carry the stereo as he made his escape from Stephanie's apartment. The basket also gave him the additional benefit of looking like he was simply heading for the apartment complex laundry room if someone spotted him walking around the parking lot early in the morning.

But at the end of the day, the stereo and the laundry basket looked like every other stereo and laundry basket in any young person's apartment in Raleigh. Police were going to be hard-pressed to find them unless they developed a solid suspect. Only one person knew where Stephanie's belongings were, and *he* wasn't talking.

Sexual deviance and control, not robbery, were shaping up to be the primary motives in the case. But still, trying to identify what might have been taken from the apartment was important, because the killer most likely held on to these items as souvenirs of the crime. Psychologists call the items taken from a murder scene for this purpose "trophies." They are seen by the murderer as prizes or awards for what he has done. They are tangible items he can take out and look at when he wants to think back on what he accomplished. Psychologists say just seeing and touching these things may give the killer further sexual satisfaction.

The media was let in on everything except the laundry basket—that detail was held back. It was the investigators' ace in the hole, something only the killer knew about, something that might ultimately trip him up. They figured if the killer didn't think the police knew it was missing, he'd be more likely to hold on to it. If they caught him, and found the laundry basket in his possession, it would only make their case stronger.

## Autopsy Revealed

Cause of death—strangulation.

On June 20, 2002, Stephanie Bennett's autopsy went

public. The gruesome details terrified the community and reignited the pressure on the police department to catch the killer.

The report from Dr. Gordon LeGrand at the Wake County Medical Examiner's Office was much more specific than the sketchy details that had been previously released to the public by police. Even the sterility of the medical terminology couldn't lessen the impact the report would have on the public.

"This one I remember more than others," LeGrand said. In all of his years performing autopsies, LeGrand said he always remembered the women and the children the most. They were always the saddest cases that touched him more deeply than others. "Here was somebody living in an apartment, going about her life and there is a psychotic deviant lurking around."

First, the autopsy report set the scene—it stated that Stephanie had been found nude, lying on her back in the bedroom adjacent to her own. She had a pair of pale blue women's underwear stuck in her mouth. The underwear had apparently been used as a gag to prevent her from screaming during the attack.

The report went on to describe the state of the body. There was a thirteen-inch ligature mark around Stephanie's neck. Her wrists and ankles also had marks on them consistent with the use of restraints. The doctor stated the double red lines on Stephanie's wrists *might* be from handcuffs, although he couldn't say for sure. The only real injury on Stephanie Bennett's body was a pronounced bruise above her right eye, but LeGrand also noted some minor evidence of self-defense, small scratches here and there. There was also clear evidence of sexual assault including dried semen on the body.

"In all likelihood, he surprised her and got her before she could do much," LeGrand said.

There were key details in the report that gave investigators clues as to how the crime was committed. They used these details to create a theory of what happened that night in Stephanie's apartment—a theory they hoped would help them eventually zero in on a suspect.

Because the maintenance employee believed the front door to the apartment was dead-bolted when he entered the day Stephanie's body was found, investigators assumed the killer most likely came through the window in Emily's bedroom. A window screen was missing from the window and placed on the ground outside, and while the window was closed when police arrived, it was not locked.

Lieutenant Morgan believed that on the night she was attacked, Stephanie—who would've probably still been tired from her weekend trip to Greenville to visit Walter Robinson—was probably sound asleep when the killer entered through Emily's bedroom window.

Investigators considered whether the killer had come to the front door and was let in by Stephanie, after which he dead-bolted the door again, but after much examination, it didn't seem plausible. In this scenario, the killer would have had to have been someone Stephanie knew well for her to open the door to him. By all accounts, she was a very careful girl who always locked the door and would never have opened it to a stranger, especially not at night when she was already concerned about safety at the apartment complex.

Investigators also considered whether the killer could have forced his way in through the front door. But, again, this seemed unlikely and too risky for someone trying to keep a low profile in an apartment complex where young people came and went at all hours of the night and could have spotted him easily beneath the light of the front door. Another theory involved the killer picking the lock on the front door, and then staging it to look as if he had come in the window. But it was hard for anyone to imagine why he would go to all of the trouble to do this. So the window, which was cloaked in darkness and hidden from the parking lot by overgrown bushes, continued to be the logical point of entry.

In addition, there was physical evidence supporting the theory that the killer came through Emily's window. An empty blue hamper just below that window inside the apartment held a handful of pine needles and leaves from the bush just outside the apartment. Lieutenant Morgan thought they could easily have fallen off of the killer's clothing as he crawled through the window.

No one knew for sure what time the killer entered the apartment or how long he was in there before he attacked Stephanie. But based on the fact that some of the items from Emily's bedroom were found to have been moved into her closet, one hypothesis was that he climbed in the window when Stephanie was still awake, and then hid in Emily's closet until Stephanie fell asleep.

In that scenario, after Stephanie went to bed, the killer would have waited to make sure she was in a deep sleep before leaving the safety of the closet. Morgan imagined the man probably then crept quietly across the hallway, so as not to disturb his sleeping victim. Like a cat pouncing on his prey, the killer then jumped onto the bed where Stephanie slept, startling her into sudden wakefulness. For a moment, she would've resisted the evil force bearing down on her; Morgan believed the bruise on her face might have come from the killer hitting Stephanie in the eye in order to scare and subdue her while he was restraining her arms and legs. He probably had a gun, a gun that he would've held to her head in order to terrify her into immediate submission.

Once Stephanie was tied up and no longer posed a threat to her attacker, Morgan assumed the killer then took her tousled covers and piled them neatly on the floor at the foot of her bed where investigators later discovered them. This chilling detail alone always gave Morgan a reason to pause and wonder what kind of meticulous freak show of a person they were dealing with. Morgan felt like the killer had a playbook that he was going by, a set of rules and rituals he needed to follow in order to feel like he was truly in control of the situation. This particular detail regarding Stephanie's bed covers further convinced him they were not dealing with an ordinary murderer, but someone who methodically planned and carried out an organized pattern of evil.

Three pillows were left on Stephanie's bare bed in a U-shape. Morgan could almost imagine the young woman fitting snugly inside this little cocoon as she dreamed about her impending move to South Carolina to be with her boyfriend. It was the protocol for how she usually slept according to family and friends. Seeing the pillows this way further assured Morgan that Stephanie must have been sound asleep when the killer slipped into her room under a cloak of darkness. Maybe he was even able to pull back the covers first and fold them neatly on the floor without being detected by his sleeping victim, which would have given him unfettered access to restrain her quickly without any obstacles or interference.

The medical examiner's report stated that when police arrived at the apartment, rigor mortis had already set in. Rigor mortis, the buildup of lactic acid in the deceased's muscles that makes a body rigid, begins to take place within three hours after death. Morgan estimated that in this case, Stephanie may have already been dead eight or more hours by the time her body was discovered. Although the autopsy couldn't pinpoint an exact time of death, it was believed to have taken place sometime after midnight.

LeGrand listed the official medical cause of death in the autopsy report as "ischemia secondary to ligature strangulation." This meant the blood flow was cut off to Stephanie's brain due to the strangulation. It caused her to go into "cardio respiratory arrest," meaning her heart and breathing stopped as a result of the ligature being placed around her neck.

The report also noted severe petechial hemorrhages, small broken capillary blood vessels in Stephanie's eyes— a calling card of strangulation. And on the back of Stephanie's neck was a crisscross mark indicating a garrote, a ligature with a stick inserted to twist the device around someone's neck, was used to cut off her air supply. None of the details of the autopsy told the police or the public *who* killed Stephanie Bennett, but they did reinforce once again that Raleigh had a truly cold-blooded killer on its hands.

## Crime Scene Revisited

In the summer of 2002, Lieutenant Chris Morgan gave the media a tour of Stephanie's empty apartment. WRAL reporter Len Besthoff and photographer Chad Flowers were invited to see the crime scene for themselves, as well as videotape the now-bare apartment.

Morgan narrated the tour with a measured tone and, once again, a stoic face devoid of expression or emotion. He simply laid everything out and let the journalists read between the lines. He wore his usual white fedora, but tipped it back slightly so that the camera could catch a glimpse of his eyes as he spoke. In many ways he wasn't actually speaking to the journalists, but to the killer who just might be watching the case unfold on the evening news.

He told the reporters that nothing out of the ordinary seemed to have happened on the day before Stephanie's murder. She'd come home from work on Monday, May 20, and followed her normal routine that evening. She'd had a conversation with her boyfriend, who was in South Carolina, before going to bed. Morgan said investigators believed the killer attacked her after she went to bed, and then took her into her roommate's bedroom adjacent to her room where he raped and killed her.

"Sometime during the night things went *very bad*," Morgan said. "We know [that] while Stephanie Bennett slept in her bedroom at the end of this hall," he gestured dramatically to a door that was ajar, but made no effort to allow anyone to enter the room, "that the intruder came into the apartment, that she was attacked probably as she slept, and that events occurred that led to her death."

Other than the smudged black fingerprint powder lining the doorways and windows, and the blocks of carpet removed by crime scene investigators, it looked like any other apartment vacated by young tenants. It was a surreal combination of everyday life mixed in with the horror of what had occurred there.

There were restaurant takeout menus strewn about the kitchen, an empty wine bottle in the sink, and a half-full container of eye drops on the counter—mundane items in a space where mundane had no place.

"What truly struck me was the Chinese food menu still held on the fridge with a magnet," Besthoff said. "It made me think about how just a few weeks ago this was just a normal apartment, with this nice young woman leading a normal life."

"It was an eerie reminder of how ordinary her life had been before she was brutally murdered," said Flowers, who, after having witnessed his share of murder scenes, was often no longer moved. But this one was different. Stephanie was different. An entire city was in mourning for her and even hard-nosed journalists couldn't help but be touched by her story.

## *Consent* Is the Magic Word

"The first six months of this were probably the hardest. We had so many theories, so many possibilities," Lieutenant Chris Morgan said.

Morgan had five detectives working under him in the Major Crimes Task Force; he could have used ten, fifteen, or even twenty. They had other murders to investigate, and with such a limited staff, they couldn't devote every moment to the Stephanie Bennett case. It frustrated Morgan to no end, but he had to work with the resources he was given.

"Morgan told me he had few leads," WRAL reporter Besthoff remembered. "You could tell right off the bat he had his concerns this was going to go cold quickly."

In December 2002, one of the department's rising young stars, Sergeant Clem Perry, was transferred from the robbery squad to the Major Crimes Task Force. Morgan was confident Perry would be a huge asset to the Bennett case. Perry had been in on the case as a peripheral player from that very first night when his squad was called to the Bridgeport Apartments to assist the homicide detectives, but now he would be in the thick of things. It was exactly where he wanted to be, working to solve a case that mattered to so many people.

Once on board, Perry and the other detectives on the task force continued to visit Stephanie's apartment complex. In early 2003, they handed out more fliers and interviewed more tenants. They even conducted traffic checkpoints around the perimeter of the complex—they would stop drivers in the area, hand them a flier, and ask them if they had any information regarding the case. Perry was amazed to discover not everyone was familiar with the Bennett homicide even after they had spent so much time canvassing the neighborhood. With all of the legwork they had done already and all of the media coverage of the case, he could not imagine anyone not being aware of the murder. He wondered what cave they must have been living in if they proclaimed not to know anything about it.

Sergeant Perry still couldn't get the memory of Stephanie's father, Carmon Bennett, out of his mind from the night Stephanie's body was identified. Perry had been the first real contact Carmon had had with the Raleigh Police Department, and he hoped the grieving father wouldn't always remember him as the man who kept him from crossing the yellow crime scene tape and prevented him from seeing his dead daughter. His heart had ached for Carmon that night. It still did.

As a robbery detective, Perry had always believed that an armed robbery was just a murder that didn't happen. Whenever there was a firearm involved in a crime, there was a chance someone might die. But now he was a homicide detective and thinking about people dying was no longer a what if, but a reality. Maybe it was because it was his first murder case. Maybe it was because he was young and ambitious. Maybe it was just because it was Stephanie— but somehow, somewhere along the line, the case became *personal* to Perry. He suddenly realized the gravity of what he was charged with. He and his colleagues were responsible for getting a random killer off the streets, someone who could strike again if they didn't act quickly. It was all he could think about.

"There was a sense of urgency," Perry said. "It was a sexual homicide of a young girl."

Perry grew up in Louisburg, North Carolina, about thirty miles northeast of Raleigh in a family he described as "the Cleavers." But despite his all-American upbringing, Perry was not sheltered. His father was a career firefighter, and Perry grew up at the firehouse hearing the firefighters' stories and interacting with the local cops who often stopped by the station. From a young age, Perry knew he wanted to be a police officer; all he'd ever wanted to do was to help people.

Perry said the parents of young women who lived in Stephanie's neighborhood were calling his unit wanting to know if their children were safe. The pressure to solve the case was increased immensely by the concern in the community that a deadly sexual predator was roaming the streets. He thought about how he would feel if he had a daughter living in the apartment complex where a young woman was killed. It wasn't a good feeling.

"There was a great deal of tension on everybody," Perry said with a furrowed brow.

Investigators had already collected a mountain of information in the case. They had compiled "lead books," which included hundreds of pages of tips that had come in through phone calls and e-mails. It was an overwhelming amount of material to consider.

Detective J. J. Mathews had recently been assigned as the lead detective on the case and would be supervising Perry and the other detectives. His first priority was to get the files organized so investigators could make some sense out of them. Perry recalled there were many meetings about how to manage all the information in the Bennett case on top of working the other homicides that continued to take place in the city. It was an unsavory balancing act for Perry to have to put aside the Bennett case to work on more recent, more solvable murders.

The leads were organized into a large notebook when they came in, and then assigned to one of the detectives. But even as they forged ahead, there was a constant feeling they were spinning their wheels, not making any real dent in the huge volume of information they had amassed.

"Everybody in the unit was completely frustrated," Perry said shaking his head. Another problem they were faced with, Perry said, was "the number of leads still coming in almost on a daily basis from the composite that was released."

Perry made it clear to everyone who would listen that he was not fond of composites. He worried they were misleading because nine times out of ten they were always a little bit off. The fact this particular one had generated so many false leads only added to his level of discomfort about using the picture. But it was all they had, so they continued to use it.

Because they seemed to be looking for the proverbial needle in the haystack at this stage in the investigation, Perry said the detectives were still concentrating on eliminating people rather than focusing in on a suspect. They used DNA tests to eliminate as many people as they possibly could. After they interviewed someone, they would then ask him to submit to a simple saliva mouth swab. They would then test the sample against the killer's DNA found in Stephanie's apartment. By the time the case was all over, they had run DNA tests on a total of 283 people. For the most part, Perry said people consented to being tested because they had nothing to hide. It was a tedious process with seemingly no end in sight. No one, including Perry, knew if it would ever pay off.

Even though solid DNA evidence is a detective's dream, it's not a slam dunk by itself. To identify the killer, his DNA had to already be on file in a criminal database so that investigators can make a match; if the killer had never been arrested before he murdered Stephanie, his DNA wouldn't be on file. It's the perfect evidence *only* if you can find a match. But the detectives kept plugging away hoping against hope that the process would eventually lead them to the right person.

"For the most part, everyone we approached consented," Perry said with his outstretched hands in the air again, his palms facing the ceiling.

Perry used to joke with his colleagues if he ever found

someone who wouldn't submit to the DNA test, he had found the killer. Little did he know how true this statement would turn out to be.

## Color Blind

While the detectives Lieutenant Morgan supervised on the Major Crimes Task Force toiled away on the day-to-day task of eliminating potential suspects, Morgan was looking at the big picture, trying to figure out what they were missing, what piece of evidence would help them complete this seemingly never-ending puzzle of who killed Stephanie Bennett.

Without a suspect, DNA couldn't tell investigators who the killer was. But just maybe it could tell them a little bit more about whom they might be looking for. Morgan felt strongly that knowing variables such as the race of the offender would help them tremendously narrow down the pool of potential suspects. Unfortunately, agents at the North Carolina SBI told Morgan that they didn't have the technology to determine race from simply analyzing the killer's DNA. Morgan wasn't sure if this issue was simply a political hot potato or a scientific truth, but he knew he didn't have the background to challenge what they were telling him. He also knew DNA science was constantly evolving and just because it couldn't be done in North Carolina didn't mean it couldn't be done somewhere else.

In a coincidental twist of fate, just as Morgan was pondering this issue, he got a call from a scientist at a local private laboratory that did DNA analysis. LabCorp often did work for law enforcement when the SBI lab was too busy or didn't have the technology or resources to handle a particular task. Morgan's friend at LabCorp told him she had been following the Bennett case religiously and had heard about a company in Florida that might be able to help him narrow down the profile of the suspect.

"They are doing things with DNA profiles that have never been done before," Morgan's friend told him with unbridled excitement in her voice.

So Morgan took her advice and called DNAPrint Genomics in Sarasota, Florida, and asked the director about the company's capabilities. He was told they could determine the race of an offender from DNA to within only a tenth of a percent margin of error. Suddenly, Morgan started to calculate the possibilities of being able to cut an entire ethnic group out of his suspect pool with this information. But Morgan was getting ahead of himself as usual. He needed to know for sure that what they were telling him was true before he could move forward.

"Prove it," Morgan said to the scientist. He was never a man to accept anything without strong evidence, and sometimes even then he was still skeptical.

The director of the company told Morgan to send him four blind samples from anyone in the police department, and they would analyze the samples to demonstrate their extraordinary capabilities. Morgan was game. He chose a white officer, a black officer, a Hispanic officer, and a Native American officer. The results the company returned were dead-on. Morgan had his answer.

It took some wrangling, but Morgan finally got the SBI to agree to turn over a sample of the killer's DNA to send to the laboratory in Florida. Three months later, he got the results from DNAPrint Genomics. It was as he expected. Ninety-two percent of the killer's genotype was similar to the typical Indo-European genotype.

"It meant he was a very white, white guy," Morgan said, not mincing words.

This piece of the puzzle didn't tell investigators who their killer was, but it definitely told them who their killer wasn't. It basically cut anyone of another race out of the suspect pool. And when your pool pretty much encompasses the whole world, anything that can narrow it down is a good thing.

## Mind Games

Stephanie Bennett's case involved the only reported combination rape-murder in the entire state of North Carolina in 2002. It was undoubtedly an unusual case for that part of the country, but Michael Teague, the police department's psychologist, had a hunch they might be dealing with a sexual predator who may have struck before and could strike again. He believed the killer might be a traveler who had left a trail of victims throughout the country and refrained from committing similar crimes in areas that were too close together in order to evade capture.

In his private practice, Teague specialized in counseling and rehabilitating repeat sex offenders. He knew from his training that sexual deviance and violence often escalated, and this knowledge increased his desire to help investigators crack the case. Teague believed police were dealing with a unique and dangerous criminal.

"Everybody watching TV thinks it happens every night, but it's *very* rare," Teague said of sexual predators who killed their victims.

Teague noticed from reading the autopsy report that Stephanie's body was lacking major injuries other than the marks from restraining and strangling her. Strangulation is a very personal way to kill someone—a mode often used in domestic killings by enraged husbands or boyfriends, yet there was no indication Stephanie knew her attacker. Teague was intrigued. He thought this was especially unusual because he assumed the killer had had a gun that he used to make Stephanie acquiesce to his demands. Using the gun to kill her would have been much faster and easier than strangulation which, contrary to what is portrayed in the movies, takes more strength and precision than most people would imagine. The scenario made little sense. Teague drew on his years of psychological research and training as he started to develop a profile of the killer in his mind.

"I couldn't figure out what kind of guy could do all the horrible things he did to her and not bruise her more," Teague said. "To do all of those extremely violent acts and not beat up on the woman is just so unusual."

Stephanie did have what could have been minor defensive wounds, slight scratches, and a carpet burn on her knee, but for the most part she had few injuries. This was not what Teague expected from a brutal rape scenario. For him, it was a red flag that immediately made him rule out previously convicted criminals. They tended to be the most violent offenders who, after spending years in prison, would be the most likely suspects to severely beat their victims and leave obvious injuries.

Teague figured that the suspect in this case fit into a category called "the power-reassurance rapist," also known in layman's terms as the "gentleman rapist."

Dr. A. Nicholas Groth, author of the 1979 book *Men Who Rape: The Psychology of the Offender,* first defined this type of sex offender by saying that the power-reassurance rapist was someone who was of average intelligence, not typically violent, and had social problems, especially with women. Groth went on to say that this type of offender often stalked his victims, forced them to engage in foreplay, and took trophies from the crime scene as reminders of what he had done. According to Groth, these offenders tended to fantasize about being in a romantic relationship with the victim.

One thing this kind of rapist rarely did was to *kill.* This detail had Teague completely "befuddled," he said of the situation. And when crimes didn't fit into a normal pattern of psychological behavior, Teague knew they were going to be much harder to solve.

Teague surmised Stephanie was one of a "pool of potential victims" whom the killer had zeroed in on and had possibly been stalking. Because her roommates were out of town, Teague figured that the killer saw a rare opportunity to commit the crime with Stephanie as the victim. He thought the killer may have even been stalking one of Stephanie's roommates as well, but chose Stephanie that night because she happened to be home alone in the apartment.

"I think he thought, 'If one of those other girls doesn't show up by 12:00, I'm going in,'" Teague said of the killer's thinking. He believed the killer may even have been listening outside Stephanie's apartment window that evening to her phone calls and realized from her conversations her roommates would not be coming home.

Investigators told Teague they believed the killer entered through Metro's bedroom window. But then why did he take Stephanie out of her own bedroom and bring her to the floor in Emily's room? Although Morgan thought it was because the killer wanted to be able to get out quickly, the same way he came in, Teague believed the suspect wanted the most amount of space to commit the crime. Because many power-reassurance rapists have a need to document their deviance in some way, Teague also felt strongly that the murderer may have videotaped the crime.

"I'm almost positive he took pictures," Teague said of the killer. It was a theory not shared by many of the investigators on the case.

Teague's belief stemmed in part from the way the bedding in Stephanie's room was meticulously pulled back and laid on the floor at the foot of the bed. It was as if the killer had wanted the bed to be free and clear of any obstructions so that he could tie Stephanie up and photograph her.

Teague believed the killer then moved the show into Emily's bedroom, possibly onto her bed for more taping or photographs, then finally onto the floor.

"I think his purpose was to create a film that he could get excited by," Teague said grimly.

There was no semen found on Stephanie's bed or on Emily's bed—only in and around the body as it lay on the floor in Emily's room. Yet items were moved from Emily's bed into the closet. This supported Teague's theory that the killer must have used the beds for something other than rape. His hypothesis was that the killer took pictures first on the two beds, and then committed the various sexual assaults on the floor.

"He was an organized offender," Teague said. "He knew what he was going to do and how he was going to do it."

Teague was also still intrigued by the multiple pairs of women's underwear found dumped on the bush in between Stephanie's building and the next building over, about twenty or thirty feet from Emily's bedroom window. At the time, investigators decided the underwear probably didn't have anything to do with Stephanie's murder, that it was just a childish prank at the hands of a young boy, but Teague wasn't convinced. His gut told him there was more to it.

"Mighty coincidental that you had a bush full of women's underwear right near where a woman was raped and murdered," Teague said. "The odds of that happening are one in twenty thousand."

It was determined that a chocolate-colored pair of underwear Stephanie's roommates said she wore frequently was also missing from the apartment along with the stereo, the laundry basket, and the money from her wallet. More than anything, Teague saw the underwear, and possibly the stereo, as trophies the killer might have taken from the crime scene, something by which to remember the event.

"I think it actually has an emotional quality to it," said Teague of the killer's trophy taking. "I don't know if it's totally sexual, or if it was like, 'Wow that reminds me of what I did.' It has power to it."

That power was frightening. Although, Teague knew that serial killers were rare, he was starting to see signs that they might be dealing with one. An organized, trophy-taking rapist and killer was without a doubt a potential candidate for being a serial murderer.

One idea to help investigators that Teague came up with was to hypnotize Stephanie's roommates and the apartment manager who had found the body. The goal of the hypnosis was to see if the women could recall any strange individuals who had been lurking around the apartment complex in the days before Stephanie's murder or if there was anyone in their lives whom they thought might be capable of such a heinous crime. Unfortunately, nothing the women said under hypnosis aided the investigation, though their thoughts did add to the complete picture the investigative team was building of Stephanie. Teague said Stephanie's roommates, Dee and Emily, were so emotional about Stephanie's murder, even under hypnosis, their grief overwhelmed any clues they might be able to offer.

"Whenever they were talking about Stephanie, you could see their faces change," Teague said of interviewing the women. "It was like you had turned on a light bulb. 'Oh, she was this. Oh, she was that.' It was very genuine. It wasn't just like somebody had died early and we're going to make her into a legend. Stephanie really touched people in a positive way."

It became apparent after talking to people who knew Stephanie she had an unstoppable magnetism. She was described as someone who was a "good listener" and someone who always put others first. These qualities in life had given her angel-like status in death. Her family and friends lamented over and over again that Stephanie's death had left such a deep void in their worlds because she had subtly infused their lives with quiet compassion and grace.

"She was very good at cuing in to people's needs," Teague said.

Now if they could only help Stephanie in death the way she had helped others in life.

# CHAPTER THREE

# Stephanie

*The pain passes, but the beauty remains.*
—RENOIR

Stephanie Renee Bennett was born on April 30, 1979, in Rocky Mount, Virginia, to Mollie and Carmon Bennett. She was their second child—a little sister to brother Jay.

Even from a young age, Stephanie's personality was readily apparent to everyone who met her. She was sometimes timid at first until she got to know people, but as she warmed up, she endeared herself to everyone who crossed paths with her. As a result of her kindness and grace, Stephanie was voted "Miss Personality" her senior year at Franklin County High School. With her brown shoulder-length hair, deep brown eyes, and pearly white grin, she looked like she could have been a spokesmodel for Noxzema. She truly had a smile that could light up a room, in a girl-next-door kind of way. Stephanie had a talent for making people feel comfortable, as if they had known her their whole lives.

Stephanie graduated from Roanoke College in 2001 and

a short time later moved to Raleigh to take a job with IBM. It was a big step for a country girl who, by all accounts, had lived a sheltered life before relocating to North Carolina. But she was smart and ambitious and had a burning desire to show her family and herself that she could make it on her own.

Stephanie's family and friends finally broke their silence several months after her death and spoke to the media. They hoped by putting a personal face on the tragedy, someone who had information about the case might be prompted to come forward.

"She was my angel," said Jay Bennett, Stephanie's older brother, to WRAL. "I was closer to her than any other person in the world."

Carmon Bennett said his daughter had a special love for the outdoors, especially for the rolling hills of Virginia and its sparkling blue lakes. In many ways, she was a typical twenty-something young woman—she liked to read books, talk on the phone, and go shopping with her mother, Mollie Hodges. Although her parents divorced when she was a child, they remained in the same area, and Stephanie was able to have a close, loving relationship with both of them, as well as with her stepmother, Jennifer.

At a vigil held in Stephanie's memory on July 1, 2002, Carmon pleaded directly with the killer for the answers he was so desperately seeking.

"I want to know Stephanie's last words. Did she say anything that would comfort the members of her family?" Carmon said choking back tears. "Did she pray? You took my daughter; please give me some peace in knowing these things. We will not quit searching until our questions are answered."

## Unfinished Love

"Steph, she listened," said Walter Robinson, Stephanie's boyfriend, in an interview with WRAL reporter Besthoff and photographer Flowers on August 9, 2002, in Greenville, South Carolina. Walter's boyishly handsome face, dark blond hair, and blue golf shirt made him look like a happy-go-lucky fraternity boy on his way to a keg party, but it was clear from the way he choked up right out of the gate that he carried a heavy burden. "She just always seemed to be able to say the right things at the right time."

"From the get go, you could tell [how] upset he was," Besthoff recalled. "Very genuine. I remember how my photographer and I felt sorry for the guy. He was in a real state of grief."

Walter decided, as Stephanie's family had done, that he needed to let people know more about the woman he loved, the woman with whom he'd planned to spend the rest of his life with before she was so brutally murdered. A DNA test had cleared Walter as a suspect in the case early on, and he was ready to let the world know Stephanie was more than just another murder statistic.

Walter and Stephanie had met at a sorority dance at Roanoke College where they were both students. They came separately to the event with other dates, but somehow Walter had mustered up the courage to introduce himself to the attractive, demure brunette across the room. He asked her to dance, and she turned him down. She told him she was afraid his date would get upset and didn't want to hurt her feelings. Robinson said that first meeting personified the woman he would soon get to know and ultimately love.

"She always cared about everyone else, she didn't think of herself," he said smiling with tears in his eyes.

The couple had planned on eventually getting married, though they had not actually gotten engaged yet. Walter had never even bought Stephanie a piece of jewelry, until Christmas 2001, when he decided to buy her a ring, not an engagement ring, but a promise ring of sorts to symbolize their future together.

Carmon Bennett more than approved of his daughter's relationship with Walter. He considered the intelligent, witty young man to be part of his family. He felt confident that Walter, whom he described as a "fine person from a fine family," would respect his daughter and take good care of her.

"Stephanie never asked for anything," Walter said. "She was always content with what she had. I know she wanted more things, but she wanted to do it for herself."

Walter's eyes welled up with tears as he struggled to find the words to describe exactly what Stephanie meant to him.

"She was always smiling," he said. "She was a happy person. She was looking forward to her life in the future, *our* life. She was excited about doing things on her own."

After the two graduated from college, Stephanie went off on her own to take a job with IBM in Raleigh. Walter headed to Greenville, South Carolina, to pursue a graduate degree in engineering at Clemson University. They continued dating, but the distance was a strain on the relationship. After a year of long-distance romance, Walter finally convinced Stephanie to move to Greenville so they could be together again. The plan was for the two to eventually get engaged, married, and live happily ever after. "We wanted to be together. It just seemed like when we were around each other, when we were together, everything was right. Everything fit," Walter said.

Walter knew he wanted and needed to be closer to the beautiful, gentle, understanding woman who seemed to find the good in everyone and everything. He said Stephanie's excitement about life and her positive outlook made him a much better person.

"She'll always be with me. She'll always be in my heart. It's just hard to grasp the concept right now that I'm not going to be able to see her, I'm not going to be able to smell her hair, hold her hand," Walter said looking straight into the camera lens.

Walter's tone changed from sweet reminiscence to anger when he was asked about the man who took Stephanie's life.

"Somebody that does something like this is just an animal," he said, his words drenched in rage. "I want him dead, and God have no mercy on his soul."

"He was very sincere," photographer Flowers said about Walter. "I think Stephanie was truly the love of his life."

Even then—back in the infancy of the investigation—those who loved Stephanie had faith the case would eventually be solved. Even Walter, who wished out loud he could trade places with Stephanie, felt that justice would ultimately be served. He had no way of knowing just how long that would take.

"I think it is a matter of time," Walter said looking off in the distance as if he was gazing into a crystal ball. "He better walk lightly in the shadows and be very careful because he'll make a mistake and when he makes a mistake they're going to *nail* him."

## Reminders

For Carmon Bennett, every day was just another day without his daughter, Stephanie. As much as he wanted to go on with his life for the sake of his wife, Jennifer, and his son, Jay, there were reminders of Stephanie's loss everywhere he turned. No matter what happened with the case, he would be mourning Stephanie's loss for the rest of his life. As the investigation continued, he shared the constant reminders of his loss during his interviews with WRAL.

For example, Carmon couldn't forget Stephanie's first car—a red Honda Prelude. He couldn't see one pass by without craning his neck and squinting his eyes to see who was behind the wheel. In his head, he knew it wasn't her, but still, his heart always skipped a beat with foolish hope when one passed.

Tulips, Stephanie's favorite flowers, were another emotional trigger for Carmon. Jennifer kept the vase on the kitchen table in their home full of tulips in honor of Stephanie.

Even Stephanie's friends who visited the Bennetts on a regular basis were painful reminders to Carmon of what he'd lost. They were so full of life and strong potential. They had everything ahead of them. He couldn't help but think Stephanie should have been with them, planning her bright future, not buried in the cold hard ground at Franklin Memorial Park beneath a sterile bronze nameplate.

"She had a personality that was outgoing and a smile that never quit. She always had a smile. Stranger or not, she had a smile for you," Carmon recalled fondly. "She was just a wonderful young lady, and it's so hard to believe [she's gone]. She never caused me and the family a minute's trouble. Always where she was supposed to be, doing what she was supposed to do."

Carmon said Stephanie was the kind of girl who worked hard in school and was proud of what she accomplished. He said she was dedicated to her job, always on time, always doing her best.

"She had such a positive attitude. When you first met her you might not think she was outgoing, but she was very at ease, had a wonderful smile, and a pleasant tone of voice," said the grieving father as he stared off into the distance at the green rolling hills Stephanie so loved surrounding his home. "She was just very easy to get to know and be friends with."

## A Mother's Sorrow

"Last Mother's Day Stephanie sent me the sweetest Mother's Day card—she wrote in there how proud she was that I was her mom," Mollie Hodges, Stephanie's mother, shared in an interview with WRAL.

Mollie replayed the things she used to do with her daughter in her mind like a home video.

"If I go to [the] mall, I think of Stephanie. She loved to shop," Mollie said. "If I go to the beach, I see her walking down the beach."

The mother and daughter enjoyed many of the simple pleasures in life together—shopping, talking on the phone, taking vacations. Mollie said even after Stephanie moved to Raleigh, they often talked on the telephone several times a day. Stephanie was constantly calling her mother to ask her questions about cooking or how to fix something in her apartment. Although she was speeding toward her adult independence, part of Stephanie was still a little girl who needed her mother's reassurance and guidance.

"Stephanie, she was so cheerful," Mollie remembered tearfully. "We always had the best of times, and Stephanie was always happy-go-lucky, smiling." Mollie had kept Stephanie's cat with her in Rocky Mount when her daughter moved to Raleigh. Stephanie would ask her to put the cat on the phone so she could hear it meow into the receiver. It was the little things like this about home that Stephanie so obviously missed, and her parents were her constant reminders that home would always be there for her. It was also the little vignettes like that, the tender moments now frozen in time that always gave Mollie a lump in her throat when she remembered them.

Stephanie's compassion for others is something Mollie would never forget about her daughter. On more than one occasion Mollie and Stephanie would pass a homeless man who frequented the corner at the stoplight near the local mall, always holding up a sign about needing money or food. Mollie said no matter how many times they drove by him, Stephanie couldn't pass the man without wanting to help.

"She would always say, 'Mom, do you have a dollar [or] two that we could put in his bucket?' " said Mollie. "Stephanie was kind. She was kind to everybody."

For Mollie, her memories of Stephanie were all she had left. She tried to focus on the good, as impossible as it seemed. She knew Stephanie would have wanted it that way. But it was hard to be positive when her daughter was dead and her daughter's killer was still roaming the streets.

"Stephanie didn't want anybody to be down in the dumps and she wouldn't want it today. She wouldn't want us to sit around and grieve. She would want us to be happy," said Mollie fighting back more tears as she feebly attempted to put on a brave face.

## CHAPTER FOUR

# The Garbage Man

Knowledge is a process of piling up facts; wisdom lies in their simplification.

—MARTIN FISCHER

"There were so many nights when I just went to bed with a sense of dread saying, is this the night when we get another victim?" Lieutenant Chris Morgan said. "Is this the night where I'm going to get a call and there's going to be another dead girl?"

Morgan couldn't sleep. He knew he needed more help than he was getting. His resources were stretched. The chief had recently downsized the homicide division to just one unit from two, and his people were already running ragged on so many cases; he couldn't ask them to do any more than they were already doing on the Stephanie Bennett case. Yet, unlike most homicides for which they had a hunch who the killer was and were working on amassing evidence against the suspect, in this case they still had absolutely nothing. In Morgan's opinion, the Bennett case deserved more attention because a killer was on the loose in Raleigh and could very well strike again.

As part of the Special Victims Unit (SVU), Detective Ken Copeland concentrated on solving sex crimes. The SVU was occasionally asked to help with unsolved murder cases, to be another set of eyes in addition to the regular detectives already assigned to the homicide cases.

Because Stephanie's murder involved sexual assault, Morgan thought members of the SVU might have unique insight into the case given the fact that they handled sex crimes day in and day out. There was speculation that Stephanie's killer might have been involved in consensual acts of bondage with other sex partners whom he did not kill. Morgan asked detectives to find women who specialized in offering sexually deviant services, like bondage, in the Raleigh area and see if they had come in contact with anyone who might be a potential suspect in Stephanie's murder.

Psychologist Michael Teague recalled that at this stage of the investigation detectives had started looking closely at anyone who was into sexual deviance, especially bondage, since Stephanie had been restrained. They even talked to a "bondage madam" in a sleepy little suburban bedroom community of Raleigh called Holly Springs whom Teague said had one of the most "syrupy southern accents" he had ever heard. He remembered her accent as a sharp contrast to the violent acts performed for money behind closed doors in her home.

The investigators also found out about a bondage club that met monthly at a local Chinese restaurant and interviewed some of its members. No sex crime, or participation in sexual deviance, was deemed too minor to investigate when it came to looking for possible links to the Bennett case.

Detective Ken Copeland remembers the spring day in May 2003, right around the first anniversary of Stephanie's murder, when his group sat around a table getting cold-case assignments from Morgan. For the most part, everyone was assigned two cold homicide cases to review on their own time in between working their regular cases. The goal was for the SVU detectives to assist the homicide detectives in their most difficult unsolved cases. During the meeting Copeland received just *one* case, the case of a homeless man named Bernard Walker found dead behind a McDonald's. He wondered why he wasn't getting the same amount of work as the other officers. *Did they think he wasn't good enough to handle more than one case?*

After the assignments were handed out, Morgan came into the investigations area and sat in a chair in front of Copeland's desk with a serious look on his face. *What have I done now?* Copeland thought. Copeland was ready to confront Morgan about giving him only one case, but he decided to hear the lieutenant out first. Maybe he had his reasons.

"Hey, what other case is Ken going to have?" Detective Amanda Salmon shouted sarcastically in Morgan's direction from her desk across the room.

Copeland remembered how the question pissed him off, because he assumed he was being passed over for some reason but, on the other hand, it was the question he had wanted to ask anyway. It was gnawing at him. She had just beaten him to the punch. He looked directly at Morgan and waited for him to answer.

"Well, he's going to be working on the Bennett case," Morgan fired back at Detective Salmon with a grin, knowing all too well that his answer would stop her sarcasm in its tracks.

It was *the* case everyone wanted to solve. Copeland was beyond excited about the opportunity to work on such a high-profile case, not to mention the challenge. The anger he had momentarily felt about getting slighted immediately dissipated.

"I was interested in the case. Everybody in the office was interested in the case," Copeland said zealously.

To this day, Morgan fondly remembers that moment—the moment he first gave Detective Ken Copeland a little piece of the pie which would later turn out to be Copeland's pie altogether.

"If I ever made a good decision in this investigation, I picked the right man to get the job done because I knew he was persistent," Morgan said.

Morgan had dubbed Copeland "The Garbage Man" because he was so detail-oriented. He'd pick up every piece of evidence no matter how small or seemingly unimportant and examine it. It was a way of operating that would ultimately serve him well in the Bennett case.

"I don't know whether I'm thorough or lucky," Copeland said. "I think I just look at what is reasonable, what is there. I can't read somebody's mind. You have to look at the facts. And when you have nothing else you have to go by the facts that are there."

## Born to Investigate

Detective Ken Copeland came to police work through hard work. A proud member of the Haliwa Saponi Indian tribe, Copeland grew up in the small rural community of Warren County about eighty-five miles northeast of Raleigh. His father, Archie, a tobacco warehouse employee, and his mother, Keasey, a stay-at-home mother, raised Copeland and his two sisters to respect authority and work hard at whatever they chose to do in their lives.

Copeland joined the U.S. Marine Corps twenty-four days after graduating from Warren County High School in 1988 and served a four-year tour of duty. He still sports a short flat-top haircut and the in-shape physique of a military man.

After getting his associates' degree from Nash Community College, Copeland joined the Raleigh Police Department in 1994. From the start, he had his eye on being a detective, but he knew he would have to pay his dues first. On December 23, 1999, Copeland achieved that goal; he was awarded the coveted gold badge with the word *Detective* on it.

"I had become what I aspired to be," Copeland recalled proudly.

His first case as a detective was an embezzlement from a Kentucky Fried Chicken restaurant on New Year's Eve. Copeland got the suspect to confess to the crime after just two hours in the interview room. He was exhilarated by his newcomer's success, but still, he knew it was a far cry from handling a homicide case.

Getting a crack at the Stephanie Bennett case, even as a bit player, was the opportunity of his career for Copeland. He started his investigation by comparing every sex crime with any potential connection to Stephanie's murder. He was sure of one thing: Stephanie did not know her killer. While most sex crimes involve someone the victim knows—an ex-boyfriend, a co-worker, an acquaintance—there was no evidence Stephanie knew her attacker. That alone motivated Copeland to want to work even harder to solve the case. Random sex crimes, let alone random murders, were not something that usually occurred in Raleigh, North Carolina, and he wanted to make damn sure it didn't happen again.

"This one was one that you could definitely look at with one hundred percent certainty and say, *this is a stranger. This was not meant to happen. And she is a true victim,*" Copeland said.

Copeland started looking closely at the city's sex crimes to see if there were any similarities to Stephanie's homicide. If there was strangulation, bondage, *anything* involved that might be linked to the Bennett case, it raised a red flag for him and received his extra attention.

The sexual component in Stephanie's murder made it

one of the most heinous crimes Copeland had ever seen. The thought that this young woman had been tortured by a pervert for God knows how long before she was killed made him physically ill. It consumed him daily as he worked on it in between all of his other cases. What made the crime even worse in Copeland's mind was that it had happened in the sanctity of Stephanie's home, a place where everyone should have an expectation of safety.

"This was a bad combination of sex and murder. It was one of the worst. It was brutal. The thought of being in your own home and being bound and gagged like that . . ." said Copeland. "I could not imagine what Carmon Bennett was going through."

If there was one thing The Garbage Man was known for, it was never giving up. As long as he had anything to do with the Stephanie Bennett case, Detective Ken Copeland vowed to live up to his reputation.

# CHAPTER FIVE

# One Year and Counting

## Spring 2003

The best way out is always through.
—ROBERT FROST

On Saturday, April 12, 2003, relatives and members of Stephanie Bennett's sorority gathered at her alma mater, Roanoke College, in Salem, Virginia, to dedicate a handmade bench in her memory. Stephanie had graduated from college in the spring of 2001 just a year before she was killed. The event was bittersweet as Stephanie's loved ones tried to concentrate on honoring her memory, but were also painfully aware that nearly a year had gone by and no one had been arrested for her murder.

The beautifully handcrafted cherry bench made in Stephanie's honor sat beneath a shady tree dappled in bright sunlight as it streamed through the branches. A large festive yellow ribbon was tied to one armrest. Someone had laid a bouquet of yellow tulips on the seat. Next to the bench on the ground at the foot of the shading tree was a plaque that read: "Time goes on, people touch you and then they're gone. But you and I will always be friends like we were then. In Loving Memory of Stephanie Bennett '01."

Reporters approached Mollie Hodges, Stephanie's mother, as she walked up to the gathering. While others in the group wore somber colors, blacks and grays, Mollie wore an almost blindingly bright orange suit. It was as if she were paying tribute to her daughter's affable personality with her color choice. But her drawn face and eyes hidden behind massive sunglasses told a different story, the story of a mother still in the throes of deep mourning.

"It's wonderful. Stephanie's sorority sisters were her greatest friends, and she would be so proud," Mollie said to the reporters. "It's beautiful. It's beautiful, and the girls did a great job."

But Mollie couldn't help but mourn her daughter's absence on this sunny spring day—alumni weekend, a weekend Stephanie would have enjoyed coming back for, to see old friends. Stephanie should have been there talking excitedly about her job, about her love life, and reminiscing with her old pals. Instead, a solitary picture of Stephanie in her cap and gown from her college graduation leaning against the tree next to the bench was the only likeness of the beautiful young woman.

"She was always so happy," Mollie said running her fingers beneath the edge of her large sunglasses to wipe away tears. "She always had a smile on her face, and if she was here today she'd still have that big smile."

The school chaplain, the Reverend Paul Henrickson, addressed the solemn crowd peacefully at first, but then infused a bit of fire and brimstone into his tone.

"These are words I shared last year on May 25 at Stephanie's funeral service," the reverend began as he turned to survey the group assembled before him. "There are three things in the world of which we can be certain beyond any doubt—there is beauty, there is evil, and there is hope. We know beauty. We've seen it. We've touched it. We've loved it. We have held it as a newborn baby. We have celebrated the beauty of a daughter, a friend, one loved so dearly. Beauty is to behold. At the same time we know evil. We know that evil can topple large buildings. Evil can create wars. Evil can destroy happiness, can take away what is beautiful and innocent, and snatch it away in the blink of an eye. Evil is real, and it is powerful, and it longs only for suffering and death. We know beauty. We know evil, but we also know hope—hope that is not just wishful thinking. Hope looks at a handful of seeds and imagines fields of flowers."

Mollie visibly choked back tears as the school chaplain spoke. She wiped her eyes beneath her sunglasses with a tissue at each mention of the word *beauty*. Stephanie's sorority sisters stood quietly behind her mother in respectful reverence with their heads bowed and arms around one another.

Stephanie's father, Carmon Bennett, stood stoically in the front of the crowd in his Sunday best—a gray blazer, a white shirt, and a striped tie. As always, his wife, Jennifer, was by his side. Like Mollie, Carmon wore dark sunglasses to hide his grief. On one side of Carmon and Jennifer stood Lieutenant Chris Morgan, like a secret service agent guarding the president. Psychologist Michael Teague stood on the other side of the couple.

One of Stephanie's friends, Amanda Gamari, read a poem about Stephanie. She struggled to get through it, pausing at times to clear her throat and accept a hug from a friend who stood at her left shoulder for support.

"What brought us all together is a mystery to this day," the young woman read. "We all had separate lives until senior year made its way."

The woman choked back tears as another friend comforted her, putting her arm around her shoulder and giving her a hug from the side. It was clear that to these young women Stephanie's death was probably the first major loss in their lives. At a time when they should have been celebrating the possibilities of their bright futures, they were instead pondering who took their dear friend from the world.

"Last year we lost a part of us, the part that made us whole. The only way to describe her is that she was the sweetest little thing, a breath of fresh air," Stephanie's friend continued through tears.

She ended by dedicating the bench in Stephanie's memory and "her beauty that was within."

After the brief service, Stephanie's family and friends spoke to the media, surely not because they wanted to, but because they wanted to keep Stephanie's story in the public eye. In unsolved murder cases, victims' families learn quickly that it's important to keep a media spotlight on the case. They go from being ordinary people to being modern-day spin doctors trying not to topple the investigation by revealing too much. But at the same time, they have a vested interest in keeping their loved ones' stories out there because it keeps pressure on the police and often leads to new information in the case.

For the first time since Stephanie's murder, her roommate and stepsister, Deanna Powell, talked to news reporters. Dee, as everyone called her, was the epitome of a southern girl with a perfectly coifed brown bob, a black cardigan properly buttoned over a simple black and white flowered dress, and a delicate silver pendant dangling around her neck.

"I think it's amazing seeing how many people have come together and supported Stephanie," Dee said. "I know she would be really honored. Knowing Stephanie, she'd probably be embarrassed, but she would be extremely honored. She had no idea how much people really thought of her."

Despite her pulled-together appearance and cherubic face, Dee had the vacant look in her eyes of someone who had witnessed death firsthand. Clearly, the year had not done much to erase the profound pain of losing her stepsister and dear friend.

After the ceremony, Emily Metro, Stephanie's other roommate, sat with her arm around Dee on the sacred bench. The friends had not been together for some time. Distance, and the pain of shared grief, had kept them apart. Emily's hair was in a messy blond ponytail, and she wore a faded denim jacket over a white sundress. It gave her an air of someone who had not wanted to think too much about her appearance on such a sad occasion.

Emily recalled how she, Dee, and Stephanie had been excited about what their futures held; they were ready to go out and tackle the world, and then *this* had happened. It had changed everything.

Emily said that the service in her dead friend's honor had touched her in a way she hadn't expected. It dredged up emotions she had buried deeply in the bottom of her broken heart.

"It gave me chills. My heart was pounding," Emily said with a tearful smile of the bench dedication ceremony. It was like witnessing a rainbow after a storm, the perfect blend of sorrow and joy. But her smile disappeared when she talked about Stephanie's killer still roaming the streets.

"Every day you think about—maybe it was someone I saw. Do I know this person?" Emily said, her voice trembling with fear. "Just the fact that he's going on living his life when so many other people's lives have been torn."

Carmon also spoke to the media after the event. He sounded confident as usual, but never removed his sunglasses, presumably to keep anyone from seeing the weight of the grief still lingering in his eyes.

"I thought it was beautiful, with the amount of people that were here, Stephanie's friends and family. It makes you feel real good. Makes you proud of Stephanie," Carmon said. "Yes, it's difficult. It has been difficult. Stephanie's birthday is the thirtieth of this month, and that's going to be a pretty tough day."

Carmon recalled the day he brought Stephanie to Roanoke College in 1997, her freshman year. It was a day no father could forget—the day he sent his little girl off into the world to officially begin her own life as an independent woman.

"She was excited the day I brought her over here and dropped her off. I was nervous and scared," Carmon said, managing a small smile at the corners of his mouth. "I was the one that cried when I left, not her."

And Carmon was still the one crying. He could not have imagined what a toll this grief had taken on his life, his family's life, and the lives of everyone Stephanie had touched. Carmon had been working closely with the police, trying to keep tabs on the investigation, but investigators couldn't tell him everything, just bits and pieces. He knew they had to keep some things private to protect the integrity of the investigation. He resisted the temptation some victims have to lash out at police when an arrest doesn't come within what they consider to be a timely fashion. Instead, in a true test of his faith in the justice system, Carmon praised the detectives for their hard work.

"I have confidence in the Raleigh Police Department," Carmon said. "They're trying to find a needle in a haystack if you will. You know how elusive that can be. We're just hoping that something like this doesn't have to happen to another young lady. I'm sure as time goes on something's going to give, and we just got to have faith and patience."

Morgan hovered like a bodyguard around Carmon during the interview. He was always ready to jump in if a reporter got too pushy or personal and upset the father of the murdered girl. He couldn't help himself. Morgan always felt the need to protect victims' families even when they didn't need protecting. As usual, Morgan had no trouble attracting television cameras himself. He took his turn after Carmon, appearing to be talking off-the-cuff, while in actuality, he delivered perfectly formed sound bites.

Morgan loved the camera, and the camera loved him. But it was more than just theatrics. Reporters, like WRAL's Len Besthoff, respected him and his dedication to the cases he handled.

"It amazed me how deeply immersed he became in the case," Besthoff said, "and how connected he was with the victim's family and friends, and the lengths he would go, to keep the case in the public eye."

"We have several thousand man-hours invested in this investigation," Morgan said to the reporters assembled before him. "It's still actively pursued each and every day by a team of very dedicated and committed detectives who won't rest until the killer of Stephanie Bennett is brought to justice."

Morgan had a way of saying things to reporters without really saying anything at all. He rarely ever showed his hand, but he could talk to a television camera until you ran out of tape.

"People who commit crimes such as this don't live in a vacuum. They're out there amongst people every day. Somebody out there may hold the vital information that we need," Morgan said. "I'm the chief investigator and this is a heinous crime that was committed in my city and we won't give up."

## Coming up Empty

One year had gone by since the murder, and there were still no real leads after countless hours of investigation by countless officers. They had tirelessly followed up on all of the tips that came in through e-mail and by phone. They had knocked on doors, interviewed hundreds of people, and taken dozens of DNA samples, but they had nothing to show for it except an overflowing case file.

"We want to find out who did it. We don't want another

family to go through what we've been through," said Mollie Hodges.

"As time goes on something has got to give," Carmon said. "You have to have faith and patience."

Investigator Chris Morgan had taken on the case as a "personal quest," one that he vowed to solve before he retired. The problem was that every time he planned to retire, another case came up, and he couldn't let it go. Morgan had formed a personal bond with Stephanie's family that amounted to a great big hole in his heart. He wanted justice for Stephanie and for her family.

"Every day we came in with the attitude, what can we do today? What can we follow up on? Somewhere, we'll find the answer," Morgan said, remembering how he and his detectives refused to give up on the case.

## Profile of a Killer

On June 9, 2003, Morgan stood outside the Raleigh Police Department and held a press briefing as he squinted beneath the direct rays of the midday sunlight. A bead of sweat rolled down his brow. The police had come up with a new profile of the killer they hoped would give the public insight and in return give detectives the leads they were so desperately seeking.

"Likely as not, this person works, [and] moves amongst other people every day. This was a person who moved in society, who blended in," Morgan said.

Morgan went on to describe the suspect as a white man in his late twenties or early thirties who may have military experience. The military experience was based on a theory from psychologist Michael Teague. He felt like the use of restraints and the ability to subdue someone completely without leaving more injuries on her body was the mark of a trained killer.

Given this theory, Sergeant Clem Perry remembers that investigators even tried to tap into military DNA databases to see if they could find a match with the killer's DNA. He made contact with several higher-ups in the military to see if there was a way to run the killer's DNA profile through their databases.

"The comment that I got was, 'If you want to determine anything about DNA from the military, when I say it's going to take an act of Congress, Sergeant Perry, it's going to take an act of Congress,'" Perry recalled with a smile.

At the press conference Morgan went on to say the killer probably also engaged in sexual fantasies including bondage and role-playing. Detectives had worked with a number of experts, including Teague, the police department's psychologist, as well as investigators in other law enforcement agencies to try and develop a clearer picture of the suspect. But it was still just a hypothesis, a hypothesis with no identity attached to it.

By this time, Perry said, they were rapidly moving away from the theory that the Peeping Tom had something to do with Stephanie's murder. The original composite, which was based primarily on a single eyewitness account of the Peeping Tom, was shelved as investigators started to focus on the new profile.

"Based on the profile we were told that the likelihood of the peeper being responsible was very slim," Perry said.

One reporter at the press conference asked Morgan how Stephanie Bennett's family was doing. He paused and looked away from the cameras for a moment before answering. It was a question he had anticipated, but still hated to answer. He knew it was something reporters *had* to ask, but it still annoyed him to no end. He also knew that they already knew the answer, but they wanted him to give them an emotional sound bite that would play well on the 6:00 P.M. news. Morgan took a deep breath and decided to give them what they wanted this time.

"The family has shown remarkable strength and re-solve," he said. "They are certainly anxious. This is a ter-rible thing for them to have to live with."

## Money Talks

August 26, 2003, was a typical sweaty end-of-summer North Carolina day. The cool autumn breezes had not yet begun to take hold in the south as they did in the northeast at this time of year. Heat literally rose from the ground as it baked from almost three months of ninety-degree tem-peratures. The air was laden with heavy humidity, which made it hard to breathe, let alone think.

Carmon Bennett had invited the media to his house for a press conference regarding a reward he was offering for information leading to the arrest of his daughter's killer. A crowd of photographers, reporters, and detectives gathered on the lawn in front of Carmon's modest ranch home. The persistent din of the crowd quieted as Carmon stepped in front of a metal stand with at least a dozen microphones haphazardly attached to it with gray duct tape.

Carmon was a country gentleman with the weathered look of a man who had made an honest living working out-side most of his life. He had a Marlboro Man mustache, sea blue eyes, and a reserved demeanor. It was clear from the way he tentatively glanced down at his notes and then up again at the crowd that public speaking was not one of his favorite things to do. After pausing for a few seconds, he then began to read his prepared statement in front of the throng of microphones and journalists:

"These have been the hardest days of my life, as it has also been for the rest of Stephanie's family and friends. We have felt such loss and grief in her death, but as the days have passed, this has strengthened us in our resolve to see the person responsible for this terrible murder brought to justice. We also fear for the daughters, sisters, wives and girlfriends that remain possible victims of this monster," Carmon read stoically in front of the massive group of microphones.

"Stephanie was such a wonderful young lady, so kind, so loving, so gentle. She gave of herself to so many, who now miss her so deeply. Stephanie had unlimited potential for good that the world has now been robbed of by the person responsible for her death," Carmon said.

Carmon proudly talked about the scholarship fund totaling more than forty-eight thousand dollars that had been raised in Stephanie's name. But he said it was now time to do more. He said the police had told him even more than a year after his daughter's death that someone out there may be holding on to information that could help solve the case. To this end, he said he was offering a one-hundred-thousand-dollar reward for any information leading to the arrest and conviction of the person who took Stephanie's life. This money, he pointed out, was in addition to the ten-thousand-dollar reward already being offered by the state of North Carolina and the local police.

"Again, we pray that if there is someone, *anyone* who has information which might help in identifying this person who so viciously took Stephanie from us, that he or she will now come forward and do what is right." Carmon ended his speech and backed away from the microphones.

Stephanie's mother, Mollie, again hid her eyes behind her large black sunglasses and blended in with the crowd as her ex-husband made his statement. After Carmon finished, Mollie agreed to speak to the media. As she took the sunglasses off in front of the cameras, she revealed red puffy eyes swollen with unending grief.

"It's hard every day to face the fact that Stephanie is not here anymore," she said, pausing to wipe a tear from her cheek. "But it is also hard to feel like someone else's daughter could have the same thing done to her."

## Thankless Thanksgiving

Holidays seem to be the hardest times of the year for the loved ones of murder victims. The loss is almost unbearable when they start planning for the big day and realize there will be an empty spot at their dinner table, not to mention a giant hole in their hearts.

Stephanie's mother, Mollie, chose November 2003 to put a letter addressed to the public about her family's tragedy in the local Raleigh newspaper. The letter to the editor appeared in the *News and Observer* just after Thanksgiving:

"It has been over a year and a half since my daughter, my best friend, was taken from me.

"A year and a half of pain and never-ending ache deep inside my soul that cannot be filled. I have lived through another Thanksgiving without the presence of her smile," Mollie began.

Mollie described the upcoming Christmas in miserable terms—a tree with no presents underneath it labeled to her dead daughter, a day without joy.

"Now imagine a lifetime of Christmas mornings. The loneliness is all-consuming, it never ends," Mollie said.

Mollie went on to say that no matter how hard she tried, she still could not face the fact that Stephanie was not coming back. She still on occasion caught herself picking up the phone to call her daughter, and then realized that Stephanie was gone. Now, all Mollie had left were the "priceless memories" of her daughter and the wonderful times they had shared together.

"Stephanie's death was so brutal and senseless. Maybe, in time, I could have accepted a car accident or disease as a reason for my loss. My heart struggles for understanding even while my mind knows that I will never find it. I know that my Stephanie isn't any different than everyone else's daughter; my loss isn't any more painful that anyone else's loss, but I need answers. Please contact me—" Mollie said, ending her emotional letter to the editor.

Mollie included her mailing address at the end of the letter. She wasn't exactly sure what kind of feedback she would get—clues to help solve the crime? Sympathy from other parents who had lost children? But she was desperate to keep the case in the public eye and saw no better way than to reach out to the Raleigh community directly in a letter asking for their help.

Mollie was amazed when she received dozens of responses from people who were touched by her letter in the newspaper. She was relieved Raleigh residents still seemed to be keeping up with the case even though so much time had passed. She received a wide variety of responses from a wide range of people—from empathetic parents to North Carolina lawmakers who vowed to do whatever they could to push the investigation forward.

"I was just really shocked at the amount of people that wrote letters," Mollie said in an interview with WRAL. "Because I did get a lot, a *lot* of letters."

But it was more than just a kind response she was hoping for; Mollie was praying her letter would prompt someone with relevant information in the case to come forward.

"There's somebody somewhere that knows who did this. To me—he's had to talk to somebody," Mollie said firmly through pursed lips. "How do you walk down the street every day knowing you've done what you've done without talking to somebody?"

Like Carmon Bennett, Mollie Hodges wouldn't rest until she saw justice done for her precious daughter, no matter how long it took.

# CHAPTER SIX

# Cold Case

## April 2004

Creativity requires the courage to let go of certainties.

—ERICH FROMM

To the public, the Stephanie Bennett case may have looked cold by April 2004, as the second anniversary of Stephanie's murder approached, but to Detective Ken Copeland, it was an opportunity to prove everyone wrong. There was nothing he wanted more than to solve the case.

Copeland had recently been assigned to the Major Crimes Task Force—the unit that handled all homicides in the city of Raleigh. Previously, he had been on the fringes of the Bennett investigation as part of the Special Victims Unit. When Lieutenant Chris Morgan had first asked Copeland to assist the homicide detectives, Copeland had worked on the cold case in between his regular duties. But now, Copeland was officially assigned to the case as a homicide detective, his dream job, and he was ready to hit the ground running.

As a patrol officer, Copeland had responded to many homicides in uniform. At that time, his job was to help maintain the crime scene by putting up yellow tape and securing the boundaries so that no one could enter except the detectives. He was literally on the outside looking in, standing on the edge of the yellow crime scene tape, watching the detectives go about their business, waiting for the day when he would be the one *inside* the perimeter of the yellow tape calling the shots.

"I always wanted to be the one putting the clues together on the other side. I am now that person," Copeland said with pride.

Copeland also had a new secret weapon to help him in the Bennett case—Detective Jackie Taylor. Taylor had transferred from Raleigh's District 21 to join the Major Crimes Task Force at the Raleigh Police Department's downtown headquarters. At forty-two years old, Taylor had become the self-proclaimed "mother" over the homicide unit. But there was nothing motherly about her skills as a cop. She was tough as nails.

Taylor was raised with her brother and sister in West Virginia by a single mother after her father died in a coal mining accident when she was just a little girl. She had watched her mother struggle to give her and her siblings the best life she possibly could. This made Taylor into a strong woman who wanted to build a strong future for herself.

Taylor came to Raleigh in the early 1980s with a roommate, not unlike Stephanie Bennett, to begin her life there. After a stint working as a receptionist in a dentist's office, another friend gave her an application for the Raleigh Police Department, and that was it. Taylor was hooked. She had found her calling in the most unlikely place—law enforcement.

Bright and personable, Taylor moved up through the ranks of the predominantly male police force with no glass ceiling in sight. After being hired as a patrol officer in 1986, she eventually became an officer in the Drug Abuse Resistance Education Unit, and then a detective in 1999, the same day Copeland, her future partner, was also promoted to detective. She had worked in the Commercial Burglary Unit until she was transferred to the Major Crimes Task Force in 2004. That's where Taylor found her niche—problem solving, figuring things out, getting people to tell her things.

Taylor became legendary for her interviewing skills. Witnesses, and sometimes even suspects, seemed to open up to her in ways they wouldn't normally for other detectives.

"She is the best in the interview room," Copeland said of his partner. "Her famous line is, 'What would your mama think?'"

With her short, blond, no-nonsense haircut, kind face, and easygoing southern drawl, Taylor had a way of putting people at ease. As the mother of two children, including a daughter, she felt compelled to seek justice for Stephanie and her family. This was exactly the kind of partner Copeland needed to help him solve the case. They balanced each other out and finished each other's sentences like an old married couple.

Taylor and Copeland had worked on a rash of burglaries together when they first became detectives. Right away, the two developed a special rapport. They watched each other's backs. They also laughed a lot, especially after a draining thirty-six-hour shift.

"She would speak what I was thinking and vice versa. It was kind of spooky," Copeland said with a grin.

As a team, along with Clem Perry's guidance as the sergeant in charge of the task force, Detective Ken Copeland felt like they finally had a shot at finding Stephanie Bennett's killer.

## Wading In

The sheer volume of information that had been collected in the Stephanie Bennett case and put into large three-ring binders was enough to send any good detective running in the other direction.

"It was overwhelming," said Sergeant Perry, who was supervising Taylor and Copeland. Perry's biggest fear was that with so many leads still coming in, they would miss the *one* lead they desperately needed to solve the case. "If we overlooked just one of these lead sheets we're going to miss the guy. You would always wonder going home in the afternoon, is that the one that's going to break this case open?"

Perry also worried that the pattern of eliminating suspects, while a good philosophy, never allowed them to focus in on any potential suspects. Perry knew the elimination process was taking its toll on investigators working the case.

"It was very discouraging day in and day out to come to work, go out and swab three people, and when you left you got the feeling they had *nothing* to do with it," Copeland said.

Taylor and Copeland decided it was time to take a look at the case with fresh eyes. They had a way of working together, picking up on what the other one missed, that made a new perspective on the case possible. They went back to the beginning.

"There was one person who lived out there that was brought to the police department's attention, and that was the Peeping Tom," Copeland said. But they didn't have a name. "They call him 'Tom.'"

The way the detectives saw the case, they had had the DNA since day one, but it hadn't gotten them anywhere. It was the perfect evidence, but it wasn't doing them any good until they pinpointed a suspect.

"Having great evidence is only as good as the suspect you have to go with it," said Taylor. "We didn't have one."

With Copeland's background in handling sex crimes, he knew it was unusual that their suspect could not be tied to any other similar crimes anywhere else in the country before Stephanie's murder. He also found it unusual that the killer's DNA was not connected to any cases that had occurred since Stephanie's murder. Copeland was baffled; in his experience people like Stephanie's killer didn't just do this kind of thing one time.

"We thought someone that could plan, actually commit it with such brutality, that surely he had done this somewhere else before," Copeland said.

The Combined DNA Index System, known as CODIS, was used to cross-reference offenders in violent crimes throughout the country. It included DNA from known offenders, and it also included DNA from crimes for which the identity of the attacker was unknown. That DNA could be used to link crimes together, even without the identity of the suspect. The DNA from Stephanie's apartment wasn't linked to *any* of these cases.

Copeland and Taylor were open to anything. They decided to go back to one of the now-retired original detectives on the case, Sandy Culpepper, and ask her if she had any notes that might help. Unlike the voluminous case files at the Raleigh Police Department, Culpepper gave her colleagues a more streamlined version of the case, including a timeline created by another detective, Norman Grodai. The timeline indicated there were interviews with six people after the murder who had spoken specifically about the Peeping Tom. This caught Copeland and Taylor's eye. Although the Peeping Tom had long ago been abandoned as the prime suspect, the detectives just couldn't shake the feeling they needed to re-visit this theory.

"What is the likelihood that you got one person peeping on this girl, and then somebody else is going to come in and murder her?" Taylor said. "You have to be reasonable."

Based on his experience in the Special Victims Unit, Copeland said, "Most sex crimes are progressive. You start as a Peeping Tom, or you start as exposing yourself, and eventually you work your way up to those things that happened to Stephanie."

The detectives picked Culpepper's brain, trying to glean any bit of information that might help them get some leverage in the case. She helped them zero back in on the Peeping Tom from what she had learned in the early stages of the investigation.

As a result, Copeland and Taylor started looking at every Peeping Tom case in the area. They also again went back to looking at every minor sex crime as Copeland had done when he worked on the Bennett case as part of the Special Victims Unit. No case with a sexual component was too insignificant to consider as having a possible connection to the Stephanie Bennett homicide. On one occasion, they even followed up on a burglary case at an adult gift store, thinking the burglar might have been after more than just cash.

To the surprise of many of the petty criminals they arrested for minor sex crimes, the detectives would bring them down to the main police station and ask them point-blank if they had anything to do with Stephanie Bennett's murder.

"They would say, 'I ain't got *nothing* to do with that,'" Copeland said. They would then gladly submit to a DNA test in order to positively eliminate themselves as suspects in Stephanie's murder. After this experience, they were usually only too happy to cop to the original misdemeanor they'd been charged with.

One warm evening in the late spring of 2004, the detectives went back to the Bridgeport Apartments and stood in the parking lot in the darkness. They wanted to see what kind of view a Peeping Tom would have from this location. They couldn't believe what they could see from their very public vantage point. Windows were open everywhere they looked. Blinds and shades were also open, offering wide glimpses directly into many people's apartments. Women sat alone on couches in their nightgowns watching television in plain view of anyone standing outside under the cloak of darkness.

"We went, 'Oh my goodness, this is unbelievable,'" Perry said.

"It was a target-rich environment for anyone who had some sexual perversions," Copeland said.

Taylor and Copeland decided it was time to get busy and find this monster before he hurt somebody else. They divided up the group of six people from Culpepper's file who had spoken about the Peeping Tom and went back and reinterviewed them. Those six people gave them the names of others to talk to. Those people in turn gave them more names. Suddenly, the case was going from freezing cold to very warm.

## Two Years

"This was the murder of a totally innocent person which made it stand out in my mind above the others," WRAL photographer Chad Flowers said as he recalled when heading to Virginia to interview Stephanie Bennett's parents two years after her murder. "Even though I don't usually get emotionally involved in the cases I cover, this one got to me."

Carmon Bennett's home in Rocky Mount, Virginia, had the living room set up as a shrine to Stephanie. Pictures of her were peeking out from almost every space.

"Every one of them showed a smiling, happy Stephanie," Flowers said, remembering the discomfort he felt every time he walked through the Bennett house, on the way to the sunroom in the back where Carmon preferred to conduct interviews.

On the kitchen table sat a vase of purple tulips, Stephanie's favorite flowers. The Bennetts always kept tulips on their table in her honor. In front of the vase was a framed picture of Stephanie in a red sweater, looking down. Stephanie had been a demure, humble young woman who shied away from attention, but attracted it nevertheless, because of her exceptionally beautiful qualities.

During the interview, Carmon sat on a faded green couch. The rolling hills stretched out in front of him endlessly, disappearing into the horizon. He wore his traditional southern businessman uniform—a yellow golf shirt, jeans, and cowboy boots. He propped one leg across the other one in what might have been interpreted as a casual move, but his serious face and weary eyes told a different story. He answered each question, but provided little or no elaboration.

"The main thing is just why? She was so undeserving of this," Carmon said as the two-year anniversary of his daughter's murder approached. "She had a life in front of her, and it's just tragically taken away for someone's sickness." One day Carmon Bennett was living a happy, quiet life in Virginia, building houses, proud of the life he had built and the children he had raised. Then suddenly, his daughter was murdered, and the life he knew was gone forever. "It's just a very tough situation to be in, and one that you never dreamed you would be in," Carmon said wearily as he reiterated a statement he had probably made dozens of times before.

No matter how this family tried to fill their lives after Stephanie's death, they would always be incomplete. They could put the pain aside for brief moments and enjoy life, but the grief was too palpable for them to ignore for any real amount of time. It weighed them down to the point that even the simplest tasks, like eating, making a telephone call, or driving, became a chore.

"Time has healed some of the wounds, not totally, I don't think it ever will," Carmon said. Stephanie's birthday, April 30, was just a few days away. She would have been twenty-five years old. "I just hope that another family doesn't have to go through and suffer what we have."

Stephanie's mother felt similarly. "People tell me all the time that time will take care of it. For me time has not helped any. Each day just gets a little harder," Mollie Hodges said, dabbing the corners of her eyes with a tissue as she talked about the case to WRAL just before the second anniversary of Stephanie's murder.

Although two years had passed, in a single second Mollie could be transported back to the day she learned her only daughter had been murdered.

"It's a nightmare. It's a total nightmare. When I got the call that Stephanie hadn't reported for work that day the most awful feeling just went through me," Mollie said. "It just tears the deepest hole in your heart, and it's a hole that will *never* be filled.

"There won't be any telephone calls saying, 'Happy Birthday, Stephanie,'" Mollie said with more bitterness than sorrow this time. "No presents, no birthday cake, no party—all I'll get to do is visit her grave and wish her a happy birthday."

Stephanie had been laid to rest between Carmon's brother and cousin in Franklin Memorial Park. She was buried beneath a flat bronze marker that held only her name, "Stephanie R. Bennett," and the dates she'd lived, "April 30, 1979–May 21, 2002." There was nothing else to say on a grave marker about a young life cut tragically short.

While the markers were all flat and flush with the ground, Stephanie's stood out because there was a small white stone statue of a praying angel next to her grave. It was a fitting tribute to a girl who by all accounts had expressed angel-like qualities in the way she had lived her life.

Mollie hadn't moved on as some people had expected her to. But those people obviously didn't know what it was like to lose a child. Sure, she got up and went to work every day and went through all of the motions of daily life, but she was a woman with a major void in her life who couldn't find anything to fill it with. There were moments she could put the pain aside and appear normal when she really needed to, but in reality, Mollie was permanently wounded.

"To lose your child," she said, "It's just unexplainable."

Mollie's biggest concern was that the killer was still out there and could harm someone else. She said it was a thought that made it difficult for her to sleep at night. Her head never hit the pillow without praying to God no one else would be killed by this evil man.

"Don't think that it can't happen to your daughter, your sister, or your mother or whoever because we never thought it would happen to us either, but it did, and he's still out there, and it bothers me a lot just knowing that he is and he could strike anybody anytime again," Mollie said. "It's hard every day thinking this person, this mean person that did what he did to Stephanie is still out roaming the streets."

## Morgan on Deck

"Chris Morgan is wonderful. He assured me he would find [the killer] and would not give up until he did," Mollie said. "I've put my faith in Chris Morgan. I've put my faith in God. I pray every night that we find him."

Once again a victim's family was relying on Lieutenant Morgan to solve the case for them. It was a big responsibility, and one he took seriously. But he always feared he would not be able to come through for them. The Bennett case was one of those cases that no matter how hard he tried he sensed might not be solved before he retired. His plans had been to leave in the spring of 2004, but the date was pushed to the summer because he was just finishing up another high-profile case in which a woman named Ann Miller was suspected of poisoning her husband with arsenic. *That* case was close to being solved. They knew who did it; they just needed the final piece of evidence. In Morgan's mind, the Bennett case wasn't even close. His gut told him to hang in there and postpone his retirement yet again, but he wasn't sure it would make a difference.

"You've done everything you can do in this case. It's been suggested to us that we wait until we get a phone call. We're not content to do that. We don't believe it's fair to the victim, or the victim's family, or to other people who might be victimized by the perpetrator in this case," Morgan said on the second anniversary of Stephanie's murder.

They were still following up on every tip on a daily basis, Morgan told reporters, but reading between the lines it was clear that they had nothing, *absolutely nothing.* They were no closer to solving the case than they had been on the very first day.

"A constant relentless pursuit of the truth and the person who is responsible for this terrible crime," Morgan said as he characterized the investigation. "We're dealing with what appears to be a very organized offender. Organized offenders don't make a large number of mistakes."

And so far it appeared the killer had made few, if any, mistakes, given the fact that he was still a free man. Like the permanent grief etched on Carmon's and Mollie's faces, there was a combination of determination and anxiety on Morgan's face too.

"It's just something that you can never put down, and you have to keep working on it out of a sense of duty to the victim and the family," he said with firm resolution.

## Angel on Tape

On the second anniversary of Stephanie Bennett's murder the Raleigh Police Department released a home video of her to the media. The goal of the release was simple—keep the case in the public eye and maybe someone will come forward with information. What better way to do that than by showing a video of the beautiful girl-next-door whose life was tragically snuffed out by a sexual predator? Nothing else had worked; why not try to tug on the heartstrings of the public in an effort to get someone with information to come forward?

The video aired on every local television station in the Raleigh area. The first clip was labeled "Summer 1996." It showed Stephanie sitting on the floor in an oversize white T-shirt with her legs crossed. Her hair was up in a short ponytail bound by a blue scrunchie. She was perched over a suitcase folding clothes, either in the act of packing or unpacking.

In the following clip Stephanie was playing a tune on an electric organ in her father's den. Her brown shoulder-length hair was down this time, and she wore a white, short-sleeved V-neck sweater, a black skirt with white flowers on it, and sandals. She looked young and carefree as she reluctantly performed for the camera.

After she finished at the organ, Stephanie stood up in front of the camera nervously clapping and snapping, never making eye contact with the person who was taping her. Finally, she said in a soft voice tinged with a strong southern accent, "Can we go now?"

The third clip was labeled "Christmas 1996." In it Stephanie and Dee Powell sat on the couch shoulder to shoulder. Stephanie wore a white turtleneck, a bright green V-neck sweater, and jeans. Her legs were crossed casually and there was a wide grin on her face. Dee was trying to coax Stephanie into looking at the camera. Ever the bashful subject, Stephanie kept turning away. Finally, she looked at the person behind the camera, giggled like the schoolgirl she was, and said in the same syrupy voice from earlier, "You look like Rudolph!"

"High School Graduation 1997" was the next title on the screen. Stephanie, wearing a red cap with a yellow tassel on it and a gown with a large white collar, made her way across the stage. In this segment of the video Stephanie's hair was now cut fashionably short in a sophisticated bob. She stood next to her father, Carmon Bennett, in her cap and gown with a smile on her face from ear to ear. It looked like she was probably posing for a still photograph while the video was rolling. Then she stood next to Dee, who also graduated that day, their arms around each other, both proudly holding their diplomas in their free hands.

The following scene was shot in Carmon's house after the graduation ceremony. It showed Stephanie looking mature and elegant in a slim black cocktail dress with white trim. She was standing idly at the kitchen counter. It captured one of those awkward moments in home videos in which no one is really doing anything, but the videographer insists on rolling tape until something does happen.

Someone then asked Stephanie from behind the camera whether she wanted to see the graduation video. In a low, breathy voice she said, "Yeah, I do."

Stephanie then joined Dee at the table to read graduation cards. The girls whispered and laughed quietly, sharing confidences as they each separately read through their individual stacks of cards. It was clear from the scene that they had shared a deep bond of friendship well before they ever became stepsisters.

The final clip was a continuation of the first one on the tape. Stephanie had her hair up, and she was sitting down as the camera moved in for a tight shot on her Noxzema-girl face. This time she was clearly avoiding the camera.

Finally, she turned toward the lens and the person behind the camera said something about her hating to have the focus be on her, and just above a whisper Stephanie said, "I do."

## House of Horrors

After the home videos, the tape contained video of the crime scene taken by a police officer in Stephanie's apartment on May 21, 2002, the day her body was found. The two-year-old tape had been in evidence since the very first day, but no one other than investigators had ever seen it before. Once again, while it had little relevance when it came to solving the crime, the goal was to get the public's attention, and it was hoped, make someone come forward with information.

The camera started outside the apartment and then went inside and moved down the hallway to Emily Metro's bedroom. The sight of Stephanie's body on the floor had been digitally covered, to prevent the disturbing image from being seen on television.

Raleigh Police Department psychologist Michael Teague said there were things the video *didn't* show. He was specifically interested in a framed photograph Emily told police had originally been facing the bedroom door. When Stephanie's body was found, the frame was on the floor at the edge of the closet facing the wall.

"There was something about the scene [the killer] liked, something he didn't like, so he put it in the closet. There was some stuff on the windowsill he put away. Some stuff on the bed he put in the closet. He was a director," Teague said. "He was staging the scene. He was definitely staging the scene."

These details only added to Teague's firm belief the crime may have been videotaped as it occurred—a theory it should be noted that Detective Copeland never bought into and that Lieutenant Morgan was ambivalent about. But Teague was convinced that the killer had documented his gruesome deeds.

"As Ted Bundy said, 'You would never go to all this trouble without taking pictures,'" Teague said.

In the video of Emily's bedroom a sheer curtain hung from the window. The bed was neatly made, with a patch-work quilt and blanket folded at the foot of the bed. Nothing obvious appeared to be disturbed or out of place. In fact, the room was so neat it was hard to believe a brutal attack had taken place there.

The videographer then moved across the hallway and zoomed in on Stephanie's tidy bedroom. The bed covers were meticulously pulled back and folded on the floor at the foot of her bed. A quick scan of the room by the camera revealed the teddy bears on Stephanie's bureau and the Harry Potter book on the night stand, further reminders that Stephanie was still in limbo between childhood and adulthood.

The video gave no answers but left the viewer with one overwhelming feeling: Stephanie Bennett didn't deserve to die.

## Civil Justice

In the absence of justice in the criminal system, families of murder victims often look for other ways to vindicate their loved ones. Some set up websites and solicit the public to help them solve the case. Others get involved in promoting legislation to change the way our criminal courts work. But the most common catharsis for these families is the wrongful death lawsuit.

The families can sue the actual suspect, if there is one, even if that person has not been charged. For example, this happened in the O.J. Simpson case when the family of Ron Goldman sued and was awarded damages from Simpson even though the ex-football player was found not guilty in a criminal courtroom.

But if there is no suspect, families sometimes choose to sue a third party whose negligence may have contributed to their loved one's death.

On May 19, 2004, Carmon Bennett filed a lawsuit against the company that owned and operated the Bridgeport Apartments, Equity Residential, based in Chicago, Illinois. In the lawsuit, Carmon alleged the complex failed to protect his daughter and was therefore negligent in her death. He cited the fact that after the Peeping Tom incident was brought to the apartment management's attention, they did not notify the residents of the potential danger lurking in their neighborhood. The lawsuit also stated that the situation was further aggravated by the fact there had been multiple crimes reported in the area around the time of the Peeping Tom incident. It alleged these crimes should have made the apartment management more concerned about security. Records showed the police had been called to the area nearly a thousand times in the two and a half years before Stephanie's murder. Not only did Bridgeport not notify tenants about the Peeping Tom but, the lawsuit said, they took no extra security measures, in light of the peeper incident and other recent crimes, to protect their residents.

The lawsuit also alleged that high shrubbery and poor lighting around the complex gave the killer an opportunity to watch Stephanie under the cloak of darkness and to break into her apartment without being noticed by neighbors.

The most specific allegation in the lawsuit involved the window in Emily Metro's bedroom where Stephanie's body had been found. Because the maintenance employee of the apartment believed the door was dead-bolted when he opened it, investigators assumed the window was the most logical point of entry for the killer. Carmon Bennett maintained the window was unlocked because the lock was in fact broken and had been broken for some time. The maintenance staff of the apartment complex had been previously notified about the window lock, but in the lawsuit, Carmon said it was never properly fixed.

Publicly, Carmon Bennett said nothing about the lawsuit. But one didn't have to be a lawyer to realize he was trying to make damn sure his daughter's death was not in vain.

## Passing the Torch

"He had become such a close friend. He had worked so hard on it," Mollie Hodges said sadly after learning of Chris Morgan's upcoming retirement. "He's so concerned."

Lieutenant Morgan had vowed to himself and to Stephanie's parents he would not retire until he got justice for their daughter. But after almost thirty years on the job, the last four years spent doggedly pursuing Ann Miller, who was suspected of poisoning her husband, Morgan was worn out and ready to go. Miller was going to be indicted for murder. Morgan's work was done on that case until he was called to testify at trial. The Bennett investigation up until this point had gone nowhere, and he knew in his heart it might never be solved, no matter how many years he continued to work on the case. Yet, he had such a close relationship with Carmon, he felt like he had to tell him about his impending retirement in person and try to make the transition as smooth as possible. Morgan felt he owed him that.

With Detective J. J. Mathews getting ready to make sergeant, Morgan needed to officially assign a new lead detective to the Bennett case before he left so he could make sure it was in good hands. Copeland had already worked on the case extensively, first with the Special Victims Unit, and then as a detective newly assigned to the Major Crimes Task Force. In Morgan's mind, it was a no-brainer—Copeland was the guy to take the reins. Morgan told Perry he wanted Copeland to take the lead on the case.

"I told Clem, 'He's a garbage man. He's going to go through every scrap, every piece of crap that we threw away and maybe he'll find something,' " recalled Morgan.

Morgan said not everyone above him agreed with his choice, but he knew it was the right one, and luckily Perry agreed. After all, it wasn't the first time higher-ups had questioned Morgan's judgment.

To make the handoff go smoothly, Morgan decided it was time to introduce Carmon Bennett to the team that would be handling the case when he retired. Carmon was not a man who easily trusted people, and Morgan needed to make sure he was going to be comfortable dealing with new investigators. Even though many other detectives had worked on the case all along, Morgan, as the leader of the Major Crimes Task Force, had always been Carmon's point person.

In June 2004, Lieutenant Morgan took Perry and Copeland with him up to Carmon and Jennifer Bennett's house in Rocky Mount. Above all else, Morgan wanted the Bennett family to know they would not be forgotten just because he was retiring. Morgan felt it was his responsibility to make sure Carmon had confidence in Perry and Copeland, if the grieving father was going to continue having a good relationship with the Raleigh Police Department.

Carmon had gotten so used to dealing with Morgan it was hard for him to imagine himself working with other detectives. Morgan was the guy he could call at 3:00 in the morning when he couldn't sleep just to talk about the case.

When they came through the door of the Bennett home, Carmon immediately made it clear that he remembered Perry from the day Stephanie's body was found. Perry was the one who had initially approached Carmon at the crime scene and kept him at bay until Morgan could speak to him directly. Perry wasn't sure if that memory would bode well for him. He represented Carmon's first contact with the police the night he found out his daughter was dead. He was nervous that Carmon would hold it against him and not give him a chance.

During the meeting in Virginia, Carmon pulled Morgan aside and asked him if the fresh-faced young cops were really old enough to be detectives. Morgan assured Carmon not only were they old enough but they were good, and they would take care of his family and the case.

"Clem is one of the most brilliant, effective detectives you could ever hope to have working on your case, and Copeland is too," Morgan told Stephanie's father.

Later, Morgan would look back on the decision to leave the Bennett case in the hands of these capable detectives as one of the best moves he ever made. As it turned out, he was right.

# CHAPTER SEVEN

# Finding the Needle

## February 2005

No question is so difficult to answer as that to which the answer is obvious.

—GEORGE BERNARD SHAW

The six people named in former detective Sandy Culpepper's file turned out to be just the leads Detectives Ken Copeland and Jackie Taylor were looking for. The witnesses all had one thing in common: they had *seen the Peeping Tom*. After years of the investigation gravitating away from the theory of the Peeping Tom as the logical suspect, it was once again slowly moving back in that direction.

The detectives interviewed the six people, and those people gave them the names of other potential witnesses who might have also seen the peeper. Quickly, they started to develop a clearer picture of the suspect.

Psychologist Michael Teague admitted he too had moved away from the Peeping Tom theory. He had been convinced the killer was someone with military experience and maybe someone who didn't necessarily live in the area, but perhaps only traveled through. Teague felt that the killer's talented use of restraints and the way he was able to subdue his victim quickly without causing her more injuries might point to a military background. Also, because the killer had been so elusive, Teague thought maybe he was someone who had been deployed for periods of time during which he could not offend. Clearly, the Peeping Tom was more likely to be someone local. After Taylor and Copeland got on the case and started rethinking this angle, Teague did as well.

"Not all peepers rape, but just about all stranger rapists do peep," said Teague in hindsight.

The most defining interview, as it related to the theory that the killer could be the Peeping Tom, was with a Czechoslovakian man named Blaze Szalay who also lived in the Bridgeport Apartments. In an early interview with police, Szalay told investigators he had seen the Peeping Tom crouched down near Stephanie's window just a few weeks before she was killed. It happened early one morning while Szalay was walking his dog. The initial description he'd given investigators was very general, not enough for them to go on. But when Copeland called Szalay back three years later, he was able to get more information out of the man with a little creative probing.

"I asked him if he remembered the case. I asked him if he remembered seeing the Peeping Tom. He said, 'Yes, like it was yesterday,'" Copeland remembered, recalling his excitement that they were finally onto something.

Szalay described a dark figure, a tall skinny man, looking into Stephanie's bedroom window on the end of the building. Szalay told Copeland that when the man saw him, the peeper then retreated out of the shadows and slid down the side of the building in an effort to sneak away quickly without being seen up close.

Szalay told Copeland he was curious as to what the man was doing, so he followed him around to the front of the building where he spotted him again. With a little light on him this time, Szalay got a better look. He said the man was wearing a dark-colored hooded sweatshirt.

Szalay then told Copeland he had seen the man *again*. It was a few days later, and he saw the same man he believed to be the Peeping Tom walking a big brown or black dog, possibly a rottweiler, through the apartment complex parking lot.

"I told my wife, you see that guy right there? He's bad news, look out for him," Szalay told Copeland.

Szalay also told Copeland that the man walked back through the woods toward the neighboring Dominion Apartments. Originally, everyone had assumed the killer had come from the trail around Lake Lynn—but now they had a new lead. The Dominion Apartments were just fifty yards through the woods from Stephanie's front door. This was consistent with what the other people who had seen the Peeping Tom had said—that he was either walking toward Dominion, or actually on the Dominion property. To get back to the lake, the man would have gone in a completely different direction, through the Bridgeport parking lot which bordered the path along the water.

Finally, they had a possible suspect, and they thought they knew where he lived. Now they just needed a name.

## Seek Local Knowledge

Good cops know they can get ten times more information by chatting with people than they will with a subpoena, not to mention getting the story in a timelier manner. Subpoenas can be used later to get the information on the record in a public document that can be used in court. But before getting a subpoena, the police have to know exactly what they're looking for. As soon as Copeland and Taylor had the lead about the suspect possibly living in the Dominion

Apartments, they decided it was time to get to know the people who worked there.

The detectives paid a few visits to the Dominion on Lake Lynn Apartments—the official name of the complex. They were always greeted warmly and would casually sit and eat cookies, drink sweet tea, and shoot the breeze with the people who worked in the main office. Since Carmon Bennett had filed the civil lawsuit against Bridgeport Apartments, investigators were pretty much banned from that office because the management had been told by their attorneys not to speak to *anyone,* not even the police.

The day Detective Copeland talked to Blaze Szalay, he decided it was time to go to Dominion and get some real answers. Copeland said he and Detective Taylor chatted for a few minutes with the ladies in the office and then he casually dropped the bomb, "Who is the white guy with the rottweiler?"

"It was like a record had scratched. It was silent. I'll never forget it. It was kind of eerie," Copeland said. Suddenly, a woman appeared out of the back room.

"His name is Drew Planten and he's a strange bird," she said.

She described Planten to detectives as being tall and skinny with long shaggy brown hair. She added he was "frail looking." The woman told the detectives Planten used to live at Dominion, but had moved out about a year ago. She said he did have a large rottweiler that he often walked around the complex.

Copeland and Taylor were excited, but they tried not to show it. For the first time in months they had a promising lead, but they had been disappointed so many times before that they didn't want to get their hopes up. They glanced at each other and their eyes locked. Without saying a word each one knew what the other was thinking. *Hold it in. Act casual. This could be it. Or it may not be. Don't blow it.*

Copeland changed the subject and casually asked the

office workers if they knew of any "nosy neighbors," someone who had lived at Dominion forever and was into everyone's business. The office staff pointed the detectives in
the direction of an older woman in the complex who had
lived there a long time and seemed to always be in the loop
on all of the latest gossip.

Copeland and Taylor moved swiftly out of the office and
headed for the woman's apartment. Once they were safely
away from the office, they both smiled, but they knew they
had to remain focused. *Keep it together. Keep cool.*

The detectives knocked on the woman's door, identified
themselves as police officers, and were cordially invited
inside. They sat on the woman's couch and chatted with her
for a few minutes to put her at ease—or maybe to put themselves at ease—before they started probing their new lead.
Then the investigators got down to business. They told the
woman they were investigating the murder of Stephanie
Bennett.

"Ya'll ain't arrested nobody yet? I thought everybody
knew the man with the dog did it," the woman exclaimed
to the stunned detectives.

Copeland remembers being so shocked about hearing
this bold declaration that he literally felt his jaw drop open.
He wanted to jump right up and run out and find this guy.
But there was work to do, a lot more work to do. First, he
had to finish hearing the woman out.

"Everybody knows the man that used to walk the dog
around here is the one killed that girl," the woman reiterated, in case they hadn't heard her the first time. She left no
room for interpretation about what she had said.

Taylor was also flabbergasted by the simple, direct way
that the woman told them the dog walker, a.k.a. Drew
Planten, was the killer. All Taylor could think about was,
*Why had no one ever looked at this guy before? If this lady
knew about him, why didn't the Raleigh Police?*

The woman went on to tell the detectives that she would

stand around with other residents in the parking lot and talk about the strange man and his possible connection to the murder. They asked her when these conversations took place—she said she wasn't sure, but she remembered one detail: The crime scene tape had still been up. Crime scene tape is only up for a few days after the murder, at best. The neighbors had been talking about this character *three years ago.*

Both detectives looked at each other in amazement. They couldn't believe they were just now hearing this critical information. Too much time had been wasted looking everywhere *except* in Stephanie Bennett's backyard. Copeland and Taylor vowed not to waste one more minute.

## Picture This

Like all good detectives who always crossed their T's and dotted their I's, Detectives Ken Copeland and Jackie Taylor then prepared a subpoena for the tenant records at the Dominion Apartments. From those records they were able to determine that Drew Planten had in fact lived at the apartment complex in May 2002 when Stephanie Bennett was murdered. The records also revealed something else— tenants had to list all pets on their leases, and Planten's lease indicated that he owned a rottweiler.

Copeland and Taylor received a picture of Drew Planten from the Division of Motor Vehicles (DMV). One immediate conflict that they had to contend with was that the original report of the Peeping Tom that led to the composite involved a man with short hair, and yet Planten's driver's license photograph showed him with shoulder-length light brown hair. Copeland slid the DMV picture next to the composite on his desk to compare the two.

"This doesn't look very promising. Look at it," Copeland said to Taylor as he put the pictures side by side.

In the DMV picture, Planten looked like someone out of a grunge rock band, but the man in the composite looked clean-cut and preppy. Once again, the double-edged sword of using a composite was revealed. Copeland said because the composite didn't have long hair, the people who had seen the long-haired dog walker never came forward because they were convinced it wasn't the same man as the Peeping Tom. It wasn't until Copeland and Taylor re-interviewed these people that they discovered there was a connection between the peeper, who could've had his long hair tucked into his hooded sweatshirt, and the dog walker.

The detectives used a computer program to shorten Planten's hair in the photograph and compare it with the original composite. But as many times as Copeland put the pictures side by side, he simply couldn't tell if it was the same person. One minute he was sure it was the same man. The next minute he was sure it was not. He wanted the pictures to match so badly that he suspected his eyes were playing tricks on him on the days when they appeared to be similar.

"It didn't excite us a lot when we saw his picture. We'd been disappointed on so many things," Copeland said wearily.

Meanwhile, several other cases cropped up that seemed to have potential connections to the Bennett case. There was a sex offender from whom they had previously taken a DNA sample who then killed himself in a field in Johnston County just outside of Raleigh. At the time of his suicide his DNA sample had yet to be tested. After his suicide, they put a rush on the test. Unfortunately, it came back with the same answer they had seen so many times before—no match.

Then there was a man who had moved out of Stephanie's apartment building around the time she was killed. Copeland said the man left behind a bunch of sex toys. They tracked him all the way to the Philippines and were able to get a DNA sample from him. The sex toys and the timing of his move were big red flags. But once again—no match.

"We had a few cases like that where we would get our hopes up," Sergeant Clem Perry said, only to have them dashed.

Copeland said Planten's picture sat on his desk for several weeks as he worked on other cases and tried not to get too pumped up about the possibilities. As long as the picture sat there, Copeland could tell himself they had not exhausted all of their leads. But the second they ruled Planten out, they would be back to what they had had all along. Nothing.

"People would walk in and say, 'Who is this guy?' I'd say, 'Nobody,'" Copeland recalled as he tried to brush off any inkling that he and Taylor might be onto something when other detectives saw Planten's picture on his desk. As long as no one had any real expectations of them catching the killer, they couldn't disappoint, right?

In March 2005, Taylor and Copeland went by Planten's apartment seven or eight times in between handling all of the other murder cases piling up on their plate. They discovered that he had moved across town from Dominion to a lower-income apartment complex called the Birchleaf Apartments on Buck Jones Road in West Raleigh. They would be out working on a current case and decide to give it another shot. They would swing by Planten's apartment, knock on his door, and leave their business cards stuck in the door when no one answered. On one hand, they were determined to talk to this guy so that they could either eliminate him or start moving in on him. On the other hand, trying to speak to him at his apartment started to feel like an exercise in futility.

When the detectives knocked on Planten's door, they would hear a dog scratching and whimpering on the other side of the door. The noise would have been too loud for

Planten to ignore if he was home, so they assumed he was simply ignoring them. But hearing the dog gave them a strong feeling that they were looking at the right guy.

"We could actually hear the dog whining behind the door," Copeland said. "So we felt like we were at the right place."

The maintenance man in the apartment complex told the detectives that Planten drove the old rusty Camaro in the parking lot that looked like it couldn't possibly pass inspection, let alone make it down the street. It was almost always parked outside Planten's apartment when the detectives knocked on the door. They went at different times of the day hoping to catch him off guard. Taylor even went by herself one morning around 6:00 and still got no answer.

Clearly, Planten intended to make it difficult for the detectives to speak with him. But they weren't giving up yet, not by a long shot.

## Angry Grief

On what would have been her twenty-sixth birthday, April 30, 2005, Carmon Bennett put roses on Stephanie's grave. He was getting ready to present the third annual college scholarship in Stephanie's name to the tune of twenty-five hundred dollars on the anniversary of her death. The money was raised through an annual golf tournament that had already netted seventy-two thousand dollars since Stephanie's murder. While this was the silver lining that had come out of Stephanie's murder, Carmon said the spring was the hardest time of year for him emotionally.

"Nobody should have to go through this at all," Carmon said, shaking his head. "I think about her on a daily basis. She was such a wonderful young lady."

It was May 16, 2005. Carmon had sat down to do what had become a ritual—an interview with WRAL on the anniversary of his daughter's death. He said even three years after his daughter's murder, he would sometimes forget she was gone. The phone would ring, and, for a split second, he would think, 'It's Stephanie.' But then reality would quickly set in.

"I kind of keep waiting for her to call, and you have that realization that that's not going to happen," Carmon said wistfully, gazing out at the lush green hills and fields in the distance.

Carmon's grief was beginning to have an angry edge to it. He was trying to be patient, to wait for the right lead that would crack the case wide open and bring Stephanie's killer to justice, but it was becoming increasingly harder for him to do with every day that passed.

"Patience, I think, is a good virtue that I don't have a lot of," Carmon said with his trademark matter-of-factness.

Despite his palpable grief, it sounded like there might be something brewing behind the scenes. Carmon said Sergeant Perry was going to release some new details at the third-anniversary press conference scheduled for the following Saturday.

For the first time in years Carmon talked specifically about the investigation and what he thought might have happened in the days leading up to May 21, 2002. In the past, he had always stuck to talking about Stephanie and steered away from the details of the case.

"I believe whoever did this to Stephanie did their home-work real well," Carmon said knowingly. He said he felt like the person was watching Stephanie, perhaps stalking her, and knew her roommates were out of town the night he struck. Carmon believed the killer knew exactly what he was doing and planned his actions very carefully. "Who-ever did this I think had just singled Stephanie out because of her looks and her personality."

Carmon and Perry had been talking. Carmon made a point of saying the press conference would be important to the case. It was clear something was happening behind the scenes. "Somebody has an answer for us," Carmon said with conviction.

Mollie Hodges was wearing a cheerful top with brightly colored stripes that contrasted sharply with her solemn face. She sat in a white plastic chair in the backyard of the daycare center where she worked framed by the swing set in the background and an acre of freshly mowed green grass. The previous year of *still* not knowing exactly what happened to her daughter and why it happened appeared to have taken a toll on Mollie. Her shoulders seemed to be slouching under the weight of her ongoing emotional pain.

"I lost my only daughter," Mollie said resolutely as tears welled up in her eyes, "and she wasn't only my daughter, she was my best friend." Almost immediately she began crying. The interview had to be stopped and started several times until she could regain her composure.

"We just celebrated her birthday and of course," Mollie said before again trailing off into more sobs. "I'm sorry, I thought I could do it," she apologized.

Mollie pulled herself together and started again. She said that she felt the anniversary of her daughter's murder was always the hardest time of year because it fell just after Stephanie's birthday, and just before Mother's Day. On these three days she felt her daughter's absence even more profoundly than usual.

"It's hard being a parent thinking you've lost your child. It's not a normal thing I don't think for a parent to give up their children," Mollie said, sharing the universal truth of all parents who lost a child. "I want them to remember Stephanie as a sweet young girl just starting her life—her life had just begun."

Even after three years of trying to process everything, Mollie still couldn't understand why a young woman with so much ahead of her could have it all taken away so tragically in an instant.

"I would just like to know why, *why* it happened to Stephanie," Mollie said, looking up at the pale blue sky dotted with white fluffy clouds. "I never dreamed anything like this would happen to Stephanie, I just never dreamed it," Mollie said, her voice cracking again as tears streamed down her face.

Mollie had always been sad, but now she too was getting increasingly angry, angry that the man who killed her daughter was still roaming the earth free to possibly hurt someone else.

"It's very frustrating that's he's still out there and that he could attack your mother, your best friend, anybody, anytime," she said with venom in her voice. "There's somebody out there who knows more than what they're telling. They need to come forward."

## Anniversary Presser

On Saturday, May 21, 2005, the third anniversary of Stephanie Bennett's murder, the Raleigh Police Department held a press conference in the hopes of reviving the public's interest in the case. The goal was, as always, to generate fresh leads.

Copeland and Taylor had not given up on Drew Planten, but they had yet to see him face-to-face and were reluctant to put all of their eggs into that one basket.

Lieutenant John Lynch had taken over as the head of the Major Crimes Task Force for Chris Morgan when he retired. Because Lynch hadn't worked on the Bennett case all along, he relied on his detectives to let him know what was important to talk about at the press conference. He asked the team of investigators what they would like to see as the main focus of the event. Based on their recent interviews with people from the apartment complex, Sergeant Perry and Detectives Taylor and Copeland unanimously decided the Peeping Tom was once again the most probable suspect. They asked Lynch to concentrate on this fact when he talked about the case at the press conference.

They now had additional details from new interviews they had done that might help the public identify the killer. They wanted to emphasize the peeper along with the fact that he might also be the dog walker. Of course, in the back of their minds, they were also quietly hoping the name "Drew Planten" might surface as a result of what they released at the press conference, but they went into it casting a wide net to see just what they might catch.

Lynch stood in front of the television cameras at the podium dressed in a gray suit, white shirt, and a gray and black checkered tie. His salt-and-pepper hair and studious-looking black glasses gave him the appearance of someone in charge, someone the public could trust and would listen to.

"The fact of the matter is that Stephanie was an innocent victim who suffered a homicide that shouldn't have happened. What we need to do is we need to bring that person to justice and prevent that person from harming anybody else," Lynch said in an almost monotone voice.

With a solemn tone Lynch told the media that the Raleigh Police Department had new detectives on the case who were trying to look at it with fresh eyes. He said they wanted the public to concentrate on identifying a man seen in the area around the Bridgeport Apartments in the weeks leading up to the murder. He gestured to a large aerial picture of Stephanie's apartment complex along with the Dominion Apartments on the table next to the podium.

"We're coming up with new ways to look at this. New ways to try and work it. We're going to refocus our energies," Lynch said. "Obviously, what we have done in the last three years has not gotten us the killer. We have to re-evaluate what's already been out there."

Lynch told the reporters that investigators were moving

away from the original composite in the case and asked the journalists not to use it anymore—not to print it, not to air it, not to post it on the web, period.

"The composite was never really a strong composite as composites are judged," Lynch said. "Although there may be some characteristics of the composite that were fairly accurate, obviously, that composite has not assisted the investigation in locating the suspect."

Lynch explained that while several people had seen the Peeping Tom and given a brief description, the composite was mostly based on the recollection of one witness with a few small details from the other witnesses thrown in.

Lynch asked the public to put aside the information the police department had previously released about the case and to consider only the new information they were releasing on this day. Perry, Copeland, and Taylor were concerned about people getting bogged down in the composite and the profile released earlier in the investigation. They asked Lynch specifically to address this issue.

"If our profile has been too narrow, somebody who knows something may have decided they simply didn't need to call because they didn't think that information was significant," Lynch said regretfully. "What we want to do is broaden that perspective. We want *any* information."

Lynch gave the new description Taylor and Copeland had come up with through their many interviews.

"The individual is described as a white male in his late twenties or early thirties, with a thin build, standing 5'10" to 6' tall, and with light brown or blond hair. He was variously described as wearing and not wearing glasses. At times he was seen walking a large to medium dark colored dog, but at other times the dog was not with him. The man was often seen wearing a dark hooded sweatshirt, even during warm weather conditions," Lynch said.

Lynch was blunt about telling the group why they were holding the press conference. He stopped short of saying people might have information they were holding back, but he implied that for whatever reason they had not come forward before, they needed to do so now, and would not be judged for withholding it.

"We hope that we get some kind of splash out of this particular coverage. We hope that it's going to trigger somebody to realize that they had something, and they just haven't told anybody yet, and they will come forward and share that information with us," Lynch said. "Somebody probably knows who he is. Somebody's probably seen him come out of a certain apartment, saw him get into a certain vehicle, or saw him in a certain area, and that could reenergize the investigation and help us tremendously."

The public already knew from the earlier information released by police that investigators had solid DNA evidence from the crime scene. This only added to the mystery as to why there had been no arrest in three years. To outsiders, it seemed like a no-brainer—the killer's DNA should have turned up a match by now. After all, it happened every night on television crime dramas like *CSI* and *Law and Order*. To this end, reporters asked Lynch if he was relying on DNA evidence to ultimately solve the case.

"That is something we're very hopeful about, but we are not simply placing our emphasis and our hopes on the fact that DNA is going to tell us who the killer is. We're going to continue the investigation from many different avenues," said Lynch.

Lynch told the media the police department had set up a forty-eight-hour tip line to see if they could once again gain some momentum in the case. He said it would be manned continuously by detectives working on the case from 7:00 Saturday night to 7:00 Monday night. After that, it would be connected to a voice mail where callers could leave a confidential message.

The journalists prodded Lynch, asking him if the case wasn't in fact cold after being unsolved for three years. He repeatedly told the crowd in several different ways that it wasn't cold. They were still working it every day. They would not give up.

"If we sat around speculating on when we were going to call it quits with this case, we shouldn't be doing what we're doing. We just keep on going. We work the case to its logical conclusion, and that will be the arrest of the suspect," Lynch said. "The case is solvable."

Whether he actually believed what he was saying or not, Lynch came across as a man who meant business.

# CHAPTER EIGHT

# A Friend of the Devil

## May 23, 2005

Fear grows in darkness; if you think there's a bogeyman around, turn on the light.

—DOROTHY THOMPSON

The third-anniversary press conference got results.

"We received dozens of calls, *interesting* calls," Lieutenant John Lynch said like a man who had a secret. "Each one of the tips that's coming in is being treated seriously. Investigators are following up on each and every one of these."

On the record, Lynch wasn't about to show his hand, but behind the scenes things were cooking.

Detective Ken Copeland said of the dozens of calls they received, some of them were very relevant to the case. The press conference had done what it was designed to do— give investigators new leads that they could run with.

One caller named Sidney Hoff, who'd lived in the Dominion Apartments at the time Stephanie Bennett was murdered, remembered a man fitting the specific description police gave at the press conference. Hoff lived above the man and said he was very skinny with long hair and

EVIL NEXT DOOR    131

walked a large dog around the apartment complex at all hours of the night. Hoff said he didn't know the man's name, but described him as being "very strange."

"He was very reclusive. He wouldn't talk to anyone or make eye contact, and he walked a big black dog, usually wore a sweatshirt with a hood over it," Hoff said during an interview with WRAL. "When you actually tried to say, 'Hi,' he would flinch away, look down, look the other way."

The clincher for investigators was when Hoff described the man's car to them. It matched the description of the car parked in front of Drew Planten's new place at the Birchleaf Apartments exactly. A raggedy old rust bucket that looked like it was about to fall apart any minute. There couldn't possibly be another clunker just like the one he and Taylor had observed in the parking lot of Planten's apartment, Copeland thought.

"His car was one-of-a-kind—an old Chevy Camaro, rusted out, looked like it wouldn't even run," Hoff said.

Another caller, a woman who lived in the building next to Stephanie's, remembered something she had overheard soon after the murder. She had spoken to police on several occasions in the months following the murder, but had neglected to share this information. She said she just now realized it might be important.

"I was spoken to in the original investigation. I'm sorry I did not tell you this, it's been on my mind for a while," the woman told Copeland over the phone.

The woman said soon after the murder she saw a tall, skinny man matching the police department's description of the suspect walking in the breezeway at the Bridgeport Apartments where she lived. She said the man was "frail, sickly looking" and was walking with a young boy. They were speaking to one another in hushed tones as if they were afraid someone might be listening to what they were saying.

She told police she overheard the boy say to the man, "I told them that I didn't do it. I had *nothing* to do with it." Then she told police she overheard the man say, "Be quiet, and don't say *anything* else."

Psychologist Michael Teague recalled the young boy that had been interviewed early on in the investigation about the women's underwear strewn on the bush near Stephanie's building. At the time, the boy reluctantly admitted to stealing the underwear from the laundry room at the apartment complex and dumping it on the shrubbery, but said he had no connection to the murder. The boy lived next door to Stephanie and his bedroom shared a wall with hers.

Despite the boy's denials about being involved, now armed with this new information, Teague couldn't help but think the boy walking in the breezeway with the suspect was most likely the same boy who had admitted to dumping the underwear on the bush, the same boy who lived right next door to Stephanie. It appeared that the boy might have been friends with this strange man who matched Planten's description. Teague started to wonder if the boy *had* been there when Stephanie was murdered. He also considered the gruesome theory that maybe the boy had even documented the crime for the killer with a video camera.

"It's the old pervert training the young pervert," Teague said of this theory.

Teague said sexual deviants liked to groom young boys and get reinforcement for what they did. In this case, if the boy had been there, Teague felt like he would have been too scared not to do whatever the killer asked him to do.

"This is a way for the killer to say, 'Look at what I'm doing. I'm the big guy,'" said Teague. "This wanting to show somebody, share it with somebody, it is part of what we called the dependant-personality traits."

Teague also considered that if the boy was involved, he was probably so horrified by what he had seen that he felt a need to "cleanse" himself by getting rid of the underwear because it was evidence of his own sexual deviance.

"He flips out. He can't handle it," Teague theorized.

Teague's close friend and colleague, Lieutenant Chris Morgan, never shared Teague's conjecture about the boy's possible connection to Stephanie's murder. Morgan was willing to consider that possibly the boy knew the killer and had some weird, inappropriate friendship with him, but even that didn't automatically mean the boy knew about the murder or had been involved in it. Morgan was part of the original team who had repeatedly interviewed the boy and his mother regarding the underwear found in the shrubbery. Morgan never got a strong sense about the boy's involvement, or found any evidence indicating he took part in the murder, though of course he also couldn't completely rule it out. Like so many facets of a complex murder investigation, some things will always remain a mystery.

Detectives Copeland and Taylor didn't buy Teague's theory about the boy's potential involvement in the murder either, but they were intrigued by what the woman had overheard. They were more interested in confirming the identity of the man—to see if it was in fact Drew Planten—and far less concerned with rehashing the boy's possible connection to the case.

The detectives brought the woman who had overheard the conversation down to police headquarters. They asked her to look at a lineup of pictures to see if she could recognize the man she saw walking in the breezeway that day with the young boy. They held their breaths as she gazed at the single sheet of paper that held photographs of several suspects who all shared similar physical characteristics. One of the pictures was of Drew Planten. It didn't take long for her to come to a definite conclusion.

"She picked him out," Copeland said excitedly. "She said, 'That's the man that I saw walking through the breezeway.'"

Suddenly everything was coming into focus for the detectives.

"We're going to *find* him," Taylor said at that moment vowing to do whatever she had to do to get a face-to-face meeting with Drew Planten once and for all.

## Face-to-Face

Fed up by multiple failed attempts to interview Drew Planten at his apartment, the detectives asked the manager of the apartment complex for the location of Planten's job.

On Tuesday, May 24, 2005, Ken Copeland and Jackie Taylor made an unannounced visit to the state fertilizer lab on Reedy Creek Road in Raleigh where Planten was employed as a chemist.

The detectives flashed their badges and asked the receptionist to tell Mr. Planten that he had visitors in the lobby. Taylor sat down for a moment, and when she looked up she saw a painfully thin man through the glass coming down the stairs toward her. *Bingo,* she thought, *he's just like they described him.*

"He came walking down the stairs, walking just like they always said he walked, his head down, not looking at anybody," Taylor said, remembering the first time she ever laid eyes on Planten.

Planten sheepishly introduced himself without making eye contact and reached out awkwardly to shake Copeland's hand.

"The first thing I noticed when he shook my hand, [was that] he had a death grip, and I mean a *death grip,*" Copeland emphasized. "He was strong."

Coming from a former Marine who looked like he could break most average men in half, Copeland's description of Planten's handshake became something of legend around the Raleigh Police Department. The handshake was in direct opposition to Planten's frail appearance. He looked like he could barely walk down the stairs without passing out, let alone squeeze someone's hand like a vise.

"He looked like he would fall apart if you touched him," Taylor said, shaking her head as she remembered that day.

The detectives told Planten they were investigating the murder of Stephanie Bennett and asked him if he had heard anything about the case. He said, "No," which was the first of many red flags for Copeland and Taylor in their dealings with Planten. It would have been virtually impossible to have lived in the Dominion or Bridgeport Apartments in May 2002 and not know *something* about the case, especially given the extensive media coverage over the past three years. After a few minutes of denial, Planten finally told the detectives he thought he might vaguely remember the case.

"We'd like to sit down and talk to you about it. Do you have some time when you could come down to the police department?" Copeland said to Planten.

"I'm not coming to the police department," Planten fired back.

The detectives then asked Planten if he wouldn't come to the police department, would he be willing to speak to them at his apartment. He told them they would have to make an appointment to see him. The word *appointment* struck them as odd. Planten didn't appear to be the kind of guy who had a busy social schedule. But nonetheless, the detectives played along and made an appointment to meet with Planten the following Thursday at his apartment after work.

"He was very hard to talk to. You had to pull stuff out of him. It wasn't like you were carrying on a conversation with a normal person," said Taylor, remembering how difficult it was just to make a simple plan to meet with Planten.

Planten answered the detectives' handful of questions with very short or one-word responses. Right away, they decided he was "odd," but not necessarily their murder suspect. Taylor and Copeland had dealt with a lot of odd people throughout the investigation; they didn't immediately think being odd qualified someone as a killer. But as they said their good-byes and turned to leave, something strange happened—*red flag number two.*

"He started shaking uncontrollably from head to toe like he was freezing cold," Copeland remembered.

"Are you okay?" Taylor asked him.

"I'll see you Thursday," Planten responded, ignoring her question and turning away.

As they walked away from the building, Taylor and Copeland could barely contain their hopefulness that maybe they were finally onto something. Once again, neither of them spoke. They just looked at each other and knew exactly what the other one was thinking.

"We looked at each other and we were like—I think we found him," Taylor said.

"I think we found him," Copeland echoed.

## And We Meet Again

Before Jackie Taylor and Ken Copeland went to Planten's apartment, they let everyone in their unit know what was going on. Sergeant Clem Perry and several other officers decided they would take a position close to the apartment complex and be ready to head toward Planten's apartment in case something went wrong and the detectives needed backup. While Planten seemed meek, not at all like someone who might pull a gun on a cop, Perry wasn't going to take any chances with his detectives' safety.

When Taylor and Copeland arrived at the apartment on Thursday, May 26, 2005, and knocked, to their great surprise he promptly answered the door. It was the same door they had knocked on so many times in the previous few weeks and never gotten an answer. But on this occasion, it was clear that Drew Planten was expecting them. He was ready to speak to the detectives as long as he could maintain control of the situation.

Taylor remembered how Planten immediately took charge of their encounter. "I walked right into the living room, [and] he stopped me," Taylor said.

"Oh no, no, stop right there," Planten told her. "We'll have this conversation right here."

Her radar went up at that very moment. What was he trying so hard to hide in the apartment? What did he not want them to see? Did it have something to do with Stephanie's murder?

Planten ushered the detectives to a small table up against the wall in the cramped kitchen surrounded by two matching chairs and a lawn chair which was just a few steps from the front door. Planten sat down at one end of the table and the detectives took the other two seats. Glancing around, Taylor and Copeland noticed that the apartment appeared to be neat and organized, not your typical bachelor pad. It looked like Planten had cleaned up for his company.

He was wearing a cotton dress shirt buttoned all the way up to his neck. His hair was combed neatly and tucked behind his ears. He folded his hands serenely in his lap and looked straight ahead as if he were about to close his eyes and meditate instead of have a conversation. He sat and waited for the detectives to begin. He was ready.

"You could tell he had prepared," Copeland said, not knowing exactly what to make of the odd man in front of him. Planten wasn't the typical street thug Copeland was used to interviewing. This guy looked more like a pitiful nerd than a killer. *Focus,* Copeland recalled thinking, *don't let his appearance fool you.*

The detectives asked Planten the same basic questions they had asked everyone else in their interviews about the case. They asked him what he knew about the murder, and whether he had ever been to the Bridgeport Apartments. He told them he had never been to the Bridgeport complex. Copeland countered with another question asking him if he was *sure* he had never walked his dog over there to which he said Planten replied, "Maybe I did." Planten shrugged off the contradiction. He acted like the detectives had simply jogged his poor memory instead of catching him in a lie.

The investigators asked Planten if he wore glasses. This was important given the fact that the Peeping Tom and the dog walker were both sometimes seen wearing glasses. Planten said, no, he did not wear glasses. *Another red flag.* Planten's driver's license included a "lens restriction." By law, he needed glasses to drive.

Detectives asked Planten whether he smoked. The peeper had reportedly been seen smoking cigarettes, but Planten told the detectives that he did not smoke.

Planten answered the questions, but offered as little information as possible. Copeland found him to be so introverted that he had a hard time believing Planten had ever had a relationship with anyone, let alone a woman. He was probably the kind of guy that was so terrified by women, Copeland thought, that he had few, if any, dating opportunities.

"I didn't think he had a relationship with females," Copeland said as a statement of fact rather than a judgment.

"He was odd," Taylor said. "He was an odd guy."

"He was a strange bird," Copeland added. He knew from the answers Planten was giving him that things were not adding up. The guy was guilty of *something*. He had to be. He was acting so weird—keeping them captive in this little dingy kitchen and lying about small details like where he walked his dog and whether or not he wore glasses.

Privately, at that moment, both Taylor and Copeland were starting to think that they had found their Peeping Tom. They didn't know if Planten was the killer, but they

Stephanie Bennett's May 2001 graduation photo from Roanoke College, shown here at a memorial service honoring her at the college.
*Courtesy of WRAL News*

Deanna Powell, known as "Dee," Stephanie Bennett's stepsister and roommate.

Emily Metro, Dee Powell and Stephanie Bennett's other roommate.

Walter Robinson, Stephanie Bennett's long-term boyfriend.

*All photos on this page courtesy of WRAL News*

Carmon Bennett, Stephanie Bennett's father, and her stepmother, Jennifer, agonized over the search for Stephanie's killer throughout the years-long investigation.

Mollie Hodges, Stephanie Bennett's mother, said she would always remember Stephanie as "my best friend."

Detective Ken Copeland, one of the leading homicide investigators in the Raleigh Police Department, known as "the garbage man" for not leaving any scrap of evidence behind.

Detective Jackie Taylor, Copeland's partner, known for her Southern gentility, ingenuity, and excellent interviewing skills.

Sergeant Clem Perry moved up in the ranks of the Raleigh Police Department with record speed, and had the privilege of calling Carmon Bennett to tell him that an arrest had been made.

*All photos on this page by Chad Flowers*

Lieutenant Chris Morgan worked the Bennett case diligently until the day he retired and handed it over to Detective Ken Copeland.

Raleigh Police Department psychologist Dr. Michael Teague.

North Carolina State Bureau of Investigation agent and scientist Mark Boodee, who was able to use his expertise to make the final DNA match that put the killer behind bars.

*All photos on this page by Chad Flowers*

Raleigh police officers gathered in the parking lot of the Bridgeport Apartments on May 21, 2002. Every available detective in the city was called in to work the murder case that night. *Courtesy of WRAL News*

LEFT: This early composite of the suspect in the case was widely circulated in the community, generating a lot of leads, but never the right one. *Courtesy of the Raleigh Police Department*

RIGHT: Drew Planten's driver's license photo was the first glimpse detectives had of the man who might be their suspect.
*Courtesy of the Raleigh Police Department*

Detectives walked Planten from the police station to a waiting patrol car for his short trip to the Wake County Jail.
*Courtesy of WRAL News*

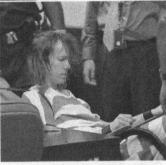

When Planten made his first court appearance on October 20, 2005, he was unresponsive and uncooperative. Top county law enforcement officials believed his apparent catatonic state was an act.
*Courtesy of WRAL News*

LEFT: Joanne Reilly, Planten's supervisor at the North Carolina fertilizer laboratory, who aided the police despite her initial belief that Planten was innocent. *Photo by Chad Flowers*

RIGHT: Wake County Assistant District Attorney Susan Spurlin, who vowed to do her best to get justice for Stephanie Bennett.
*Photo by Chad Flowers*

If not for Stephanie Bennett, Rebecca Huismann's murder might never have been solved. Once Planten was arrested, he was also linked to her murder, and the six-year-old cold case was finally put to rest.
*Courtesy of Glenna Huismann*

Detective Joseph Dionise of the Lansing, Michigan Police Department, who never gave up hope that Huismann's murderer would be found. *Courtesy of Joseph Dionise*

had independently gotten a strong feeling that he was the kind of person who might be inclined to watch a woman through her window under the cloak of darkness—a woman whom he would never have had the courage to talk to in daylight.

Even with his idiosyncrasies that day, Planten was a far cry from the man whom the detectives had met in the lobby of the fertilizer lab just two days earlier. He looked at them directly, and answered their questions without hesitation. He did not fidget or make dismissive gestures the way he had during their first encounter. On this day, Planten appeared calm, almost tranquil.

"I won't say rehearsed," Taylor said, "but he had obviously decided he was going to carry on a conversation with us. He was a lot different than when we first met him because when we first met him he was very noncommunicative."

They worked up to the big question of whether he would give them a DNA sample. Of all the questions they had asked him, they knew this would be the most important one, so they saved it for last in case he decided the conversation was over at that point.

At this juncture in the investigation, they had already interviewed and taken samples from nearly 250 people. Not one of those people had refused to give DNA when it came right down to the moment of truth. Taylor and Copeland told Planten that it would be simple, just a quick swab of saliva from his mouth. But it wasn't the procedure itself that Planten was afraid of; it was the result.

"We're only using this to eliminate you so we won't have to come back and bother you again," Copeland told Planten.

"I don't feel comfortable giving you that," Planten said to them.

Copeland basically told Planten it was obvious that he didn't enjoy talking to the police. Who did? He said giving them the DNA sample was the easiest and quickest way to make them go away forever.

The detectives said Planten seemed to know a lot about DNA. He countered their pitch with his concerns about what they might do with the results of the test.

"I know about the databases and you're going to put my name in a database and it's going to be compared to a bunch of stuff," Planten told the detectives with growing agitation in his previously calm voice.

Copeland assured Planten that would not happen with his DNA sample; it would be used to compare with DNA only from the Stephanie Bennett crime scene.

"My first line to a normal person would be, 'Hell, if you ain't got nothing to hide then don't worry about it.' But I wasn't going to say that to him," Copeland said, knowing he wasn't dealing with a regular Joe on the street corner.

Copeland and Taylor had done their research on Planten. They knew his mother, Sarah Chandler, was an attorney in Charlotte, Michigan. Given that fact, they knew he was likely to be wary of giving a DNA sample for legal reasons, fearing his privacy would be violated. To put his mind at ease, the detectives encouraged him to call his mother and get her input on the situation. The harder they tried to convince him giving the sample was no big deal, the more resistant Planten became.

"First he just shut me down and said, 'No.' And then we said, 'How about you give it some thought?' Because we wanted to come back again," said Copeland, not wanting to permanently close the door on their conversation. "We wanted a reason to talk to him again."

The detectives told Planten to consult with his mother about giving the DNA sample. They told him once he made his decision, he should e-mail Detective Copeland about whether he was willing to submit to the test. They gave him a deadline of 5:00 P.M. on the following Tuesday, May 31.

The detectives left Planten's apartment that day with more questions than they came in with. Even after spending more than an hour talking to the strange man, the truth of who he was and what he *might* have done remained elusive.

## The Moment of Truth

Detective Copeland constantly checked his computer that Tuesday waiting for the e-mail from Planten. Every time he passed it, he would click on his in-box. Sitting there was like watching a pot and waiting for water to boil while constantly wondering if the burner was really on. He was up and down all day long, taking little walks and then always ending up right back in front of the blank screen. *No new messages.*

"The talk around the office had always been when you get the one who won't give you the DNA, then you've got your suspect," Detective Taylor said.

Copeland finally decided Planten was simply going to ignore the deadline. He couldn't figure out what kind of game this guy was playing, but he didn't like it one bit. First, he had ignored all of their previous visits to his apartment. When he finally let them in, he forced the detectives to sit in the tiny kitchen and did not allow them to venture farther into the apartment. Something about this guy scared Copeland in a way the street thugs never had. Street thugs were predictable; Planten was clearly in his own bizarre league.

Around 5:00 P.M. on May 31, Copeland and several other detectives were standing around his laptop watching the screen, waiting for the water to boil. They had pretty much given up on Planten replying, and were chatting among themselves about what to do next. All of a sudden, *there it was.* An e-mail from Planten popped up on the screen.

Copeland immediately clicked on it, barely able to contain his excitement in front of his colleagues. It was one simple line. It read:

> I appreciate your consideration, however, I respectfully decline.—Drew Planten

Copeland stared at the black words on the white screen in disbelief. Even in their simplicity, they seemed to be mocking him.

"Oh boy," Copeland yelled after he read the single line of text out loud to his colleagues one more time.

Planten had technically made the deadline, but in Copeland's mind, Drew Planten's time had just run out.

# CHAPTER NINE

# Catch Me if You Can

## June 2005

*Without courage, wisdom bears no fruit.*
—BALTASAR GRACIAN

Detective Ken Copeland contacted North Carolina State Bureau of Investigation Agent Mark Boodee and consulted with him regarding how they should go about getting a DNA sample from Planten now that he had refused to co-operate. After years of testing what amounted to elimination samples, Boodee felt an instant adrenaline rush when Copeland let him know they might finally be onto an actual suspect.

"They said, 'We've got this guy who we really think is kind of hinky. He won't give us a sample,'" Boodee recalled police telling him. "I thought, that's kind of weird, let's try and get a sample from him."

Boodee suggested the detectives try to swab Planten's steering wheel, the door handle on his car, or the door-knob on his apartment door. He even suggested trying the handlebars on Planten's bike. But the Raleigh Police Department's legal staff shot these ideas down. They were worried about the legal liability of violating Planten's right to privacy. Because they had no search warrant, they feared they would be treading on shaky ground if they didn't play by the rules.

Boodee countered their concerns by saying why not get one of Planten's trash bags from the communal Dumpster at the apartment complex. By law, once you throw something out, it no longer belongs to you. Boodee figured that there might be something useful inside one of Planten's trash bags that he could test for DNA. But the detectives told him they had recently learned from some sources at the apartment complex that Planten *never* threw out his trash. Nobody had ever seen him leave the apartment with a garbage bag or go near the Dumpster.

"I was like, what the hell is going on with this guy? This guy is seriously whacked," Boodee said.

## Watchful Eyes

In June 2005, after more meetings about how they were going to get Planten's DNA, the Raleigh Police Department's Fugitive Task Force was assigned to follow Drew Planten twenty-four hours a day for a week. Their goal was to get close enough to him to get a credible DNA sample, but not so close that he would spot them. They wore street clothes and drove unmarked cars, but following Planten in his old rusty Camaro became a real challenge because it went up to only about thirty miles per hour. This made it virtually impossible for anyone to get behind Planten unnoticed because they always ended up practically attached to his bumper.

The officers then decided it would be better to post up in strategic locations around the fertilizer lab on Reedy Creek Road and watch Planten come and go from work. Sergeant Clem Perry said this was when investigators started to witness Planten's truly bizarre behavior.

"He would come outside at lunch and sit inside his car and it was just *smoking hot*. It had to be a hundred and some degrees inside the car," Perry said. Planten sat there with the windows closed, the car off, and no air-conditioning when the temperatures outside the car were well above ninety degrees. During these times, he never ate, drank, or read anything. He simply sat in the driver's seat staring straight ahead and appeared to do nothing at all.

Another odd thing investigators witnessed was that the car was in such bad shape, Planten had to place a pan beneath it to catch the leaking oil while he was inside working every day. At the end of the day, they said he would open up the hood and pour the oil from the pan right back into the car, presumably in order to make it home again.

Sergeant Perry and Detectives Copeland and Taylor were instructed to stay away from the task force while they were doing their surveillance. They couldn't risk being spotted because Planten already knew the detectives. Still, there were some days they couldn't help themselves. They would find their own covert locations on Reedy Creek Road and watch the action from a distance just to see how things were going. Mostly they just listened to the radio traffic in order to monitor what the other officers saw and what Planten was doing. After all, it was *their* case. Who could blame them for wanting to know what was happening?

"One time the sergeant on the fugitive task force actually caught us doing surveillance ourselves," Perry said with a grin. "We were scolded and chastised a little bit for joining the surveillance unofficially. We were not close enough to be seen. We were just wanting to get out and listen to what was being said over on the police radio."

So far the week had been a bust. The surveillance team had failed to come up with any reliable sources where they could get Planten's DNA. Finally, on the last day of the surveillance, officers got their chance. They saw Planten get into his car on his lunch break with a water bottle. After a few minutes, he got out of the car and threw the empty bottle into a nearby Dumpster in plain sight of the officers. They knew it would be easy to retrieve, and they were right. *Bingo, this is it,* thought Copeland and Taylor when they heard about the water bottle. Suddenly, they imagined all of their hard work was about to pay off, and their gut feelings would be rewarded with a perfect DNA match. *Case closed.*

The water bottle was sent to Mark Boodee at the State Bureau of Investigation crime lab for DNA analysis. There was a rush put on the test. Boodee gladly sped up the process. He was almost as excited as the detectives to finally have a real prospect.

The surveillance team also sent a cigar butt found on the sidewalk after Planten and a friend were seen smoking outside the building. This intrigued the detectives because Planten had clearly stated in his interview with them at his apartment that he did not smoke. Maybe it was just a little white lie, but it was a lie nonetheless. If he lied about this, what else had he lied about?

As exciting as this development seemed to be at the time, neither sample gave the investigators what they were looking for. It was like a kick in the gut for Boodee, who, like Taylor and Copeland, had thought that this time they might really be onto something.

"First of all, the samples didn't match each other, and then they didn't match up with the profile [of the killer] as well," said Boodee after analyzing the cigar butt and the water bottle. "Either your 24-7 surveillance didn't pick up the right stuff, or they were from someplace else, and he's just trying to throw you off the track."

The cigar butt not matching had a logical explanation.

"As fate would have it, we got the friend's cigar because we weren't close enough to actually see where it landed, so it was kind of a shot in the dark," Perry said with regret.

Copeland and Taylor were floored. There started to be

rumblings among the cops at the station that they obviously had the *wrong guy*. But the detectives weren't ready to give up yet. Their guts told them something was wrong with the samples, not with their suspect. They could explain away the cigar butt snafu, but the DNA from the water bottle not matching made absolutely no sense to them.

"Sometime after that," Perry said, "one of the officers assigned to the fugitive squad admitted they were not a hundred percent certain Planten had actually drank from the water bottle."

Given this information, it was possible Planten either didn't drink from the bottle at all, or he switched it with a clean bottle before he got out of the car and threw the decoy into the Dumpster.

"He very well may have made the surveillance detail on him," Perry said. He added this didn't reflect on the quality of the team, but on the fact that Planten was already anxious about police after having been visited by the detectives twice. As a scientist, he obviously knew the ways in which investigators might go about trying to get his DNA. So when the water bottle came back negative, Taylor and Copeland decided it probably wasn't an accident after all.

"At that point we thought, Drew really was smarter than we gave him credit for. He pulled one over on us," Copeland said.

Despite some skepticism from within the police department, Boodee was still on Copeland and Taylor's side. He encouraged them to keep trying to get a good sample for him to analyze.

"Those two were like dogs with a toy. They would not let go," said Boodee. And neither would he.

## Three's a Charm

"We were told it's not him, move on," Jackie Taylor said, recalling their marching orders from the top brass.

While many people at the Raleigh Police Department now doubted Taylor and Copeland's hunch about Drew Planten being the one who killed Stephanie Bennett, they were not deterred. The detectives decided it was time to pay Planten another visit. They would ignore the naysayers until they had exhausted every possible means to get a good DNA sample from Planten.

This time Taylor and Copeland went unannounced to Planten's apartment without an appointment as he had required for their second meeting. They stayed out of sight and waited for him to get home from work. They watched him go inside his apartment briefly, and then leave again to walk his dog. When Planten left with the dog, the detectives got out of their car, stood by his front door, and waited for him to return. They hadn't rehearsed what they were going to say, but they had agreed it was time to be brutally honest with Planten about where this investigation was going and what role he played in it.

When Planten rounded the corner and saw the detectives hovering around his front door, his expression turned dark. It was obvious he was surprised and unsettled to see Taylor and Copeland standing watch in front of his home. With a shaky voice he told them he needed to put his dog up and would come right back out and speak to them. He was gone so long, they wondered if he was really coming back. Seconds stretched into minutes as they both nervously glanced at their watches. He finally reappeared, but on this visit, Planten did not invite the detectives inside. They were unwelcome visitors. The three of them stood awkwardly outside Planten's apartment door and waited for someone to speak first.

"This interview was a little bit more argumentative and confrontational," Taylor said. "It showed us just how smart he was because he could quote exactly what we had said to him in the first interview."

Taylor said she believed Planten had taken notes regarding what they talked about during their encounter with him a few weeks earlier in May. This was probably at his mother's advice, seeing as she was a lawyer who was no doubt concerned about police interviewing her son. It was as if he had not only taken notes on their first meeting but had also memorized those notes. He spit back things the detectives had said to him *verbatim* whenever he spotted a contradiction in what they were saying now.

Gone was the calm man who had politely answered question after question, waiting patiently for the next one to be lobbed at him. This time around, Planten challenged and corrected almost everything the detectives said to him and threw it back in their faces. Gone was the subdued, shy, buttoned-up man they had met just a few weeks ago.

"People have seen you over at Bridgeport," Copeland said to Planten firmly.

"That's their opinion," Planten replied.

"That's not an opinion, Drew, that's a fact," Copeland retorted.

It was a long shot, but once again the detectives asked Planten for a DNA sample. They told him this was the easiest way to get them out of his hair for good.

"No, you're not getting that. You trick people. I know what you do. I know how the police work," Planten said defensively to the detectives.

At that point the detectives laid it on the line. Copeland told Planten because he had refused to cooperate with them he had "graduated to the class of suspect" and they would be "looking at him *hard* now." Planten seemed to bristle at this suggestion. Rather than retreat, he took an even more combative stance. He bowed up his thin chest and crossed his arms.

"You've gone from a person of interest to a suspect," Taylor told Planten in no uncertain terms.

"Once you've elevated yourself to a suspect, there's a whole lot more I can do with you," Copeland added, picking up where Taylor left off. But nothing they said seemed to move Planten. He simply glared at them and folded his arms with hostility even tighter into his body.

Realizing nothing they could do or say was going to break this man, the detectives decided it was time to go. They shook Planten's hand awkwardly and said an abrupt good-bye. From this day forward there would be no more handshaking. Things were about to change dramatically. The gloves were off, and as far as Taylor and Copeland were concerned, the game was on.

## Inside Job

One of Ken Copeland's gifts as a detective was developing relationships with ordinary people in the community who might be able to help him with the investigation. He looked like a regular guy and spoke like a regular guy, not like some tough-talking detective you see in the movies or on television. People trusted him and spoke to him like they were chatting with an old friend over a beer.

When Drew Planten shut them down hard on the third visit, Copeland knew it was time to up the ante. He needed someone inside Planten's little world who could watch him and maybe assist in helping detectives get a good DNA sample. Given his introverted personality and the fact that the surveillance team had noticed no friends coming and going from Planten's apartment, Copeland felt like Planten's office was the only hope of finding such a person.

After talking with several people who knew the hierarchy in Planten's laboratory, Copeland zeroed in on Joanne Reilly, a section supervisor of several chemistry laboratories in the fertilizer division. In November 2004, she had been promoted to supervise the lab where Planten worked. Reilly was an accomplished state employee who had worked for North Carolina's government off and on for the better part of two decades.

When she inherited Planten from the former supervisor, she didn't know him other than to say good morning or hello. Before Reilly took the promotion, Planten had barely spoken to her, only in passing and only when she spoke to him first. In the beginning, because of his long hair and effeminate features, Reilly wasn't even completely sure whether Planten was a man or a woman. She would see Planten from behind walking down the hallway and do a double take.

But Reilly, a gracious older woman with gray hair, a kind smile, and an affable way about her, made an effort as a supervisor to get to know all of her employees, including Planten. She was old enough to be his mother, and sometimes she felt her motherly instincts kick in when she was around him. Reilly pitied the reclusive young man who appeared to be afraid of any human interaction or contact.

"I would ask him about his family, what was he going to do that night, how was his dog doing? He would talk a little bit, but you had to drag it out of him," Reilly said, recalling their early conversations.

To Reilly, Planten looked like a young hippie, tall and extremely lean with long, thin hair. Despite his unusually long hair, she felt he always appeared clean and well groomed at the office. Reilly considered herself a pretty good judge of character, and felt like Planten was a harmless young man who just needed some love and attention in order to come out of his shell.

"He had a really gentle face, just a really gentle face with the most beautiful eyes I'd ever seen on a man or a woman. They were bright green," Reilly remembered, her voice trailing off.

Joanne Reilly said people who worked in the office felt sorry for Drew Planten because he seemed so painfully shy and even more painfully thin. It wasn't unusual for co-workers to bring in food for him. They wanted to fatten him up, but Reilly said she rarely, if ever, saw Planten eat anything.

In many ways, Copeland knew approaching Reilly was a risky move that could backfire badly. If she told Planten the police were onto him or told anybody what was going on, he might run. But, on the other hand, Copeland was out of bright ideas and losing ground on the case fast. The "water bottle incident," as it was dubbed, was constantly being thrown back in his and Taylor's face as proof they were on a witch hunt. But they knew better and were out to prove everyone wrong.

Copeland called Reilly one day at her office and set up a meeting with her for after work. He decided it was best to try to get her cooperation face-to-face instead of over the phone. In person, he could better assess her reaction to what he was asking her to do.

"He said he wanted to speak to me about an employee of mine," Reilly said, intrigued. "He said it was totally confidential, and I was not to tell anyone. I agreed."

When Copeland told her the man they wanted to talk to her about was Drew Planten, a "person of interest" in a murder case, she was speechless.

"I thought oh my God, he would be the least likely person, he looked so weak," Joanne said of the frail, meek young man.

Copeland also told her that he wanted to make sure Planten had left the building before they met with her because he didn't want to risk running into him.

Around 4:30 P.M., when Planten normally left for the day, he was instead on his stool hunched over his lab table working. Reilly said good night and called Copeland on his cell phone to tell him Planten was still hanging around in the building for some reason. She left the laboratory and drove across the street to the North Carolina Museum of Art to make it look as if she were going home for the day. When she returned a few minutes later, Planten and his bike were gone. (Recently, Reilly said, Planten had been riding his bike to work because, no surprise, his car was out of commission.) *The coast was clear.*

Reilly let Taylor and Copeland into the building through the front door and led them back to a small library where they could talk privately. Once everyone shook hands and sat down, the detectives told her they were investigating the Stephanie Bennett murder and Planten's possible connection to the case.

"We went in there the first day to get a feel for her," Copeland said. "Just to see if she was tight with Drew. We were dancing kind of a fine line."

Reilly was devastated at the mere thought that one of her employees could be involved in such a brutal crime. As an avid news watcher, she had followed the Stephanie Bennett case closely and knew just about every detail. *It couldn't be him, no way. It's not possible.*

"It just really hurt my heart," Reilly said of the murder. She recalled the beautiful pictures of a smiling Stephanie splashed across the television screen and on the front page of the local newspaper. She remembered seeing tearful interviews with Stephanie's family pleading for the public's help in solving the heinous crime. It made her tear up just to think about it.

"We explained to her that we had spoken to Drew, and Drew had not cooperated," Copeland said.

"They said out of 246 people so far, he was the only one who had consistently lied to them and refused to give a sample of DNA," Reilly said.

Knowing how shy Planten was and that his mother was a lawyer, Reilly wasn't immediately swayed into thinking Planten was guilty just because he refused to give a DNA sample.

"I could see him saying, 'That's private, you need a warrant to get that,'" she said.

The detectives asked Reilly lots of questions, questions to which she didn't have the answers. While she supervised the laboratory where Planten worked, she did not directly oversee him on a daily basis. But because Planten was painfully shy, even those who worked with him more closely knew little about him. Reilly figured she had as much of an opportunity as anyone to help investigators learn more about Planten.

The detectives told her that they needed more information about Planten, information his acquaintances and coworkers might be able to help them get. They told her the only way to eliminate him as a suspect at this point was by comparing his DNA to the killer's DNA.

"We told her we wanted to make sure he didn't kill himself or hit the road," Copeland said. "We said, 'if he doesn't come to work one day would you call us?' He appeared to be a little emotionally unstable."

Reilly told the detectives Planten had a very solid track record in the fertilizer laboratory and generally kept to himself. She said he came to the lab on time and completed his work accurately and efficiently. While she didn't think there was any way this quiet, timid man could have had anything to do with such a violent crime, in her heart, she felt it was her duty to help clear his name even if it meant working behind his back with police. The end result would be the same, she thought. They would eliminate Planten as a suspect, and he would never even have to know what she had done.

"I was so sure he was innocent, I was willing to work with the police and exonerate him," Reilly said with confidence in her voice.

## Private Eyes

Reilly took her new role as an undercover liaison to the Raleigh police investigators very seriously. There was no task too tedious or too challenging that she wasn't willing to tackle. She decided not to let her managers in on the situation yet, preferring to go it alone until she had a compelling reason to reveal the situation to them. Her motivation continued to be clearing Drew Planten's name and having the police move on to the *real* killer.

Detective Ken Copeland asked Reilly if she could get them a good phone number for Planten. Copeland was sure Planten had multiple numbers, and the investigators needed access to all of them. In order not to raise his suspicions, Reilly created a form on her computer and sent it out to all of her employees asking them to update their contact numbers. The plan worked, and she turned over Planten's phone numbers to Copeland. *Mission accomplished.* Reilly was proud she could deliver on what the police were asking her to do.

On another occasion, Reilly said Copeland asked her to get Planten's e-mail address. Again, Copeland suspected Planten had several e-mail accounts, and he wanted to know the address for every single one. This time Reilly enlisted the help of Planten's direct supervisor for this mission even though investigators had specifically told her not to tell anyone what was going on. But Reilly felt like she needed help to do what was being asked of her, and she knew she could trust her colleague.

When Planten was on the computer, his supervisor would call Reilly, and she would casually come down and chat with him while looking over Planten's shoulder in an effort to get his e-mail address. During one of these encounters, she was able to see the address clearly and memorize it. Reilly was so excited, she immediately called

Copeland with the information. She was disappointed to find out it was the address Copeland already had. *Mission aborted.*

The detectives also asked her to try to get Planten's timesheet from May 21, 2002, the day Stephanie was found dead in her apartment. They wanted to find out whether he had shown up for work that day, and if he had, whether he was on time. Copeland knew asking Reilly for a state employee's personnel record was no simple request.

"We knew that would take a little finagling," Copeland said with a grin, knowing all too well the bureaucracy they would have to go through to get information out of a government office through normal channels. But he had a feeling his newest honorary detective was up to the task.

Once again, even though investigators had asked Reilly not to tell anyone in her office about what she was doing, she knew she would not be able to get the timesheet without some help. So she asked a co-worker with connections in the human resources division if she could get the document. The co-worker told her it would have to come from downtown, meaning that the officers would have to get a warrant to search Planten's employee records and wade through a mile of red tape in the process. But to Reilly's surprise, the next day the co-worker called her down to her office and told her there was something for her on the desk. She said she would leave her office, and Reilly could take it if she wanted to. Having Reilly pick the document up off of her desk eliminated the co-worker from any direct responsibility for the act.

When Reilly opened the envelope and saw Planten's timesheet from May 21, 2002, the day Stephanie Bennett's body was found, her heart dropped. It showed that he'd been *one hour* late that day. This wouldn't have been so unusual expect for the fact that in Reilly's experience with Planten, he had *never* been late for work.

Reilly was starting to feel a pang of doubt about Planten.

It wasn't a persistent, threatening feeling but more like an uneasy voice in her head telling her things were not looking good for him. But then she realized it was not up to her to decide anything. She was not an investigator. It was up to the detectives to figure this puzzle out. She slid the timesheet back into the envelope and called Copeland to let him know she had something he needed to see.

## Sightings

Detectives were still getting calls from people who had lived in the Bridgeport Apartment complex and the Dominion Apartment complex at the time Stephanie Bennett was murdered. Some of the callers were just now remembering things that might pertain to the case. Others had been holding on to information for all of these years and only now realized it might be relevant.

"Now we're looking at Drew, and we're trying to see if what these new people were telling us fit Drew," Ken Copeland said.

One woman told the detectives she was walking her dog in the breezeway of the Bridgeport Apartments one morning when the dog stopped and started growling intensely at something in the nearby bushes. She had to pull back hard on the dog's leash to keep him from leaping into the shrubbery.

"Her dog started growling at the cedar bushes right there by Stephanie Bennett's window and, lo and behold, a man stepped out of the cedar bushes, but he didn't look like the composite," Copeland said, recalling what the woman had told him. He said because the man didn't fit the composite, she hadn't bothered telling anyone about the incident when she found out that Stephanie had been killed. But once investigators broadened the description of the suspect, she thought it might be important information for detectives to have.

This woman introduced investigators to another woman who also had a strange encounter with a man near the Dominion Apartments. She too had been walking her dog early one morning—but instead of in the apartment parking lot, she was walking around the lake.

"And when she turned around, a man was just standing right up on her. He had the hood over his head, and he was right in her face," Copeland said. The woman described the man as tall and skinny, just like Planten. She said he quickly left the path bordering the lake and walked away in the direction of the Dominion Apartments.

A third woman told detectives she moved out of the Bridgeport Apartments because she felt like a man who lived in the area was stalking her. The woman was now living in New York. It took investigators about a week to track her down. She told them that back when she lived at Bridgeport, she would sit on her patio, and a tall, skinny, sickly looking man with long, grungy hair would sit on a picnic table across from her apartment and stare at her.

"That was important," Copeland said, "because that picnic table sat *right behind* Stephanie Bennett's apartment."

Copeland then told the woman that a young girl had been killed at the Bridgeport Apartments after she moved out. He explained that they were trying to figure out who killed the victim, and whether he had stalked other women in the area. For a moment, the line went silent, and then Copeland began to hear a sobbing sound on the other end of the receiver that was growing in intensity.

"She got so upset she wouldn't talk to me anymore. She busted up crying and hung up the phone," Copeland said.

He called the woman back, and she told him that she was just so upset she couldn't talk about it at that time, but would call him later. He told her he understood. As much as he desperately wanted to hear what the woman had to say, Copeland knew from experience that he had to be patient when it came to delicate situations like this one.

As promised, a few days later, after she had calmed down, the woman called Copeland back and told him the rest of her story. She said the man on the picnic table made her so anxious, she would move inside her apartment from the patio. Then he would start peering through her windows from what he obviously must have thought was a safe distance until she finally closed her blinds. The situation made the woman so nervous, she ultimately moved to another apartment complex on the other side of the lake.

With new details like these starting to emerge so many years after the crime, Jackie Taylor and Ken Copeland continued to pore through the hundreds of pages of reports, thinking they might have missed something. They were looking for anything to absolutely confirm or definitively rule out Planten as a suspect. They knew it was often the smallest details that made no sense at the time, but later proved to have the most relevance to a case.

In the reports, the detectives found an interview with a woman who had been walking through the breezeway at Dominion with her son. A man passed them wearing a hooded sweatshirt and sunglasses. The woman recalled her son saying hello to the man, but the man didn't speak to the child.

"Who is that guy you're speaking to?" the woman asked her son. She was startled that her young son was talking to someone who was a stranger to her.

The boy told his mother the man was the uncle of one of his friends. When the interview was first recorded, everyone assumed the boy was speaking about a man who did live with his nephew on the top floor of this particular apartment building.

But then Copeland and Taylor went back and re-interviewed the boy. They discovered that he was actually talking about a man who lived on the bottom floor of the building. The man had hung out with a young boy he referred to as "his nephew," when in fact he was not really related to the child. The "nephew" turned out to be the same young man who had admitted to stealing the underwear and throwing it on the shrubbery the night Stephanie was murdered.

Putting all of the witness statements together, Taylor and Copeland determined the man this woman had seen, and the man who another woman witnessed in the breezeway talking to a little boy, both had to be Planten. There was just no other logical explanation. The description fit, and the building where he had lived at the time was just on the other side of a narrow patch of woods from Stephanie's apartment building.

"And that's when we said," Copeland said banging on the table with a fist, "he's right there at her front door."

## E-mail Buddies

Joanne Reilly felt uncomfortable talking to the detectives on the phone at her office. She just knew at any moment Drew Planten might walk in, and she would be caught talking about him behind his back. Given her feelings, Ken Copeland suggested they start communicating through e-mail.

Reilly had started to notice strange things about Planten. He rarely if ever ate or drank and was constantly wiping down things he touched or putting them in his knapsack after he used them. It was if he knew that someone might be trying to get a DNA sample from him. But how could he know? Reilly didn't think she had done anything to tip him off, but she also knew he was very bright and probably paranoid after his last visit with detectives.

By this time, Planten's direct supervisor and Reilly had started talking about ways they could get a DNA sample from him for police. Every day one of them would stay late and look for strands of Planten's hair around his workstation. They thought that surely, with such long hair, he was bound to leave a strand or two behind, but every day they came up empty.

"He used to comb his hair, and save it, put it in his pocket," Reilly said. "And apparently, he would clean it up off the floor before he left every day."

Reilly confided in Copeland that despite her strong initial feelings that Planten could not be their suspect, his unusual behavior had started to make her nervous.

On Thursday, August 25, 2005, at 7:30 in the morning, Reilly wrote an e-mail to Copeland:

> Hi Ken. Nice to hear from you. I was thinking about you yesterday. Do you have fingerprints from the scene? I have some paperwork that your person of interest personally placed on my desk. I picked them up with a piece of paper and they are in a plastic bag. I have also been thinking about bringing in some ice cream or something since our fertilizer season is winding down. I may be able to get a used spoon for you without being too obvious. I would probably need your help planning that. Would that help? Joanne

In another attempt to get Planten's DNA, one day Reilly gave Planten a can of Pepsi. After he left for the day, she and Planten's supervisor searched his workstation and all of the trash cans inside and outside the office for the can. It was gone. It had simply vanished. The only explanation they could come up with was that Planten was obviously onto them and was making sure he left nothing with his DNA on it anywhere in the laboratory. Still, Reilly reassured herself that this didn't mean he was necessarily guilty; it only meant that he didn't want anyone to violate his privacy by testing his DNA.

One night Reilly was working late when she ran into Planten standing alone awkwardly in the office thirty minutes after he was supposed to have gone home. She had no idea he was still there and was startled. For a moment, she was frightened by his sudden appearance, but then she looked at him as he meekly slinked away, and she told herself once again the police had to be wrong. *This gentle man could not be a killer.*

Eventually, Reilly decided it was time to tell her managers what was going on. She had been so sure she could handle it by herself that she had been reluctant to bother them. But things were getting serious now, and she felt like she had already taken too many risks that could have gotten her into serious trouble. It was time to come clean.

"I probably could have gotten fired for all of the stuff that I did," Reilly said.

Reilly knew her managers would want to protect the reputation of their division first and foremost. They wouldn't want the public to think the state of North Carolina had knowingly hired a killer. But she also knew that without their blessing and cooperation, she couldn't go on helping the police and trying to stay beneath the radar. It was too risky. She felt strongly that they would understand the importance of the situation and agree to allow her to continue working with investigators.

Reilly first told the director of the division the extent of what was going on and the extent of her involvement.

"His mouth stayed open for a period of time," Reilly said, remembering his reaction to the news.

The director called in other administrators to discuss the situation. She explained to them she wanted to help the police by staging a luncheon where they might be able to get a DNA sample from Planten. They told her she could plan the event, but added it needed to be off state property. They didn't want to host a party at the laboratory for the specific purpose of trapping one of their employees.

Reilly agreed to the terms of the luncheon, and agreed to keep her managers in the loop about all of her future dealings with the Raleigh Police Department regarding Drew Planten. She had gone out on a limb this time and there was no turning back.

## Banana Pudding

On Monday, September 12, 2005, Joanne Reilly e-mailed Detective Ken Copeland and told him their end-of-the-fertilizer-season office luncheon was scheduled to be held at the Golden Corral on Glenwood Avenue at 11:30 A.M. the following Thursday. She typed up an invitation asking everyone on the floor to attend. Everyone, including Drew Planten, was expected to be there.

The wheels were in motion. Sergeant Perry decided to send two plainclothes detectives to the restaurant that day, George Passley and Dale Montague. As far as Perry knew, Planten had never seen either of these investigators before. Their mission was single-minded: *Get his DNA.* While Planten had consistently avoided eating and drinking at his workplace, investigators couldn't see any possible way he could avoid eating or drinking at a restaurant.

Copeland told Reilly that she wouldn't know who the detectives were in the restaurant. They wanted her to be able to act naturally and not call attention to them.

On the day of the luncheon, the employees from the fertilizer laboratory piled into several vehicles in order to caravan to the restaurant. Planten was in the backseat of a white state-owned van in front of Reilly's car. As soon as she got into her car, she got a call from Detective Montague checking in to make sure everything was on go. He wanted to know exactly what Planten was wearing and what kind of vehicle he would arrive at the restaurant in. Reilly assured him that Planten was so unique looking the detectives would not have any problem spotting him.

"Drew turned around and stared at me the whole way,"

Reilly remembered. "And here I am on the phone talking about *him*."

It literally gave Reilly the chills seeing Planten peer out the back window of the van with his sad, gentle face. She wondered in his heart if he knew she was the Judas who would ultimately betray him. She hoped not. She hoped he would never have to know what she had done, that once he was cleared the police would move on and never reveal she had helped them.

Once the group arrived at the restaurant and was shown to a large table, Reilly was careful to pick a seat where she could observe Planten without being right next to him. She didn't want it to look like she was watching him even though she really was.

"I tried to not pay attention at all," Reilly said. But she couldn't help herself. Her eyes kept wandering across the table to see if Planten was still doing the weird stuff he did in the office, wiping things down, putting trash in his pockets. And he *was*. It deflated Reilly's hopeful demeanor. Not only did it make her more suspicious of Planten, but she worried that investigators would find nothing useful to test because he was cleaning everything he touched.

For the most part, Planten ate finger foods, a cheeseburger and fries, things for which he didn't need utensils. He did use a straw, but every time he got up from the table to go to the restroom, he would put the straw into his pocket.

"He blew his nose at one point and I thought, yes, maybe he'll leave that," Reilly said. But to her dismay, the used tissue also went into Planten's pocket, along with the straw and everything else he was hoarding.

Even though she had been warned to keep her cool, Reilly casually scanned the restaurant looking for the undercover detectives. *There they are, bingo! The guy in the denim jacket and his friend in the baseball hat, cops trying to look like regular folks.* But every time she would think she had found them, the men would get up and leave, and then she would realize she was wrong. Detectives Montague and Passley blended in so well that Reilly never spotted them. She hoped that meant that Planten didn't spot them either.

Passley and Montague knew what Planten looked like from his DMV picture that had been passed around the Major Crimes Task Force multiple times. Their prodding of Reilly for a description of her co-worker's clothing turned out to be unnecessary. They quickly spotted Planten sitting with the large group of employees from the fertilizer laboratory as soon as they entered the restaurant. The undercover detectives decided to sit at the table directly across from Planten's so that they would be close enough to see what possible sources of his DNA might be available.

At the time, Sergeant Perry and Detectives Copeland and Taylor were busy working on a kidnapping case in North Raleigh. Passley excused himself from the table and went outside to call Perry to update him on how things were going.

"I have never seen anything like this in my life," Passley told Perry.

"George, you've got to be kidding me," Perry responded with agitation, wanting Passley to get to the point. "Tell me what you got."

"This guy is completely weird. He is wiping off every utensil. He's gone to the bathroom several times. It looks like he's throwing away napkins. He put a straw in his pocket," Passley said.

Perry of course wondered if the reason for Planten's strange behavior was that he had spotted the undercover detectives in the restaurant. Passley told Perry he didn't think Planten had any idea they were there. Perry then wondered if the detectives were messing with him, pulling his leg. He even hung up and called Montague to get his version of the story. To his surprise, it matched Passley's in details and sincerity.

"He had become so concerned that we were trying to capture his DNA, that [this behavior] was probably just an everyday thing for him," Perry concluded regarding Planten's odd cleansing rituals. Bottom line—Planten was *always* on guard.

And it worked perfectly—well, almost perfectly. At the end of the meal Planten, who had been eating mostly finger foods, broke format and decided to try a bowl of banana pudding. The detectives watched with guarded amusement wondering how Planten was going to pull off eating this one without a utensil. He took two bites of the pudding with a *fork* and then vigorously wiped down the fork with a wet napkin. It was as if he didn't care who witnessed this bizarre behavior, and clearly, his colleagues had become so numb to this that no one paid him any mind. All the undercover detectives could think was *Boy, he must have really wanted that banana pudding.*

"They said he spent five minutes wiping the fork," Taylor said in disbelief.

"At that point we said he may not have killed Stephanie, but he's done something," Copeland said.

And apparently he didn't do a good enough job wiping down the fork.

"That's what did him in," Copeland said.

"Banana pudding did him in," Perry added.

As they were leaving the restaurant, Reilly was hopeful the undercover cops had seen Planten use the fork, but she didn't know for sure since she was never able to pinpoint who they were. She literally crossed her fingers as they walked out of the restaurant hoping the operation had been a success.

Planten followed Reilly and the other employees down the sidewalk in front of the restaurant on the way to their cars. She turned around to ask him how he liked his meal, and suddenly, he was gone. Reilly froze, wondering if Planten had figured out what was happening and had decided to run. She rushed back inside the restaurant just in time to see the back of his head as it disappeared around the corner into the men's restroom. At that point, Reilly was sure Planten was getting rid of more things that might have his DNA on them—maybe even the fork. She panicked and ran back outside to call the undercover officers on her cell phone. Reilly was reassured by Montague that he was aware of the situation and had sent his partner into the bathroom to see exactly what Planten was doing.

"He's already been flushing his napkin and straw and everything else he has down the toilet," Montague told Reilly.

"He said they had the fork, but he didn't know if it would be of any use," Reilly said with obvious disappointment in her voice.

Montague was lucky enough to snag the fork Planten used to eat the banana pudding. He had no idea whether or not it would contain Planten's DNA given all of the wiping down, but it was worth a shot. The fork was taken immediately to the State Bureau of Investigation laboratory for DNA testing. Their go-to guy, SBI Agent Mark Boodee, agreed to put a rush on the test once again.

As Copeland waited for the test results later that day, he had a permanent smile on his face. *Things were finally coming together.* He e-mailed Reilly who wanted to know how everything had gone on their end at the restaurant.

Copeland replied to Reilly on September 15, at 4:16 P.M.:

I'm quite sure you will remember this day for awhile.

## Putting It to the Test

Detectives told Agent Boodee about Drew Planten's strange behavior at the restaurant, not leaving his straw or napkin, instead flushing them down the toilet. They told him it was very difficult to get a DNA sample for this reason; the fork was the best they could do.

"He was clearly someone on the fringes of society," Boodee said. "The guy was a molecular biologist. He knew ways he could be tripped up, and he was being very careful about what to do and what not to do."

Boodee said the detectives were so pumped about the possibility of the fork being the definitive thing to cement Planten's fate, they hand-delivered it to him personally.

"It's like, here's the trophy," Boodee recalled thinking when he received the fork.

Boodee was also thrilled about the potential that this might finally be the evidence investigators needed to solve their case. He once again worked through the weekend isolating and analyzing DNA from the fork. He hadn't been this excited about the case in years. Finally, there was a chance he would get a match and not just be eliminating another poor dude who happened to live near Stephanie Bennett.

Boodee told the detectives the fork had probably not been washed well before Planten used it, and thus had already been contaminated with another diner's DNA when he put it in his mouth at the restaurant.

"On six out of fifteen chromosomes that I looked at, I got matches, but with the other chromosomes that I tested, I have mixtures with this other female," Boodee said. "We can't hang our hats on this. You've got to do better."

But he also told them that the partial match they did get was *very* promising. He said they should not under any circumstances give up on this potential suspect yet. He really felt like the detectives were onto something this time. He didn't want them to lose hope simply because they hadn't nailed it on the first try.

"Part of the mixture was really, really strong," Perry said. "The closest we'd ever gotten."

And for the detectives, *close* meant they had no choice but to keep going. They had come this far and weren't about to throw in the towel at this late stage in the game. Boodee wasn't ready to give up either.

"I felt like they had the right guy. They just had to get the right sample," Boodee said definitively.

# CHAPTER TEN

# If the DNA Fits

## Fall 2005

Conscience is the chamber of justice.
—ORIGEN

Unlike any other scientific marker, our DNA is unique to us as individuals. The only time someone's DNA is going to be strikingly similar to another person's DNA is if the two people are biologically related, and even then, it won't be *exactly* the same unless they are identical twins.

As it turned out, Detectives Jackie Taylor and Ken Copeland had discovered through their research that Drew Planten had an older brother in Asheville, North Carolina, named Donald Planten. And that wasn't all—Donald Planten had previously been convicted of secret peeping in February 2004. Asheville police reports revealed that Donald had rigged up a video camera in the women's bathroom of the architectural firm where he worked in order to watch women in various states of undress.

"I think the two brothers compared notes," psychologist Michael Teague said of Donald and Drew Planten and their apparent shared proclivity for sexual deviance.

Teague said the bond the brothers probably shared involved something called "the risky shift phenomenon." According to psychologists at ChangingMinds (changing minds.org), this is defined as: "When people are in groups, they make decisions about risk differently from when they are alone. In the group, they are likely to make riskier decisions, as the shared risk makes the individual risk less. They also may not want to let their compatriots down and hence be risk-averse."

In other words, if one of them did something deviant, it made it okay for the other one to also engage in similar behavior. Drew Planten may have looked to his older brother as a mentor when it came to his peeping behavior.

Given the sexual nature of Stephanie's murder and the fact that the killer might have been a Peeping Tom, investigators couldn't totally rule out the very remote possibility that Donald Planten may have visited his brother, Drew Planten, in Raleigh and committed the murder himself. Donald Planten also bore a striking resemblance to the original composite, even more so than Drew Planten. Knowing the brothers' DNA would be very similar, Sergeant Perry thought it was imperative that investigators get a DNA sample from Donald as well as from Drew to compare to the killer's DNA. This comparison, he thought, would ultimately eliminate Donald Planten as a potential suspect and erase any lingering shred of doubt in anyone's mind.

"It was decided that we would have to get DNA samples from both of them in the interest of being thorough," Perry said.

Detectives Jackie Taylor and Ken Copeland were sent to Asheville with instructions to do their best to get Donald Planten's DNA. They hooked up with the Asheville Police Department because they were out of their own jurisdiction and asked for their investigators' assistance—assistance the Asheville detectives were more than happy to give.

Unlike the hunt for Drew Planten's DNA, Taylor and Copeland had no problem getting Donald Planten's DNA. Boodee said Donald worked as a waiter in a local restaurant and bar in the small western North Carolina city. Copeland and Taylor went into the bar pretending to be visitors. They talked Donald into socializing with them after work and were able to get several beer mugs he drank from and a pen he used on the job. Boodee remembered with a chuckle that Taylor had even taken a turn or two on the dance floor with Donald in order to distract him so Copeland could take the glasses from the table without his noticing.

Boodee told the detectives he would wait and test the DNA from Donald Planten and Drew Planten at the same time. As they left Asheville with Donald Planten's DNA evidence in hand, they knew they were halfway to their goal of finally having an answer in this gut-wrenching case. One down, one to go.

## Watchful Eyes

Detective Ken Copeland continued to maintain his e-mail relationship with Joanne Reilly, the manager of the laboratory where Drew Planten worked. He had told her that the Golden Corral DNA sample was close, but not close enough. He was thankful that she was still on board with him, willing to help with the investigation in any way she could.

On Monday, September 19, 2005, at 3:12 P.M., Copeland wrote Reilly an e-mail:

Hello Joanne, Just hollering at you to see if there are any "Drew" events occurring. As always, he is the first person that comes to my mind when I sit down at my desk.

At 3:42 that same afternoon, Reilly responded to the investigators in her own e-mail:

> Hi Ken. Not really. He is sitting in front of his chromatograph as always, but he is shaking from head to toe, which I have never seen before, but maybe it is a nervous mannerism of his. I glanced at him a couple of times when I went through the lab looking for his supervisor, and his whole body was shaking. He did not respond to my greeting. I just decided to leave him alone . . . Joanne

Even though her managers now knew what was going on with the investigation, Reilly was still nervous about talking to police on the phone at work or using her work e-mail to relay information to them. She felt more comfortable and communicated more freely with Copeland from home through her personal e-mail.

On September 20, 2005, Reilly wrote a long letter to Copeland from her personal e-mail account:

> I don't know why he was shaking. I asked his [direct] supervisor if he had seen him do that before and he had not.
>
> His supervisor also told me that Drew had been acting a little more strangely lately. Ordinarily, he sits on the stool in front of his ion chromatograph 9 hours a day—straight through lunch—and the supervisor told me he didn't ever see Drew leave his seat, even for the bathroom. Now he is spending 20-30 minutes each day in the bathroom/locker room, where he keeps his knapsack.
>
> Last Friday [the day after our lunch] the supervisor saw Drew bring the knapsack into the laboratory and get some antibacterial soap from the cupboard. He watched Drew pour the soap into a beaker. Then he

got busy and didn't notice Drew again until he heard him rinsing the beaker out in the sink. He was wondering if Drew had a container in his knapsack now full of antibacterial soap or what??? The supervisor also said that he noticed yesterday that Drew is not leaving used paper towels or tissues in the bathroom, but is flushing them.

Now, what can we do to help? The guy is starting to make me nervous. What do you need to get a search warrant that you haven't been able to get yet? Is there any way he could leave DNA on his bike, which is parked here? Would hair help? We will watch out for long hair around his stool, but if it falls out naturally there is less chance of DNA right? We also have a pair of safety glasses identified that his supervisor says he wears occasionally. No one else wears them. Do you want those? I saw him polishing them the other day, (like the fork?), so perhaps they wouldn't help. Outside of getting my ring caught in his hair and giving it a good yank, I don't really have any more ideas. I am starting to dream about him. Help!

Reilly also engaged Planten in conversations at work in order to learn about him and his family. She eagerly passed on what she learned to Copeland. She felt most of it was benign information that further revealed Planten was just a regular person with a normal, mundane life. At this point, she was the *only* person on the inside, the *only* person who was talking to both Planten and the police. As Copeland saw it, she was his *only* hope of getting Planten's DNA.

On Thursday, September 22, at 3:23 P.M., Reilly wrote to Copeland again from her personal e-mail:

Hi Ken. Any News? I did find out that Drew did not have a dad in the picture, at least from the time he was a young-to-mid teen. He grew up in New Jersey, and he, his mom, and brother and moved to Michigan so that his mom could go to law school.

Reilly was getting anxious. She wasn't a lawyer or a cop. She didn't know exactly what authorities needed in order to make a move on Planten or to eliminate him as a suspect, but she desperately wanted to help. One way or another, she wanted a conclusion to what had become a daily obsession for her. It was an overwhelming distraction from her work, her personal life, from everything. She was in deep, and she knew it.

One afternoon Reilly decided to take matters into her own hands and throw an ice cream party at the office to see if she could get the elusive DNA sample from Planten. The failure to get a good sample at the Golden Corral had continued to haunt her even though investigators assured her it was not her fault. Yet, it was still eating away at her. She was *determined* to make it right.

So Reilly brought ice cream bars on popsicle sticks to the office with the hope that Planten might throw his stick away and then she could grab it for police. She knew it was a long shot given his history of not throwing away anything that he had touched, but she decided it was worth a try. She planned it for the same day as the division director's retirement party, thinking that distraction might give her an opportunity to slip away and be alone in the fertilizer laboratory for a few moments and score something with Planten's DNA on it.

"I ate [an ice cream bar] that had a red stick to match the red stick that he had, just in case I was able to switch them," Reilly said sheepishly revealing her well-crafted plan. She figured everyone, including Planten, would find it hard to resist the offer of a special treat during their mid-morning coffee break. And she was right. Even Planten, who rarely ate anything at work, helped himself to several popsicles.

Reilly then left the lab and called back a few minutes later to talk to Planten's direct supervisor. He told her that, as usual, Planten was holding on to his popsicle sticks instead of throwing them away. She told the supervisor to keep an eye on them and let her know where Planten put the sticks when he was done. Eventually, the supervisor called her back and told her that Planten had put the popsicle sticks in his drawer. *Score,* she thought. *I can do this.*

When the group from the fertilizer lab, including Planten, moved upstairs for the retirement party, Reilly went back to the laboratory alone. She practically crept, walking quietly on the balls of her feet, scanning the room carefully for people as she moved closer to Planten's work area. Ever so slowly she slid open Planten's drawer. Immediately, she saw what she came for. The popsicle sticks were laying there wrapped in a paper towel right in front of her. Her heart skipped a beat as she reviewed the plan in her mind. She felt a sudden sense of panic rising in her chest.

"I just felt scared at that moment," Reilly said. "I didn't think I could do it fast enough. I knew he was upstairs at the retirement luncheon, but I also knew that he suspected me of trying to get things from him by the way he looked at me."

Reilly couldn't help but think that if Planten was in fact innocent and found out that she had intruded in his personal space, he would never forgive her. She felt ashamed of herself for snooping in his drawer, but she had little time to dwell on this feeling. Suddenly, Reilly heard the back door to the lab swing open on its squeaky hinges. As quietly as she could, she slid Planten's desk drawer shut. *Houston, we've got a problem,* she thought. She was still holding her own red popsicle stick in her hand, the one she had planned to switch with Planten's, and had no pockets to hide it in. She knew it would look suspicious for her to be standing there holding the stick so long after they had all finished their ice cream. Thinking quickly, Reilly shoved the stick into the waistband of her pants beneath her shirt concealing it from view. She turned around and walked away and almost crashed right into Planten who simply stood there and stared at her. She knew she must have looked flustered, but she managed a weak smile and a half wave as she mumbled "excuse me" under her breath and kept on walking.

Reilly turned around slightly to glance at Planten as he passed her without saying a word and went right to his drawer. She turned away quickly so that he wouldn't think she was watching him. That's when she heard the drawer open. Reilly heard paper crinkling as Planten apparently took something out of the drawer. She heard the drawer close and then the faucet turn on in the sink. She tried to busy herself with a computer on the supervisor's desk, acting like she was looking up something. *He was washing something.* She could hear intermittent sounds as he ran something underneath the stream of water. *It had to be the popsicle sticks,* she thought. Reilly glanced up just in time to see Planten putting something into his knapsack when he was done.

On Monday, October 3, 2005, Reilly e-mailed Copeland:

Any news? We had our reception/ice cream party. I had an opportunity to get something, but felt very uncomfortable about it and backed off. Let me know when you hear something and if we need to, I will decide if/when we might set something else up.

Thanks Ken . . . Joanne

## Gloves On

Agent Mark Boodee felt strongly that the best place for investigators to get a sample from Drew Planten was inside the state fertilizer laboratory where he worked. He felt like there would be multiple possibilities in and around Planten's workstation that might yield a strong DNA sample. Boodee suggested swabbing Planten's computer, his chair, and his desk. He said the best sample would come from something Planten had had close contact with for a period of time that no one else would have touched. Being a scientist himself, Boodee knew people who worked in laboratories often wore gloves when they performed certain experiments. He recommended getting Planten's laboratory gloves as he felt like they would yield the best opportunity for getting a good DNA sample.

At the same time, Sergeant Clem Perry was in constant discussions with the Wake County District Attorney's Office, as well as the police department attorney, Dawn Bryant, about how they could legally obtain Drew Planten's DNA. Assistant District Attorney Susan Spurlin was the prosecutor now officially assigned to the case.

Spurlin, a no-nonsense, tough-talking litigator, had been with the Wake County District Attorney's Office off and on since 1980. She left briefly in 1984 for several years to work as a criminal defense attorney, but the pull of being the one to get the bad guys off the streets was too powerful for her to ignore. So she returned to her first passion, criminal prosecution.

"I missed the courtroom. I missed trying cases. I missed working with the victims. I missed working with law enforcement," said Spurlin of her brief stint in criminal defense work with esteemed local attorney Joseph Cheshire. "I'm one of the very fortunate people who loves her job, loves coming to work."

Spurlin was a thin woman with glasses who always wore very traditional, tailored business suits and kept her brunette hair cut sensibly short. In the courtroom she was a pit bull who had successfully convicted many murderers in her two-plus decades as a prosecutor. But in her spare time, she was an avid horse rider. On her horse, out in the country, was where she really let herself be free. When she climbed on top of a horse, she said she was at peace. It was the one place not even the bad guys could creep into her mind and ruin her day.

When Spurlin first heard about Stephanie Bennett's murder, she reacted emotionally like everyone else who had heard about the case. *What kind of a monster could do this to a young woman?* she thought. Even before it was officially assigned to her, she'd followed the case with great interest.

"I was aware of it from the sense that it was so tragic, because you had a victim that did not put herself in harm's way," Spurlin said. "Everyone ought to be safe in their home. This was a terrible, violent crime. I was aware early on that once they identified the person it would be conclusive because of the evidence that was left at the scene."

Spurlin had been kept up-to-date all along and consulted with investigators throughout the summer about what they were trying to do in order to get Planten's DNA. The detectives wanted to make sure their actions were legal and wouldn't get them into hot water down the road if the case went to court.

"They did it in ways that you legally can collect DNA. They didn't invade his privacy. They didn't take anything for which he had any expectation of privacy," Spurlin said firmly.

They considered every possible idea that was brought to the table for getting Planten's DNA. For example, investigators discovered Planten had failed to change the address on his driver's license when he moved from Dominion to the new apartment complex across town. They considered doing a traffic stop and arresting him on this minor violation simply in order to get his DNA, but after consulting with attorneys, they decided this might be considered entrapment.

Boodee kept the pressure on investigators to go forward with his plan to get Planten's work gloves, which he wore when he performed experiments. He insisted the best place for them to get the DNA was from the fertilizer laboratory. Boodee reasoned that because Planten was employed by the North Carolina Department of Agriculture, the lab was state government property. According to Spurlin, this gave law enforcement carte blanche to search the area without Planten's permission because it was owned by the state of North Carolina.

"Our legal advisors informed us there would be *no* expectation of privacy for him there," Perry stressed.

But before they went into the lab, investigators wanted to make sure they had the best possible items to choose from that might contain his DNA. With Planten's history of sanitizing his work space, they knew it was going to be a challenge to find usable samples.

Detective Ken Copeland talked to Joanne Reilly about things she saw Planten touch in the lab on a regular basis. He wanted to glean what locations might offer the investigators their best shot at getting a credible DNA sample. Reilly told Copeland that yes, sometimes Planten wore his lab gloves when performing experiments, and that all of the scientists had personal sets of gloves assigned to them. But Copeland had also learned from Boodee that the DNA in the gloves had to be fresh in order for it to be a good sample. He needed Planten to have worn the gloves just before the State Bureau of Investigation agents entered the lab to collect the DNA.

Reilly cleared the SBI agents' visit to the lab through top administrators with the North Carolina Department of Agriculture. They were now running the show when it came to Planten. Reilly said they had become somewhat reluctant but were, nonetheless, participating in the unfolding drama. She had agreed to help the investigators with the glove issue, to make sure Planten wore them at some point on the day of the search.

On Monday, October 17, 2005, at 10:07 A.M., she e-mailed Copeland:

> I have reassigned ten limestone samples to Drew, stating that they were brought to my attention as being in question by my supervisor. He is upset at having to repeat his work. We cannot guarantee that he will use the gloves, but he usually does when he is running limestones . . . Joanne

Because limestones are rough on the hands, chemists in the laboratory usually wore gloves when performing experiments involving them. Reilly hoped Planten would wear the gloves while he reevaluated the ten limestone samples she had assigned him to review. There was no guarantee, but it was their best shot.

At 10:39 A.M. on that same day Reilly wrote an e-mail to Copeland again. There was just one simple line:

> Gloves are on.

## Swab the Gloves

The entire investigative team had met on the previous Friday, October 14, 2005, and decided the search of the fertilizer laboratory would take place the following Monday after work. Detective Ken Copeland was working off-duty security at the North Carolina State Fair that same week and would not be able to participate in the search. It was an annual stint that paid so well he couldn't pass it up. Besides, he knew the Bennett case was in the capable hands of the scientists now. He had done all he could do. *This was it.*

On Monday, October 17, Sergeant Perry, Detective Taylor, and two agents from the SBI, including Boodee, waited for Drew Planten to leave the laboratory. They sat in their cars across the street waiting for Reilly to give them the all clear that Planten had left the building.

Reilly hustled across the parking lot of the art museum around 6:00 P.M. to tell them that Planten had *finally* left. Boodee said she was sweating profusely as she told the investigators that Planten had lingered that evening for some strange reason. The security guard had found him uncharacteristically sitting alone in the break room of all places, two hours after he was supposed to have left for the day. Finally, the security guard told Planten he was locking up the building. Planten reluctantly got on his bike because his rusty old Camaro was still out of commission and left.

"What they thought is that he was waiting for everyone to leave so he could clean and get his gloves," said Boodee.

Reilly accompanied the team of investigators into the lab and showed them where Planten worked. Boodee said they swabbed Planten's computer, his wooden stool, and the dial on a radio near his workstation.

"It took a long time. They swabbed *everything* that he could have possibly touched," Reilly said, sounding exasperated at the mere recollection of the search.

But Planten's gloves were what they'd really come for. The gloves were made of thick rubber and looked like the kind of gloves people wore to wash dishes.

"What is the best item of evidence?" Perry asked Boodee point-blank as they stood together in the laboratory assessing the situation.

"Those gloves are," Boodee said without missing a beat.

The question everyone had was whether to simply take samples from the gloves and leave them, or to take the gloves themselves and replace them with a similar pair. Planten's gloves were of a particular style and color not made anymore. They had also become stained and worn in specific places from so much use. The concern was that Planten might notice the differences if they switched the gloves, and even with a rush job, it would take at least a day or so to do the DNA test. If he noticed the gloves had been switched, he was more likely to run.

They also thought about simply taking the gloves and then not replacing them in the hopes that Planten would think he had lost them. But given his meticulous nature, it was unlikely Drew Planten had ever misplaced anything.

Perry wanted the agents to swab the gloves; Taylor wanted them to take the gloves. Boodee told investigators the best way for him to test the gloves would be to take them back to the lab where he could cut them up and test the individual pieces of the gloves for DNA.

"I want the gloves," Taylor said over and over.

"I was worried about taking them, the whole expectation of privacy thing. [Detective] Jackie [Taylor] was not as concerned as me," Perry said.

Taylor and Boodee won the debate. They took the gloves. Investigators replaced them with a similar pair, hoping that Planten wouldn't notice, at least right away, and it would buy them some time. They knew they were taking a chance. Their biggest fear was that if he learned they were definitely closing in on him, he might take off or try to hurt himself. They decided it was a risk they had to take if they were going to solve this case.

The team left the laboratory that night feeling like they were sprinting to the finish line. Finally, identifying the man who might be Stephanie's killer seemed within reach. They were determined not to let him go.

"We're feeling very, very strong that we're cooking with gas," Perry remembered.

## Cooking with Gas

On Tuesday, October 18, 2005, Agent Mark Boodee began analyzing the samples he'd obtained from Planten's workstation. While he was on an emotional high believing he might just have the literal key to the case at his fingertips, he knew the true job of a scientist was to deal only in facts. Scientific facts don't lie. It is the most credible evidence you can have in a criminal trial. It is also what jurors expect to see. In a day and age when television crime dramas solve cases in an hour, jurors want everything, including DNA, handed to them on a silver platter.

Boodee ran all of the samples from the lab and studied what are called *electropherograms*—peaks on a chart that show whether the sixteen specific areas on a chromosome are the same as those same areas on the suspect's chromosomes.

He was hopeful that they had been able to retrieve good samples from Planten's lab, but he also knew that in public spaces, it was always a gamble trying to get a clean DNA profile with no contamination from another person. Yet, right away, the computer showed Boodee that he had taken several clean samples from Planten's work space, primarily from the gloves and from the dial on the radio.

There was one unusual configuration of a chromosome Planten had that matched with an unusual chromosome in the killer's profile. Boodee had rarely, if ever, seen this particular chromosome configuration before in any sample he had analyzed previously in his career.

"I was like, I can't believe it. It's either him or it's a very *close* relative," Boodee said.

By itself, the unique chromosome configuration meant

nothing, but it was a promising start to the process. Next, Boodee clicked on the rest of the profile analyzed by the computer program and, voilà!, there it was.

"Then I looked at all the rest of them, and they *all* matched up. I was like *holy shit!* I can't believe we got the right guy. I can't believe this is finally coming to an end," Boodee said excitedly.

At the same time, Boodee also ran the samples taken from Drew's brother Donald, which had been obtained from a blue ballpoint pen, two brown Newcastle Ale mugs, and the door handle of his car. While they were similar to Drew Planten's profile, they did not match the killer's profile.

"At that point I was like, that's it! I know we have the right guy," Boodee said.

Boodee told his supervisor, Bill Weis, about the results of the tests. Weis immediately got on the phone with Raleigh police chief Jane Perlov to tell her what they had found.

" 'Look, we've got the right guy. It's time to take him down,' " Weis said to the chief.

Boodee said that up until that point, everyone at the State Bureau of Investigation had been sworn to secrecy about the latest development in the Stephanie Bennett case. But the rush of knowing that they finally had a match was almost too much for Boodee to keep to himself. *It was really happening.* He hoped an arrest would be imminent so he could share the good news with the world.

"I always knew that this case would be solved eventually, simply for the fact that I know that DNA is such a great tool," Boodee said with a smile from ear to ear.

The science had worked. It was now time to sit back and let the police do their work.

## Gotcha

On Wednesday, October 19, 2005, Sergeant Clem Perry and Detective Jackie Taylor were walking around in a daze at the police station. They were physically and emotionally drained from the case, and from waiting for the DNA test to come back. Detective Ken Copeland was still working security at the State Fair, waiting patiently for his colleagues to call him when the results of the DNA test came in.

They knew Agent Boodee had put a rush on the test, but they also knew science took time. After all the time they had put into the case, what were a few more hours of waiting? Who were they kidding? *It was agony.* If the DNA didn't match this time, they were right back where they had started—nowhere. It was unlikely they would get any more chances. If Planten's DNA didn't match, it was over. The investigators' anxious haze was interrupted by a call from Bill Weis, the director of the State Bureau of Investigation laboratory.

"Okay," he said to Perry. "Are you sitting down?"

"Give it to me, Bill," Perry said anxiously.

"You got him," Weis said matching Perry's level of excitement through the phone. "Now we have a question for you: Which one do you think it is? Is it Drew or his older brother?"

This debate had been an ongoing discussion between Perry, Copeland, and Taylor. Even though they had gone through the motions to get Donald Planten's DNA, Taylor and Copeland never had any doubt in their minds that Drew was their killer based on everything they had learned in the past few months. They never really considered Donald a viable suspect.

"It's Drew," Perry said to Weiss definitively.

"Yeah," Weis said. "Let everyone know."

It was a surreal moment for the detectives who had

waited so long for this day. Taylor was literally jumping up and down in the Major Crimes office unable to curb her excitement. After taking a breath, she immediately called Copeland on his cell phone at the fairgrounds to tell him the good news.

"It's Drew, it's Drew," Taylor shouted into the phone at Copeland.

"We *knew* it was Drew," Copeland said as his partner confirmed what they had believed for some time now.

The excitement of the DNA match was quickly replaced by the seriousness of planning the next step—the arrest. The detectives didn't want Planten to spend one more minute on the street where he might be able to hurt someone, but at the same time, they needed the blessing of the district attorney to move forward, even with the damning evidence they now had.

"That's when the stress started," Taylor said.

At first, the group decided they needed to do some more follow-up investigation before they made an arrest, just to be thorough. But then they came to the consensus that they couldn't sit on this information for long. If it leaked, they might lose Planten forever. This was a risk they were not willing to take.

"We decided right then and there to go ahead and get an arrest warrant," Perry said.

Perry and Taylor headed to the Wake County District Attorney's Office. Luckily, given the new information, prosecutor Susan Spurlin gave them her blessing to move forward as they'd hoped she would. She helped them prepare the arrest warrant. Chief Resident Superior Court Judge Donald Stephens then signed the warrant, making it official. Everything was on go. Now all they had to do was to plan Drew Planten's takedown.

At the same time they got the arrest warrant, investigators also prepared search warrants with Spurlin and had Stephens sign off on them as well. They wanted to be ready

to search Planten's belongings for more evidence as soon
as he was in handcuffs. The warrants gave them the legal
authority to search his apartment, his car, his work space,
and to take a DNA sample directly from him. They would
need a DNA sample taken in a controlled scientific setting
to use at trial. The initial sample from the fertilizer lab was
simply used to establish the probable cause needed to make
an arrest. But the sample taken in a controlled environment, as directed by the search warrant, would be the one
used in court to link Planten beyond a reasonable doubt to
Stephanie Bennett's murder.

With the arrest warrant in hand, Detective Ken Copeland, Detective Randy Miller, and Officer David Green
loaded into an unmarked van and headed to Planten's laboratory. Copeland's heart was beating out of his chest. He
couldn't believe this day had finally come. They had suc-
ceeded. He couldn't wait to see the look on Planten's face
when he told him he was under arrest.

The building was surrounded by officers in preparation
for Planten's exit from any door that he might choose to
leave through. They were taking no chances in case he saw
them and decided to run. One way or another, Planten was
going to leave work that day in handcuffs.

## Countdown

Wednesday, October 19, 2005, was cleanup day at the state
fertilizer laboratory. Large Dumpsters were placed outside
the building, and employees spent the day going through
drawers, closets, and storage areas throwing out what they
didn't need. They also took stock of their inventory and
took notes on what supplies needed to be replenished.

Reilly had grown fond of Drew Planten in a motherly way despite everything that was going on behind the
scenes. The more time she spent with him, the more she

pitied him and worried about him. She was torn between a sense of guilt about what she had done behind Planten's back, and an overriding need to help investigators find justice for Stephanie Bennett. Still, in her heart, she felt that if she cleared him, all would eventually be forgiven or, even better, Planten might never have to know what she had done. The police would simply walk away when the DNA didn't match.

On cleanup day, Reilly chose to work side by side with Planten. She knew the DNA test could be completed at any moment, and that police might swoop in and arrest him. They had not shared with her what the plan would be if Planten's DNA matched the killer's. But she figured they would act quickly. She realized that this might be her last day with Planten.

Together, Planten and Reilly went through the inventory of chemicals in the laboratory, cataloging what they had and what they were running low on. They chatted casually. Ironically, Planten seemed to trust Reilly more than his other co-workers. He was still painfully shy, but with her, he shared a small amount of personal information that he didn't with anyone else.

Around 4:20 P.M., just as Reilly went back to her office and was getting ready to leave for the day, Major Dennis Lane of the Raleigh Police Department called her on her cell phone. Lane was in charge of all of the investigators in the Raleigh Police Department. A thirty-year veteran of the police force, he very rarely got involved directly in cases, but this one was different. This was the case everyone in the department wanted to solve, including Lane. Perry, Taylor, and Copeland had been briefing him on the case since his promotion. It was after the detectives paid Planten a visit at his apartment that Lane felt like they were truly onto something.

"When they told me about that visit it made the hair stand up on the back of my neck. To me at that point there wasn't a doubt that we were headed in the right direction," Lane said.

So on the day of Planten's planned arrest, Lane decided he would be the one to contact Reilly. When he called her, he asked her in a very serious tone if Planten was still at work. Without hesitation, she put the phone down and went into Planten's lab where she spotted him in his usual spot on his stool hunched over his desk. She got back on the phone and reported this to Lane.

When Reilly returned to the phone, Lane told her the building was surrounded by police officers.

"I guess the DNA was a match?" Reilly asked solemnly even though the fact that the building was surrounded had given her the answer already.

"It was a *perfect* match," Lane told her. He didn't want Reilly to panic, nor did he want Planten to run. He knew he was walking a delicate tightrope act. He also had a responsibility to protect anyone in the building, including Reilly, from a man whom detectives now believed was a cold-blooded killer.

Lane asked Reilly what door Planten usually used to exit the building. She told him Planten left through the back door and would be riding his bike home again because his clunker of a car was still out of commission. Lane then asked Reilly to call him and let him know the moment Planten was leaving the office. The last thing Lane wanted was for them to exit the building together. There would be many guns drawn on Planten as he left work that day; Lane didn't want any citizens anywhere near the action, including Reilly. Because they were unsure of what Planten might do, the officers had to take every possible precaution to protect themselves from this man no matter how fragile he appeared to be.

Reilly's heart started racing after she hung up the phone with Lane. An overwhelming feeling of deep sadness came over her. Her months of trying to do the right thing, hoping the test would confirm her belief Planten was *not* the person responsible for this heinous crime would now end with his arrest. It was a scenario she hadn't planned for in her mind or in her heart, but she also knew there was no denying the absolute credibility of a DNA match. Like a good soldier, she would follow through with the major's orders.

"Here I am running around, trying to be invisible, trying to watch when he's going home, and hoping my cell phone won't bug out on me down in the basement," Reilly recalled hysterically.

At that time of day, few people were left in the building. Reilly could hear flushing in the men's bathroom and assumed Planten was in there. She called Lane back and told him Planten was in the restroom, and she thought he would be out momentarily. She tried to look busy at her desk. When she heard the bathroom door swing open and shut, she got up to look for Planten. She couldn't find him anywhere. It was like he had simply vanished.

"I couldn't find him," Reilly said. She peeked into the back hallway and saw that his bike was still there. "I know *he knew*. He had to have known."

Reilly got fed up after a while thinking Planten had to be hiding from her. There was nothing more she could do to make him come out. She was also admittedly a little concerned about being alone with him in the building knowing that he was now officially accused of murder. She was weary. She was *done*. So, at a few minutes before 5:00 P.M., she decided the police would have to take it from here. She ignored police orders, left the building without calling Major Lane, and went directly to her car.

Reilly scanned the parking lot for police as she left and saw no sign of them which she thought was strange, but decided they must be keeping a low profile. No sooner had she gotten into her car when her cell phone rang again. It was Major Lane telling her to go back into the building and find Planten. A million thoughts went through her mind: *Drive away; let them handle it; it's not your problem anymore.* But then something else went through her mind, a picture of Stephanie Bennett from the news flashed in her head. Stephanie's beautiful, innocent smile edged its way into Joanne Reilly's conscience. She knew what she had to do. She had come too far to let Stephanie's family down now. She had to do the right thing. Reluctantly, she got back out of her car and headed for the building wondering just how all of this was going to end. She hoped not with a gunfight and hoped not with her in between Planten and the police.

"As I did, he was coming out, and I held open the door while he maneuvered his bike through it," Reilly said, her voice cracking with emotion as she replayed the moment in her mind. She tried to act casual as Planten nodded good night to her in their brief passing. She tried not to look back because she knew she wouldn't like what she was about to see. Suddenly, she heard commotion behind her, loud voices, the clanking sound of the metal bike hitting the sidewalk. She stopped and forced herself to look back. "I turned and looked over, and they had his head down on the ground with his hair spilling over his face and guns pointed at him."

As hard as she has tried, Joanne Reilly has never been able to erase this image from her mind. She barely glanced at Planten on the ground before turning away, but it was enough of a look for the moment to be indelibly etched in her consciousness forever. It was a bittersweet moment, one of justice, but at the same time, one of loss, *her* loss. She lost the person she had come to believe Planten was— a meek, sensitive introvert who just wanted everyone to leave him alone. Yet, at the same time, she gained the satisfaction that in some small way she had helped police get a cold-blooded killer off the streets.

Detective Ken Copeland remembered the moment vividly as well, but his recollection included no regrets. Only one feeling arose in his mind about that day: victory.

As Drew Planten walked down the sidewalk away from the front door of the fertilizer laboratory, Copeland and his crew jumped out from their hiding place, an old beat-up van, and took him down to the ground. He let go of the bike, and it fell to the ground as investigators handcuffed him behind his back. It was seamless.

"We just pulled right up beside him in the covert van, slid the door open, jumped out and grabbed him," Copeland said, shuddering as he remembered the adrenaline rush.

Copeland patted Planten down and, to his surprise, found a loaded handgun in his right cargo pants pocket. Both buttons on the pocket were fastened, but the detectives felt sure that if Planten had had any advance notice they were coming, things might have turned out differently.

"I think if we had walked across the parking lot things might have gotten ugly," Copeland said, shaking his head.

Lane agreed that the gun was a red flag. In his mind Planten had a plan—suicide by cop.

"We got on him so quick he couldn't get to his gun," Lane said. "But, if he could have gotten his hand in that pocket to his gun on the day that we arrested him, we would have had to shoot him. There's no doubt in my mind."

The detectives were assisted in the takedown by the Raleigh Police Department's Fugitive Task Force. Per department protocol, the team was told only that they were going to participate in a "high-risk arrest." They were not told what the suspect was accused of doing or to what case he was connected.

"Drew, you are under the arrest for the murder of Stephanie Bennett," Detective Ken Copeland said in a booming voice after he picked the handcuffed Planten up from the sidewalk and brushed him off.

With those words, the members of the Fugitive Task

Force went wild and started cheering. They hadn't known what Planten was being arrested for, and to hear it was the Bennett case blew their minds. This was one of those cases that was *personal* to the Raleigh officers. Almost everyone in the department had worked on the case at one point or another, and if they hadn't, they surely knew enough about it to know that this was a big day.

The detectives gingerly placed Planten into the back-seat of a waiting police car. Throughout the entire arrest, Planten didn't say a word. He just stared past the officers as if his mind were on a completely different planet. Cope-land told Officer Allen Place, who sat in the backseat of the police car with Planten, to observe him throughout the ride to the police station. He told Place not to carry on a conversation with Planten per se, but to write down any-thing Planten said. Yet true to his original form, Planten said nothing at all on the way back to the station. It ap-peared that he wasn't just shutting out the detectives; he was shutting out the world.

## A Father's Prayers Answered

Another major step: Sergeant Clem Perry needed to call Carmon Bennett and share the news with him. Perry and Copeland had become the points of contact for the fam-ily after Lieutenant Chris Morgan retired. Throughout the investigation, Perry had dreaded having to call Carmon month after month to say the same thing, "We're working on it, but we don't have anything." Perry said that before every call that he would try to come up with different ways to say "we don't have anything." This well-intentioned mis-sion to keep Carmon hopeful left Perry feeling exhausted and disingenuous.

On occasion, Carmon would call the detectives and mention how he noticed that they had solved another murder case in Raleigh, yet his daughter's case remained unsolved.

"I've seen on TV that you guys have had another murder and you've made an arrest," Carmon would say.

"It was just so difficult. I'd look at Ken sometimes and say, 'Ken, what are we going to tell him?' " said Perry.

Carmon was a get-to-the-point kind of guy who immediately saw through Perry's thinly veiled attempts to sound positive in light of the situation. But on this day, Perry finally had something positive to tell Carmon Bennett. He could change his mantra and give Carmon the good news that he had always hoped that he would be able to deliver. It was something Perry had thought about doing since that first night when he met Carmon at Stephanie's apartment complex. He never actually dreamed he would be the one, however, to deliver it.

"I've got some very important news I've got to discuss with you," Perry told Carmon.

Carmon had company at the time and was getting ready to sit down for dinner. Perry told him he might want to ask his company to leave. Perry was anxious about how to approach Carmon with the information. He knew in light of Carmon's no-nonsense personality that he should just come right out with it, but Perry wasn't sure how Carmon would react. Of course, Carmon had always wanted an arrest, but now he would have to deal with the ugly truth—there would be a face and a name attached to his daughter's killer.

"He is a very matter-of-fact man, and I was hemming and hawing with him," Perry said, realizing he should have just gotten right down to business.

"We have some very important news we'd like to tell you," Perry reiterated.

"Clem, just go ahead and spit it out. Tell me what's going on," Carmon said with growing agitation in his voice. "Get to the point here."

"We got a match," Perry said clearing his throat nervously.

When Perry finally told Carmon that the police had a suspect in custody in connection with his daughter's murder, there was silence on the other end of the phone line. Carmon was in shock. It was the call he had been waiting for, for three and a half years. Perry could hear Carmon tell his wife, Jennifer, the news in the background. She started to cry. For a few moments all Perry could hear was Carmon's heavy breathing and Jennifer's sobbing. He imagined Carmon must have been comforting his wife while he waited patiently on the other end of the line.

Perry went on to tell Carmon that he didn't have a lot of details for him yet because everything was still unfolding, but he promised to fill him in on what he could later. For Perry, the conversation was a fitting ending to the conversation he had started with Carmon on May 21, 2002, the day Stephanie's body was found at the Bridgeport Apartments.

"It made me feel good because I had been the one to tell him *we thought* it might be Stephanie in there. I think he knew she was dead, but I had basically confirmed it. So telling him about the arrest was good for me," Perry said, remembering his overwhelming feeling of redemption on the day Drew Planten was arrested.

## Silence

Drew Planten sat in the interview room at the Raleigh Police Department with detectives for almost six hours. It was a tiny, plain room with a long Formica table, three mismatched leather and metal office chairs, white cinder block walls, and a small observation window on the wall overlooking the table. The investigators went in and out of the room, taking turns trying to get him to speak to them.

At first, he simply ignored their questions, played with his handcuffs, and fidgeted around in his chair. But as time went on, he became completely still and continued to be nonresponsive.

Sergeant Clem Perry asked police psychologist Michael Teague to come up and observe Planten's interview through the one-way window into the interrogation room. During his brief observation, Teague didn't get the feeling that Planten was mentally ill. Planten acted like the investigators were not there—almost as though he were in a trance. Teague had seen people pretending to be crazy before. Crazy was not what he saw when he looked at Planten. What he saw was a smart man who realized his time had run out, and he had no more options.

"Planten knew the game was up. Planten knew that he had left his DNA. He was a chemist. He knew that," Teague said. "I think he was beginning to get his courage up to kill himself. He knew that life was not going to be fun from here on out."

Investigators had been startled to find the loaded handgun in the pocket of Planten's cargo pants when he was arrested. They wondered how long he had been carrying a loaded weapon to work with him on state government property. They had assumed the gun was probably for self-defense against the police, but Teague thought otherwise.

"I think the handgun was not to fight police. I think the handgun was to kill himself," Teague said. "I think he was going to use that to blow his brains out."

While Teague's instincts told him Planten was "ready to cash his chips in," he obviously didn't know for sure what was going on in the man's mind, since Planten wasn't talking to anyone. Teague told the detectives the Wake County Jail should be notified that Planten might be at risk for suicide and should be watched closely.

As a detective, Copeland usually wore a jacket and tie, but on this day he was still in his police uniform because of his stint at the State Fair. He was afraid the outfit might intimidate Planten.

"Uniforms just don't tend to work too well in the interview room," Copeland said. "We knew he was savvy enough that what we were about to do was going to be important. With Drew, we knew his mind was like a tape recorder."

Detective Copeland borrowed street clothes from another detective before he entered the interview room. Copeland will never forget the large red button-down short-sleeved shirt he was forced to wear because he didn't have backup clothes at the station. It was all he had to work with, though, so he reluctantly put it on.

The detectives' guts told them that Planten wouldn't talk, but Copeland and Detective Jackie Taylor had been in situations like this before where suspects faced with overwhelming evidence had broken down and confessed. They decided it was definitely worth a shot.

At first, Taylor and Copeland went into the interview room together, then Taylor went in alone. She was known for her strong interviewing skills, plus there was a thought that a woman in this situation might be able to get through to Planten in a way a man could not. Not unlike the way he warmed up to Reilly, investigators thought Taylor might be able to make him do the same, but Planten didn't budge, not even an inch.

"What do you want us to do with your dog, is there someone we should call?" Taylor said to Planten hoping to get a rise out of him. *Nothing.*

"He was acutely depressed," said Teague—his professional assessment of Planten that night. "I think he knew the world was closing in on him, and why he didn't run earlier, I'm not sure."

Teague wasn't sure what had made Planten stay in the area after Stephanie's murder. Was it because he felt like he would have a hard time getting another job? Was it because he was stalking other local women, potential victims? Or was it simply that he was in denial that he could be arrested? Had he thought he was smarter than the cops?

Investigators weren't as hung up on the "why" as Teague was. To them, Planten was in police custody, *period*. There would be plenty of time to answer the other questions later. It was now time for them to brave the bright lights of the television cameras waiting outside the Raleigh Police Department and take Planten to the Wake County Jail. It was just after 10:00 P.M. and the detectives knew that the media was chomping at the bit to get the story ready for the 11:00 news. They just needed one thing: video of the accused killer. While the Raleigh police generally avoided parading suspects in front of television cameras, this was a case for which they didn't mind the media being there. They wanted them to document this historic moment.

The investigators paused and all took collective deep breaths as they walked off of the elevator and saw the glare of the bright yellow television lights gleaming through the glass front doors of the police station. *Here we go.*

Taylor had a serious look on her face as she gripped Planten just beneath his right shoulder. In her blue blazer, white shirt, and khakis she looked every bit of the tough, no-nonsense female detective. Her blond hair was neatly pinned back, and she looked straight ahead ignoring the throng of distractions as she steered Planten through the crowd of photographers to the waiting police car about twenty feet from the front door of the station.

Copeland held Planten just under his left arm. The detective's oversize red shirt that he had borrowed from another officer seemed to glow beneath the powerful television lights against the backdrop of the black sky. Like Taylor, Copeland moved toward the blue and white patrol car with no expression on his face, mindful the video would probably be repeated multiple times on every local television station in the days and weeks to come. He didn't want to regret *anything* about this night.

Planten wore a white T-shirt and baggy green pants. His gangly arms were handcuffed behind his back. His hair hung limply in his eyes, almost completely obstructing his face from view. His body appeared so frail it looked like he might just collapse to the ground if it wasn't for the two detectives on either side of him supporting his weight. Drew Planten never looked up at the cameras. It appeared he was determined to remain a mystery, not just to the police, but to everyone.

# CHAPTER ELEVEN

# Searching for Answers

## October 20, 2005

All actual heroes are essential men, and all men possible heroes.

—ELIZABETH BARRETT BROWNING

On October 20, 2005, the Raleigh Police Department's top brass, Chief Jane Perlov and Major Dennis Lane, held a press conference to officially announce the arrest of Drew Planten in the murder of Stephanie Bennett. A sign in the building's lobby read: "WAY TO GO MAJOR CRIMES." Planten's mug shot was pasted in the middle of the sign with the police radio code "10-95" beneath it, which means "suspect in custody." It was a fitting tribute to all of the hard work done by detectives and an example of just how much solving the case meant to the entire department.

"I'll tell you in all my years in this business, and there have been quite a few, this stands out as one the best pieces of dogged dedicated work that I've ever seen anywhere in *any* community," Perlov said. Coming from a chief who was as tough on her people as she was on crime, this was the highest possible praise.

The petite, blond chief with her pixie haircut stood behind the podium beaming like a proud parent as she congratulated the detectives who had worked so hard on the case. Behind her, retired Detective Sandy Culpepper, Sergeant Clem Perry, and detectives Ken Copeland and Jackie Taylor stood solemnly listening to her with rapt attention. They were no doubt so excited by the outcome of the case that they wanted to jump out of their skins, but instead, they controlled their emotions and appeared like reverent parishioners in church on Sunday morning listening intently to the preacher, a.k.a. the chief.

Perlov bragged about how Taylor and Copeland had gone back to basics and spent countless hours poring over the evidence in the case again, knocking on doors, and re-interviewing people.

"They worked hard and they worked smart," Perlov said proudly. "I cannot say enough about their dedication and their commitment to solving this crime, but I can sincerely say thank you from everybody for all you have done."

The attorney general of North Carolina, Roy Cooper, also spoke at the press conference about the role that the State Bureau of Investigation crime laboratory, which he oversaw, had played in solving the case. One of Cooper's pet projects had been to get more funding from state lawmakers for extra agents at the SBI lab. Before he did this, the lab had become so backed up it often took months to get DNA tested, if at all. To Cooper, the Bennett case was proof that his lobbying had been well worth the effort.

The handsome, affable politician was never one to shy away from a television camera, especially when his office had a credible reason to take credit for something positive.

"This case shows that it often takes DNA to close the deal," Cooper said. "Once again it's DNA to the rescue. Once again this incredible technology has helped assist determined police officers to solve a murder case and make a community safer."

Major Dennis Lane, the supervisor in charge of all of the detectives in the Raleigh Police Department, then took the podium, with an expression of pride not unlike Chief Perlov's.

Lane wasn't one to show much emotion. His neatly parted hair and Inspector Clouseau mustache screamed *serious cop,* but on this day he lauded his detectives and the incredible job they had done.

"It's a very rewarding feeling to solve a case this old, I can tell you that," said Lane with uncharacteristic enthusiasm. "This is where the old-fashioned police work meets new police work. This is where the shoe leather pays off, and the DNA pays off," he said. "It's a meeting of both worlds."

Inside, Lane was bursting. He could barely contain his excitement. The case had gone on for so long, and while they had never given up on finding the killer, there were days it had felt unsolvable. At the podium, Lane kept his feelings in check, but years later he admitted his *real* feelings from that day.

"Thrilled is probably an understatement. It's probably one of the best feelings I ever had when I was on the police department," Lane said without reservation. "Drew Planten was a conniving, sneaky predator who scouted and picked out people and was going to do what he was going to do," he added with disgust. "Once he identified who his target was going to be, he would get to that target one way or another."

But at the podium on the day of the press conference, Lane didn't get into his emotions about the case. He skirted the details saying he didn't want to compromise the integrity of the investigation by revealing too much at this early stage while preparing the case for trial. He also pointed out that the investigation was continuing, and the police still needed the public's help with information, specifically information about Planten.

"We are looking at any other unsolved crimes in our jurisdiction and other jurisdictions," Lane said.

Detectives Taylor and Copeland, who had spent most of their careers behind the scenes in the police department, were suddenly touted publicly as heroes who had solved the case with their relentless perseverance. After the press conference ended, the cameras surrounded them like a tornado and microphones were shoved in their faces from every direction. The investigators had dressed up for the occasion—Copeland in a tan blazer with an olive shirt and a beige and burgundy speckled tie, Taylor in a navy blue blazer and a blue and white paisley shirt buttoned up to her neck. They seemed as though they had properly prepared for the media circus that was suddenly being thrust on them. As bright lights shone in their faces, and reporters rapidly fired questions at them, they stood side by side and answered confidently. The first question was whether they thought their "old-fashioned police work" paid off.

"It is the best way in the world to do police work," Copeland said with a grin.

"It's the only way," Taylor chimed in off-camera, finishing his sentence, as she was prone to do.

"There's a lot of paperwork, but if you don't knock on people's doors and talk to people, you'll never get what you need, and that's what you have to do," Copeland said.

"Exactly," Taylor said, punctuating the end of her partner's sentence with a smile.

Copeland thanked all of the other investigators who'd worked so hard on the case before he inherited it. He thanked his family and Taylor's family for their support throughout the long and arduous investigation during which the detectives spent many hours away from home. He also thanked the Bennett family for their unlimited patience. Reporters then asked Copeland how Stephanie's loved ones were reacting to the arrest.

"They're very emotional. They're very happy, and

there's no way I can say I know how they feel, because I can't," Copeland said sincerely.

## Family Reax

In television news there is always the primary story that is referred to as the "nuts-and-bolts," and then there are sidebars that are additional stories related to the main story. The bigger the story, the more sidebars there will be. One predictable sidebar to an arrest in a murder case is always getting reaction from the victim's family which in the television news business is slugged "reax."

Reporter Melissa Buscher of WRAL was a veteran, straightforward, responsible reporter whose innate nurturing instinct would strike just the right tone with Stephanie Bennett's family. So, while the press conference was going on, Buscher headed up to Virginia to get reaction from Stephanie's father, Carmon Bennett, and her stepmother, Jennifer.

Unlike other marriages that had buckled under the weight of grief, it appeared that Carmon and Jennifer's bond had only gotten stronger as Jennifer supported her husband through this unimaginable tragedy. Their collective strength was evident the day they spoke to Buscher about Planten's arrest.

"Shock, quite a shock, we had no idea that they were this close to solving this thing," Carmon said as he sat on the bench on his front porch in front of the camera. He was shoulder to shoulder with his wife. "We knew they'd been working very hard on it."

"I just started crying," Jennifer said of receiving the phone call from Sergeant Clem Perry regarding Drew Planten's arrest. "I just wasn't believing what I was hearing."

Investigators had tried to keep Carmon and Jennifer in the loop over the previous weeks, but they were also mindful not to give them too much information. The last thing Perry wanted to do was get this man's hopes up only to have them dashed again if Planten had not been a match. They also didn't want to blow the case by possibly allowing the information to leak out and somehow tip Planten off they were onto him.

The couple had tried to have hope over the past three years, but their resolve was wearing thin, and there were many times they considered the fact that the case might never be solved.

"We were up and down and just a couple months ago we said, you know, I bet they never find this person, and then we'd tell ourselves we can't think like that, we've got to think positive," said Jennifer as tears rolled down her face, and she held on tightly to Carmon's arm.

Inside the house, Carmon allowed the photographer to take a shot of Stephanie's old bedroom which had basically been left untouched since her death. It was not uncommon for the parents of children who died to leave their rooms just as they had been at the time of their death. It had become a sacred space to them. Stephanie's bedroom was decorated in a typical frilly girl style with a blue and white gingham spread on the bed and teddy bears adorning every available space. There were also mementos, details of the life lost—for example, a prized diploma from Roanoke College and a poster full of pictures of Stephanie and her friends with the words "We love you Steph" written in the middle.

Carmon and Jennifer marveled at how they were able to get through the agonizing three and a half years while there seemed to be very little hope of resolution. They concluded it was Stephanie herself who'd made their unlikely optimism possible. Not a day went by when Carmon didn't think of his only daughter and the joy she had brought into his life.

"Someone just last week said, 'Did she ever not smile?'

She always smiled. She had a smile on her face continuously. Didn't have any enemies in the world," Carmon said with tears in his eyes. "I think she would be happy to know he's been caught. Stephanie was a wonderful person and a very strong young lady, and a lot of our strength comes from Stephanie."

The investigators had told Carmon and Jennifer a little bit about Planten, but the couple still had many questions. Carmon was more sure now than ever that the killer had stalked Stephanie and waited for the right time to attack. He hoped the court process would allow him to finally get the answers he had been seeking since his daughter's death.

By accident, Jennifer had seen a picture of Planten online when she was searching the Web for information on the arrest. She hadn't meant to look at it, *not yet,* but she couldn't help herself. There was a part of her that desperately needed to know who this person was so she could begin to understand what had happened to her family.

"A lot of anger," Jennifer said of seeing Planten's photograph. "I'm just dwelling on thinking of him sitting down there. I can't get it out of my mind."

"It's just takes you back to day one," Carmon piped in.

"*Why?* I don't understand," Jennifer said, her voice cracking as she continuously wiped tears from her eyes.

Jennifer's daughter, Stephanie's roommate and stepsister, Deanna Powell, was also at Carmon's house that day. Dee wore a simple black T-shirt and had heavy bags under her eyes as though she had been up crying all night long since news of the arrest.

"It's somewhat of a relief. I have a little bit more faith in the police, but still, it's really hard. Brings up a lot of things that I hadn't dealt with in a long time," Dee said swallowing audibly. "I'm disgusted, sick, it's *hard.*"

Dee said she was sure that Planten was not someone she or Stephanie ever knew, that the crime was completely random. As Carmon believed, Dee surmised Planten had been stalking Stephanie and had waited for the right opportunity to strike.

"I'm angry at him. I keep thinking about [how he's lived free] for the last three years. He just gets up and drives to work every day," said Dee incredulously.

In the front window of the Bennetts' home was a single electric candle, the kind often seen in windows at Christmas. Carmon explained that Christmas had been Stephanie's absolute favorite time of the year. After her death, he just didn't have the energy or enthusiasm to decorate the house with lights anymore. He had decided that instead, a single candle would burn in their window year-round in honor of Stephanie's memory. In an ironic way, it would be a solemn reminder of the light that was so tragically snuffed out.

"The candle in the window says it all," Carmon said in a weary voice.

## Bittersweet Justice

Investigator Chris Morgan hadn't been invited to the press conference at the Raleigh Police Department, but this didn't keep the media from wanting his input. The cameras found him out at the State Fairgrounds where he was supervising the security detail.

He had been working at the State Fair on the day Drew Planten was arrested. He knew something was up when Copeland, who was supposed to be working for Morgan as a security officer, got called into work at the police department and had to bow out of his duties at the fairgrounds. A little while later, Morgan got a call from a friend of his on the force telling him that the case had been solved.

"For two-and-a-half years I had tried everything in my bag of tricks," Morgan said bitterly, "but I couldn't find this son-of-a-bitch no matter what I tried." He added, "I was happy they had done better than I could do."

Morgan wanted nothing more than to see justice done for Stephanie Bennett, but at the same time, he had always hoped *he* would be the one to find justice for her. When he retired, leaving the case unsolved, it continued to eat away at him and often kept him from sleeping at night. He counted it among his failures as a detective. But on this day, under the clear blue October skies of the North Carolina Indian summer, Morgan finally made peace with the positive resolution, whether it came with or without his help.

Later that night, Carmon Bennett called Morgan and thanked him for all of the hard work he had done on the case despite the fact he had not actually solved it. Mostly, he thanked Morgan for his compassion and his friendship throughout the investigation.

Morgan said Detective Copeland also called him the next day and thanked him for giving him the opportunity to work on the case. Copeland acknowledged that he knew others above Morgan's head had been skeptical of Morgan's decision to put the case in his hands, and Copeland appreciated the fact that the retired investigator had had enough faith in him to ignore the naysayers.

"It's a good day. It's a very good day," Morgan said. "This is maybe the day when some things start to heal. There are some things that never will, but maybe this is the beginning."

Morgan said when he spoke to Carmon the previous evening it made him reflect on the first conversation he had had with him on May 21, 2002, the day they found Stephanie's body in her apartment.

"This was a much better conversation," Morgan said with a chuckle. "We knew that there was a monster out there. I always felt like if we didn't get him sooner or later, he'd do it again. There's a sense of relief."

Morgan said the case was never really cold; the work never stopped. He gave all of the credit to the detectives who solved it—Jackie Taylor and Ken Copeland—saying they were the real heroes. They put the pieces of the puzzle together and figured out who killed Stephanie. He was just a bit player in their magnificent triumph.

"They just busted their humps on this case from day one and never gave up, never put it down, never let it go," Morgan said shaking his head.

Morgan knew one thing for sure—Planten's arrest gave him back something he had lost for several years.

"I slept a lot better than I have in the past three and a half," he said with a grin, referring to the night of the arrest.

And it was true that Chris Morgan did look well rested for a change.

## Courtroom Drama

Shortly after the press conference at the police department ended, Drew Planten was scheduled to have his first court appearance. He had been in jail just about fifteen hours, but his physical appearance had already changed drastically. When Planten was brought into the Wake County District Court at 2:00 P.M. on Wednesday, October 20, 2005, he looked like something out of a freak show. He had refused to talk, walk, or eat since arriving at the Wake County Jail the previous evening. Deputies wheeled him into court strapped to a wheelchair. His head hung limp like a rag doll, though partially supported by a brace attached to the back of the chair so he wouldn't completely fall over. His forearms were tethered to the arms of the wheelchair with plastic cuffs. His legs were tied to the foot-rest of the wheelchair. Wake County District Court Judge Anne Salisbury was told by Assistant District Attorney

Susan Spurlin that Planten was being handled this way because he appeared to be in a "catatonic state."

Judge Salisbury watched the drama unfold as Planten, surrounded by multiple deputies and jail administrators, was wheeled directly in front of her bench. Salisbury, with her short brown curly hair, glasses, and powerful voice, always commanded authority in her courtroom. On this day, she had the determined expression of someone who was seeing something disturbing, but had decided not to publicly acknowledge the horror of it.

"Mr. Planten, you are here today charged with first degree murder. I'm appointing you counsel to represent you in this matter," Salisbury said from the bench with complete professional detachment from the bizarre circumstances. The formality of the court's rigid procedures juxtaposed against Planten's crazy appearance that no one was acknowledging made it look all the more ridiculous. Yet, somehow the formality of the courtroom transformed the weird moment into something that approached normalcy.

"I'm not sure his physical condition is such that he can fill out that information," the judge said referring to the paperwork that would declare that he didn't have enough money to pay an attorney and was in need of a public defender. This statement was the judge's only public acknowledgment of Planten's strange appearance. "Out of an abundance of caution for the moment, I'm going to find that he is indigent."

Even though it was obvious he was not going to respond to her, Salisbury ended the brief court appearance with a direct statement to Planten. "Thank you, Mr. Planten, I understand you have an appointment you need to make," the judge said in closing, as though speaking to a totally coherent individual.

The appointment in question was Planten's move from the Wake County Jail to North Carolina's maximum security facility, Central Prison, just down the road. Central Prison had a hospital where Planten could receive medical care unavailable at the local jail. Central Prison was also the home of the state's death row and housed a majority of the first-degree murderers in North Carolina who were serving life sentences. Planten was preemptively being moved to the place where he would most likely spend the rest of his life if he was convicted of Stephanie Bennett's murder.

The ultimate decision to move him came from Wake County Sheriff Donnie Harrison, who was in charge of the local jail. Harrison said his officers simply could not handle someone in Planten's state, someone who would not eat or care for himself.

When Harrison talked to the media in the hallway after the court appearance, he scoffed at the suggestion that Planten was actually catatonic. In his opinion, Planten's bizarre behavior was all just a well-rehearsed act.

"You've got to remember, for three years he's walked around. All of a sudden when he gets arrested, he's in this state, so you figure that out for yourself," Harrison said through gritted teeth, in his strong southern drawl. "But he's been this way since he's been in our custody. [Although] he has gotten up and used the bathroom, so like I said, you can read between those lines."

Harrison said his officers had had no choice but to bring Planten into the courtroom the way they did, tethered to the wheelchair. By law, everyone who is arrested in North Carolina must have a first court appearance within the next business day.

"That was because he didn't want to get up on his own," Harrison said without apology. "He would not pay us any mind, so we just put him in the chair."

Harrison also confirmed that Planten had been on suicide watch at the Wake County Jail given both the severity of the crime he was charged with, and also the unusual way in which he was acting.

Wake County District Attorney Colon Willoughby also showed up for Planten's first court appearance. He had been overseeing the case, as he did all high-profile cases, even though it was officially assigned to one of his most experienced prosecutors Susan Spurlin. While Willoughby let his assistant district attorneys handle their own cases independently, he was always in the loop about what was going on and was always available to assist them when they needed him.

The dark-haired DA with a boyish face that belied his years was not his usual jovial self this day. Like Sheriff Harrison, Willoughby was skeptical about the way Drew Planten presented himself in the courtroom.

"It's interesting they brought him in a chair," Willoughby noted, with true grit in his voice, "but they've been watching him for weeks, and he's been functioning perfectly well. No sign of any of this until after his arrest, so the whole thing is a ruse." He continued, "This is America; you can behave any way you choose. You're still accountable for what you do and the fact that you lay down on the floor and act crazy doesn't really change things."

Willoughby characterized Planten as a "very dangerous man." He said the case had been solved because of the relentless unwillingness of the detectives to give up, and reiterated that what the public saw of Planten in the courtroom had very little to do with the realities of the case as he knew them to be.

"I'd say that's drama suitable for television; that's not real life," Willoughby concluded.

## Drew Planten

"He was a good person, an upstanding citizen. I didn't know of him ever doing anything inappropriate," Drew Planten's mother, Sarah Chandler, told WRAL reporter Julia Lewis in a phone interview the day after her son's arrest.

Drew Planten was born on March 7, 1970, in Paterson, New Jersey, to Sarah Chandler and Robert Planten. He was the third of what would end up to be a family of four boys. Planten had two older brothers, Ronald and Donald, and would eventually have a younger brother, Duane. Robert Planten was a municipal works supervisor who was convicted of official misconduct in 1985 for taking a vehicle hood ornament as a bribe in return for his approval on site plans for a local development project.

Sarah Chandler, who worked at a daycare at the time, said in published reports that her husband was verbally and physically abusive to her and her sons. For this reason, she ultimately left him. Chandler took an extra job waitressing to support her four children. She also enrolled in paralegal school, falling in love with the law and believing she could use it to help people.

To pursue her dream of going to law school, Chandler moved her family to Michigan so that she could attend Thomas M. Cooley Law School. When Chandler graduated, she set up a law practice in a charming old Victorian house on Cochran Avenue, in Charlotte, Michigan. The small salt-of-the earth midwestern town, with just under eighty-five hundred residents, wasn't far from Lansing, the state capital. It seemed like the perfect place for a single mother to raise her four sons.

Chandler also wanted to give back to the community after all she had endured in her abusive marriage. She helped open a domestic violence shelter in Charlotte so that women who had gone through what she had would have a safe place to go for help.

Drew Planten attended East Lansing High School where he excelled at academics, but was not involved much in student life like clubs or sports. People who knew Planten back then said that he didn't appear to have many friends or any girlfriends, and mostly kept to himself.

"He's a very quiet man," Chandler admitted to Lewis.

Planten graduated from high school in 1988 and then took pre-veterinary classes at a local community college before transferring to Michigan State University in 1990.

"He was a good student, always made good grades all through school and even in college he got good grades," his mother said, sounding like she was mustering up as much pride as she could, given the circumstances. "He was always interested in science from the time he was a young person in grade school."

On April 9, 1993, Planten's father, who was fifty-four at the time, died in a house fire in Cheyenne, Wyoming. By that point in their lives, Drew Planten and his brothers had had little contact with their father. The local fire marshal ruled the flames started in a stove and that the deadly blaze was accidental. Still, Raleigh detectives always wondered if there wasn't more to the fire, given Robert Planten's violent history. There was no doubt the man had enemies who might have wanted him dead.

Drew Planten graduated from the university in 1995 with a degree in zoology. For the majority of the time he attended college, Planten continued to live with his mother in Charlotte, about twenty miles from the campus.

After graduation, Planten had difficulty finding a job. He worked briefly as a laboratory technician for a company called BioPort, which developed the anthrax vaccine, and for a short period of time he also worked for a company called Neogen, a food safety testing company. In spring 2000, he headed to Oregon for a seasonal job with the U.S. Department of Agriculture counting salmon as they swam upstream. Finally, in July 2000, he landed a permanent job as a chemistry technician with the North Carolina Department of Agriculture after a single phone interview.

Although moving from Michigan to North Carolina seemed like a long way to go for a job, Planten's brothers had ties to the Tar Heel state. Older brother Donald was already living in Asheville and working for an architectural firm. Donald had married Martha Grainge in Raleigh on May 16, 1992, and oldest brother Ronald had attended North Carolina State University, also in Raleigh.

At the North Carolina Department of Agriculture, Drew's job was to analyze fertilizer samples; he was paid $31,713 a year by the state—not much for a scientist, but he needed to work and hoped it might lead to higher pay down the road. He moved into the Dominion on Lake Lynn Apartments— just fifty yards through the woods from Stephanie Bennett's apartment at the adjacent Bridgeport Apartment complex.

Planten lived at the Dominion Apartments from the fall of 2000 to about a year after Stephanie's murder and then moved to a cheaper complex across town on Buck Jones Road, which is where he was living when he was arrested. By all accounts, Planten had had a pretty unremarkable life, living well beneath the radar of the people around him until October 19, 2005.

## Head Games

According to psychologist Michael Teague, research shows the most common trait in a rapist is an "avoidant personality." In his opinion, Drew Planten fit this description unequivocally.

"He avoided people he wasn't perversely attracted to," Teague said. "I was told by one of the women we interviewed if a woman was overweight, he wouldn't talk to her."

Yet, Drew Planten was unusually kind to older women, like Joanne Reilly at the fertilizer laboratory, who, Teague thought, probably represented a mother figure to him. Teague surmised Planten's mother was probably the only woman who had ever shown him unconditional love, and thus if he was going to trust anyone other than her, it was going to be someone *like* her. But when it came to physical attraction, Planten wanted young, pretty women, women who wanted nothing to do with him, women who were way out of his league.

" 'These young women have turned me down and made fun of me so much I have a right to unload on them,' " Teague said, imagining what might have gone through Planten's mind regarding the women he admired. Teague felt like it was this consistent negative treatment of Planten by women that made him want to punish them physically.

The avoidant personality disorder is defined by the *Diagnostic and Statistical Manual of Mental Disorders* (published by the American Psychiatric Association) as:

> characterized by a pervasive pattern of social inhibition, feelings of inadequacy, extreme sensitivity to negative evaluation and avoidance of social interaction. People with avoidant personality disorder often consider themselves to be socially inept or personally unappealing, and avoid social interaction for fear of being ridiculed, humiliated, rejected or disliked. They typically present themselves as loners and report feeling a sense of alienation from society.

Based on Joanne Reilly's observations of Planten at the fertilizer laboratory, Teague figured Planten had learned just enough social skills to get by in a work setting but not enough to keep him from being labeled as "strange" by the people who interacted with him.

Teague suspected that childhood physical and sexual abuse most likely played a role in causing Planten to turn out the way he did, but he also pointed out that one in seven boys are sexually abused in the United States, and the majority never kill.

Teague also theorized, based on the manner in which Stephanie was sexually assaulted, that Planten suffered from a sexual disorder known as a "paraphilia." The term was coined in the 1920s by psychologist Wilhelm Stekel, an early disciple of Sigmund Freud. The *Diagnostic and Statistical Manual of Mental Disorders* characterizes the condition as:

> recurrent, intense sexual urges, fantasies, or behaviors that involve unusual objects, activities, or situations and cause clinically significant distress or impairment in social, occupational, or other important areas of functioning.

This theory went hand in hand with Teague's powerful belief that Planten may have staged or posed Stephanie in front of a video camera. Again, it's a theory that was never supported by tangible evidence and was not shared by most of the detectives who worked on the case. Still, Teague to this day believes a videotape or pictures of the crime may have been destroyed or hidden somewhere and never found.

"I think his mind was completely pornographic. Sex was not at all about relationship to him. It was all about lights, color, action, positions," said Teague.

Planten's mother, Chandler, on the other hand, said she couldn't comprehend what people were saying about her son. She had never heard him speak of Stephanie Bennett, and she had never known him to do anything violent to anyone.

"I'm in shock because he's never been in trouble before. It's hard for me to believe that he's even suspected of something like this," she said, her voice laden with deep sadness in the phone interview with WRAL the day after her son's arrest.

## The Blame Game

With an accused killer behind bars, Carmon Bennett and his attorney, Charles Bentley, refocused their attention on the civil lawsuit against the Bridgeport Apartments. In it, Carmon alleged that the apartment complex had been negligent in providing a safe environment for its tenants and thus contributed to Stephanie's murder. Bentley spoke in an interview for WRAL on October 26, 2005, about how the criminal case might affect the civil case.

"It's really a combination of having a vicious criminal attracted into this environment that acted as sort of a magnet for something like this," Bentley said.

The lawsuit contended that the apartment complex should have done more to make their tenants secure—like trimming back bushes to keep them from obscuring windows, having better lighting, and hiring a security guard. It maintained that the height of the bushes allowed Planten to sneak into the apartment undetected because the windows could not be easily seen from the parking lot. They also said the apartment complex should have notified its residents about the original Peeping Tom report in April 2002 so that tenants could have been more aware of the potential danger.

Bentley said he felt Planten's arrest supported the lawsuit's contentions and made the civil case even stronger.

"Our case is really centered on the fact that there was a suspicious person out there, and there were unsafe conditions—that the unsafe conditions attracted someone like this into that area that was then provided with the physical opportunity to commit the crime," Bentley said. "Really, his arrest confirms a lot of the thoughts that we've had."

Drew Planten's arrest also confirmed a lot of people's thoughts about what someone who would do something like this might look like. In his mug shot, on video, and in newspaper photographs, he did in fact look like the bogeyman. But there were still more surprises to come, such as the secrets that the bogeyman's apartment held.

## CHAPTER TWELVE

# Organized Chaos

### October 20, 2005

It is the spirit and not the form of law that keeps justice alive.

—EARL WARREN

The day after Drew Planten's arrest, investigators executed the search warrants for his apartment, his 1976 Chevrolet Camaro, his financial records, his state personnel files, his computers, and his person. The warrant for his person allowed investigators to get a fresh DNA sample from Planten in a controlled environment. This would allow them to double-check the match. The new DNA sample obtained through this warrant would be used in court to prove there was no doubt that Planten was the one who had been in Stephanie Bennett's apartment the night she was murdered.

Investigators approached his apartment on Buck Jones Road with extreme caution. His dog had already been removed and taken to a shelter, so that was not the issue. The issue was whether Planten had booby-trapped the apartment. Based on how careful Planten had been not to leave his DNA anywhere, they now assumed that Planten had in fact realized that they'd been following him. Because of this, police were concerned he might have left them a little surprise in the apartment in the increasingly likely event that someone searched it. Given this concern, the Raleigh Police Department's bomb squad went into the apartment first to make sure that Planten had not left anything dangerous that could harm the officers who were about to conduct the search. They found nothing. Once the bomb squad deemed the apartment safe, the detectives got down to business.

"The first day, it was overwhelming," Detective Jackie Taylor said.

Officers from the Raleigh Police Department and the North Carolina State Bureau of Investigation were divided into teams with assignments to search and catalog items in specific locations within the apartment. Taylor remembers that the small apartment was so full of stuff and people, it was almost impossible to get any real work done.

Because of his continued involvement in the case, SBI Agent Mark Boodee was also invited to help with the search. As an agent who spent most of his time in the laboratory analyzing DNA samples, Boodee jumped at the chance to work in the field and to maybe learn a little more about Planten.

Boodee described his initial impression of the apartment as a "crappy bachelor pad." "That was like no other place I'd ever seen before," he said, shaking his head. There was nothing on the walls, and old beat-up furniture filled the den. There appeared to be nothing of real value in the apartment other than a television and a VCR. Surrounding this rather depressing setting were boxes of assorted items including magazines, clothes, shoes, and video games, crammed into just about every possible nook and cranny.

One of the first pieces of evidence investigators found was the laundry basket that had been taken from Stephanie Bennett's apartment.

The laundry basket was a significant find because along with Planten's DNA, it made the connection between him and Stephanie even more tangible. There was no logical, innocent reason for Stephanie's laundry basket to be in Planten's apartment.

The last time this basket had been seen, it had been full of laundry and sitting on the floor of Stephanie's bedroom. The laundry had been found in a pile on the floor, and detectives had theorized that the killer had probably dumped the laundry out in order to use the basket to carry and conceal Stephanie's portable stereo as he left the apartment. The stereo, however, was not found in Planten's apartment.

The investigators did find, however, newspaper clippings about Stephanie's murder from the local paper, the *News and Observer.* This, investigators considered, was evidence that Planten had gloated privately about what he had done and what kind of attention his evil deeds were getting in the media.

Investigators also found guns, nice guns, expensive guns. The arsenal included nine handguns and two shotguns, and a stockpile of ammunition. And there were knives, *lots* of knives. Forty knives, one sword, and a machete were discovered in Planten's apartment. They also found unusual items that might be used in the commission of crimes, such as a lock-pick set, duct tape, and handcuffs.

Planten had cut a path through his towers of stuff in order to get into his bedroom. There were cardboard boxes stacked shoulder-high all around his bed, filled with items such as brand new, apparently never worn clothing with the tags still attached.

There was plenty of evidence of hoarding—seventy-six pairs of men's shoes, twenty-five jars of spaghetti sauce, and hundreds of video games. The shoes, mostly sneakers, were stacked in their original boxes in the bedroom closet. Like the clothing, most of the shoes had never been worn. At least half of the three hundred or so video games were still in the wrappers. Many of those were crammed into the kitchen cabinet above the microwave.

There was a mountain of evidence illustrating what appeared to be Planten's sexual deviance—pornographic videos, photographs, books, magazines, and sex toys.

"He had tons of porn, like I'd never seen before. Like he'd have three copies of the same *Penthouse* still in the plastic," Agent Boodee recalled. "He had milk crates full of porn, magazines, stacked from the floor to the ceiling." The material was not all recent. Detective Copeland said Planten had classic editions of *Playboy* dating back to the 1970s stacked up neatly in the corner of his room, still in their original plastic wrapping. They had never been opened or read.

"There was underwear, tampons, *used* tampons," said Copeland as he recalled some of the more disturbing items belonging to women found in Planten's apartment.

Prosecutor Susan Spurlin joined in the search as well. As someone who had handled many high-profile murder cases, she knew it was important for her to get the best understanding she could of the suspect—something she couldn't get from simply reading the case file. She needed to see how Drew Planten lived firsthand. She wanted to gain insight into who this man was so that she would be able to relay the full picture to the jury.

"I was hoping that somewhere there would be an answer to the question, 'Why?'" said Spurlin. "At that point there is so much to learn. Just because officers make an arrest, doesn't mean it's over."

Spurlin was amazed by how many items Planten had been able to stuff into the tiny little apartment. She was also confused as to why someone would choose to have so many duplicate items with very little real monetary or practical value.

"There didn't seem to be any rhyme or reason," Spurlin said, throwing her arms in the air.

Psychologist Teague saw the hoarding component of Planten's lifestyle as part of his "obsessive-compulsive personality." Teague said this trait fit right in with the rest of Planten's psychological profile.

According to a paper published in the December 2003 issue of *Clinical Psychology Review,*

> Compulsive hoarding (or pathological hoarding) is the acquisition of, and failure to use or discard, such a large number of seemingly useless possessions that it causes significant clutter and impairment to basic living activities such as mobility, cooking, cleaning, showering or sleeping.

No one who saw the apartment could imagine how anyone could have functioned in such a small space with so much clutter. It was so tight, it looked like the stuff would literally keep closing in on a person until he eventually disappeared, which may have been exactly what Planten wanted to happen.

"If he had one of something, he had ten," Taylor said. "It was an organized mess."

Teague also believed what he perceived as the killer's obsessive-compulsive behavior may have manifested itself in the *way* Stephanie was sexually assaulted. He believed the crime probably followed a detailed, ritualistic pattern involving specific sexual acts performed in a rigid order— that it was less about lust, and more about following certain steps.

Probably the most disturbing thing investigators found in the apartment were the references to other women who detectives thought might have been intended as future victims. Investigators found directions printed to the home of a woman who lived in Kenly, about thirty miles from Raleigh. At one time she had worked with Planten at the North Carolina Department of Agriculture.

During a separate search of Planten's work space at the fertilizer laboratory on Reedy Creek Road, investigators found a document bearing the name of a woman who had moved to the Dominion Apartments and into the same building as Planten just after Stephanie's murder. Police also found a two-page list of other women's names.

"Any female name we found, we set it aside to research," Copeland said. " 'Who she was; was she dead?' " Police ultimately contacted every woman referenced in Planten's apartment that they could find.

One thing they learned from researching the women on whom Planten seemed to focus was that he appeared to have a type.

"He had a thing for very, very petite, skinny women," Copeland said. "If you were not the perfect girl, he considered you fat, and he would not have anything to do with you."

There was no doubt in the detectives' minds that Planten had been stalking other women—and maybe even preparing to rape and kill them, as they believed he had done to Stephanie.

## By the Grace of God

There was one particular woman named Angela Smith* who had rented an apartment on the third floor of Planten's building when he was still living at Dominion after Stephanie's murder. Investigators discovered a videotape taken of her at a party with friends.

When Smith had decided to move into the Dominion Apartments in the fall of 2002, her mother's friend had called her and told her there had been a murder in the area

---

*Denotes pseudonym.

just a few months earlier and that she was concerned about Smith's safety.

"That means the rents are going to be low," Smith recalled telling her mother's dear friend flippantly. "Bad things happen."

Smith was not the type of woman to let anything scare her. She had even taken a self-defense class and felt like there was very little she couldn't handle. So, despite the warnings from her mother's friend, she took the apartment.

She loved being on the third floor because it seemed like a safe location for a young woman living alone, but she had a new puppy, and she didn't love traipsing up and down the stairs with him. It seemed like she was always running up and down those damn stairs at all hours of the day or night. In her tired stupor, she would often pass her first-floor neighbor walking his dog. That neighbor was Drew Planten.

Smith had noticed Planten immediately after moving in because of his strange appearance and extreme antisocial behavior.

"He was just kind of a very creepy looking guy," Smith said. "He'd never make eye contact with you. He never said hello. He was just kind of an oddball. He was very quiet. He had this beat up old car." She told her friends he made her feel uncomfortable. Smith was a cautious young woman who always paid attention to her surroundings. One thing she didn't always pay attention to, however, was locking her door when she stepped out to walk her dog.

When Raleigh Police contacted Smith after searching Planten's apartment, they told her that Planten had stolen items from her apartment at Dominion. By this time she had moved in with her fiancé and was living in Hickory, North Carolina, a town about 175 miles west of Raleigh. The investigators explained they had found the videotape, as well as some photographs of Smith and some mail belonging to her. They told her that Planten, the man who was in possession of her belongings, had been arrested for Stephanie Bennett's murder.

"Your heart just kind of skips a beat," Smith said of her feelings the day she first spoke to police. "You're just freaked out. Just felt thankful. I just felt really lucky that none of it had ever happened to me. Obviously, he had the ability and was the kind of guy who could go that far and do really horrible things, and for whatever reason, he didn't do that to *me*."

The videotape, Smith explained, was actually a tape full of high school memories made by her friends. She had always kept it in the trunk at the end of her bed. The photographs came from an album that she had kept in a chest in her bedroom. She knew the tape was still in the trunk because she had looked at it recently. Detectives then concluded Planten must have somehow gotten into Smith's apartment, stolen the tape, copied it, and then returned the original to its original location so that she would not know it had been taken.

As for the photographs, at one point, she *had* noticed there were gaps in the album, missing pictures here and there, but she thought maybe she had removed some of the pictures at one point to make a collage and simply forgotten about it. Detectives told Smith they believed Planten had also taken some of her items from the trash, like her mail and even her used tampons.

Smith's fiancé's quiet strength and support helped her get through the ordeal. Her parents, who lived in the Washington, D.C., area, were understandably very upset after they learned that a killer may have been stalking their daughter.

"It was just a scary thing for everybody to realize that— to even go into the realm of what could have happened," Smith said.

Smith had lived at the Dominion Apartments for three years, and she remembered police officers passing out fliers in the neighborhood, looking for more information to help them solve the Stephanie Bennett case. She remembered stories on the news on the yearly anniversaries of Stephanie's murder. All she could think about after finding out that Planten had been in her apartment was, *Why not me?*

"I've wondered why didn't he take those steps," Smith said. "What was I giving off that he didn't go that far with me?"

The police told her they believed there were several factors that prevented her from becoming a victim—that she lived on the third floor, had a dog, and had an alarm system. Investigators told her all three probably helped save her life. Smith was also a young woman who exuded a kind of inner-strength, the kind of strength that might scare a potential attacker away. After all, if Teague was right about Planten's personality, he seemed to be a person who would have shied away from a woman he thought would put up a good fight.

While Smith was very shaken after learning that Planten had been in her apartment, she decided almost immediately that she wouldn't let the situation define her life. She wouldn't be the girl who almost got killed. Instead, she would be the girl who survived.

"When something like this happens you can either decide the whole world is just evil waiting to happen, or you can decide this was a really bad man who could have done a really bad thing, obviously did do a really bad thing," Smith said. "But there's no point in dwelling on it. All that matters is that I never did walk in and he was there. I never did wake up and have him looking at me. Nothing like that ever happened. I was totally unaware."

Smith vowed not to let what Planten could have done to her change the way she approached the world. She refused to give him that kind of power over her life.

"Compared to what happened to Stephanie Bennett, nothing happened to me, *nothing*," Smith said.

## Another Needle in the Haystack

On Friday, October 21, 2005, Detectives Ken Copeland and Jackie Taylor were finally alone in Planten's apartment. They took the opportunity to go through things slowly and methodically. Without all of the chaos and distractions of the other investigators, they could finally get down to the detail work they felt still needed to be done. Planten's apartment, like his life, was one big puzzle, and it was a puzzle they needed to figure out *before* they took the case to trial.

Maybe it was because they could finally see a clear path through the clutter or maybe it was because all the noise was gone or maybe they just got lucky—but on this day they found a 1998 Social Security refund check inside a video game box on a shelf in Planten's bedroom. The check was written to a woman by the name of Rebecca Huismann. There was also a postcard found addressed to the same woman in Lansing, Michigan. At the time, the name didn't raise a red flag. It was just another woman whom Planten had probably admired from afar, investigators thought. Just another name for them to check out.

On Saturday, October 22, 2005, the detectives came into the office to research the names they had found in Planten's apartment. They started by looking up the names online on various websites, including that of Rebecca Huismann.

"We ran her name and it came up with a 'D' beside it which means deceased," Taylor said with a bewildered look as she remembered the moment she realized there might be another victim.

Sergeant Perry called police in Lansing, Michigan, and asked if the name was familiar to anyone there.

"As a matter of fact it's an unsolved homicide," the Lansing cop who answered the phone told Perry.

"Jackie and I went, *wow*," Perry recalled.

The officer who answered the phone told Perry it was Detective Joey Dionise's case, and he eagerly gave him Dionise's cell phone number. Dionise was in the car on his way to his daughter's track meet when he got the call. Dionise was all business, no time for chitchat. He immediately cut to the chase and wanted to know why investigators in Raleigh, North Carolina, would be interested in a cold case from Lansing, Michigan, nearly eight hundred miles north of their jurisdiction.

"I'm getting goose bumps just thinking about it," Dionise said of the phone call. "I can still remember that day. So what does that tell you? *There is a God.*"

When Perry told Dionise what they had, he pulled over to the side of the road and asked his wife to drive so that he could concentrate on the call. Dionise hopped into the passenger seat, pulled out his briefcase, and started furiously taking notes on what Perry was telling him. Then it was Dionise's turn to tell Perry about Rebecca's case.

Dionise told Perry that Rebecca had been shot and killed in Lansing on October, 19, 1999. Ironically, it was the very same day Drew Planten would be arrested six years later—on the anniversary of Rebecca Huismann's murder.

That was a night Dionise would never forget, the night his city was under siege. Rebecca's was the third unrelated murder in Lansing the night of October 19, and Dionise had handled every single one.

It was 5:55 in the morning, and Dionise was finally on his way home after a grueling night. Lansing detectives had a suspect in custody in the first murder case, and Dionise had interviewed him earlier in the evening. Dionise got the call about murder number three just as he was walking out of the jail after interviewing the suspect in the second murder case. The third victim was a woman who had been found shot in her car at 121 Lathrop Street less than two miles from the Michigan State University campus, he was told.

"You've got to be kidding me," Dionise said to the dispatcher calling him back to work.

In a city with maybe a dozen-plus murders a year, this night was one in a million for Lansing investigators, including Dionise.

"What the hell happened here in the city? Three in one night, it was unheard of," Dionise remembered.

Dionise knew the neighborhood where the third murder had occurred well. It was on the east side of Lansing, in an area populated mostly by college students. Dionise went to church almost directly across the street from the house where the young woman had been killed. He had grown up around the corner just off of Michigan Avenue.

At this point, Dionise had been on the clock for twenty-four hours straight, but he knew he still had to go to the murder scene. This was how it worked in homicide. Detectives didn't clock out until the job was done. And on this night it seemed like the job was never going to be done.

Dionise said twenty-two-year-old Rebecca Huismann had been found shot in the head with one foot set just outside of her Ford Escort. The rest of her body was slumped over the steering wheel of the car. Dionise figured the loud garbage trucks that cruised up and down Michigan Avenue at that time in the morning must have muffled the sound of the single gunshot.

It looked like Rebecca was just getting out of her car when she was approached by the killer. She was shot just one time in the left side of her face with a .45-caliber handgun—the only good news was that it was an unusual caliber. Dionise hoped that fact might help investigators identify a suspect. A statewide APB went out immediately for any handguns of this type confiscated by law enforcement.

The detail about where exactly on her body Rebecca was shot was leaked to the press early on by an eager police captain; something Dionise said set the investigation back tremendously. It was something Dionise had wanted kept close to the vest, because it was a detail only the killer knew. But once it was out of the bag, he couldn't exactly reel it back in and lock it up again in a vault, so he just tried to ignore it.

Rebecca had been a dancer at a men's club called Dream Girls on South Pennsylvania Avenue, about a twelve-minute drive from her house. It was easy to see why the attractive brunette with a great figure and a megawatt smile was a hit at the club. But outside the club, everyone police interviewed said she lived a clean life. There was no indication that Rebecca was involved in anything untoward outside of her job description as an exotic dancer. People who knew her from the club said she simply did her job and went home. Her family said it wasn't what she wanted to be doing, but it paid the bills for the time being. She was saving up to go to college—and the money at the club was good. "She was a nice girl. She danced, big deal, nothing illegal," Detective Dionise said with a thick Michigan accent.

The night Rebecca Huismann was killed, her purse had been found on the ground next to her car with eighty dollars in cash inside, so investigators ruled out robbery as a motive early on in the case. But this left the lingering question—if robbery wasn't the motive, and rape wasn't the motive, what was?

"Somebody wanted her dead; why?" Dionise said. Immediately, investigators started canvassing the neighborhood, talking for the most part to college students who lived in the many rental homes and apartment buildings. Rebecca's boyfriend, Ernie, had been asleep inside the house when she was shot. He had come running outside and found her slumped over in her car. He was the one who'd called 911 and identified her for the police.

"He was a wreck," Dionise said.

Detectives then notified Rebecca's parents, Glenna and Bernard Huismann, of their daughter's murder. They were obviously devastated and shocked by their child's death. Not unlike Stephanie Bennett, Rebecca Huismann was a young woman who had been just starting her life and was not ready to leave the world.

The first thing investigators had to do was eliminate Rebecca's boyfriend as a suspect. Dionise said Ernie cooperated on a limited basis early on in the investigation, and then he got a lawyer and stopped talking to them. This made it difficult, if not impossible, for police to clear him.

"We had to go through a lot of hoops," said Dionise of trying to eliminate Ernie as a suspect.

And then, Dionise said, "the case went cold." The Michigan investigators interviewed everyone who worked at Dream Girls or who patronized the nightclub on a regular basis. At first, they considered that an obsessed customer at the club might be responsible for the murder, but nothing along those lines panned out. Detectives found no connection between Dream Girls and Rebecca's murder.

"Every lead we followed, it ended," Dionise said with frustration in his voice.

Dionise wasn't used to having cold cases in Lansing. Even the cases that were technically unsolved, the cops *knew* who had committed them, but just didn't have enough evidence to make an arrest. But in Rebecca Huismann's case, they had absolutely nothing. It was as if the murderer had simply vanished without a trace.

The Lansing police then decided to create a task force along with other local law enforcement agencies that had unsolved homicides of women in the same general area to see if there was a pattern. The East Lansing police and Michigan State University police compared notes on their unsolved murder cases with Dionise's department, but there seemed to be no common thread linking any of the local unsolved murder cases together.

Before Rebecca's murder, another young woman had been killed in an East Lansing apartment complex hallway. A velvet bag meant to hold jewelry was found stuffed inside the victim's mouth. The case seemed to have few similarities with Rebecca's case, but it was still looked at closely to see if there might be some underlying connection that wasn't immediately obvious. Still, no matter how hard they tried, investigators found nothing tying that case to Rebecca Huismann's murder.

Throughout the investigation, Lansing detectives tried to keep Rebecca's story in the media so the public wouldn't forget about her. On the anniversary of her death every year they would remind people about the case in the unlikely hope that someone might come forward with new information. That's the way it went for six long years.

"We never closed it," Dionise said as he remembered how the files sat on one of his detective's desk for six years. The files were never actually put away into the file cabinet where they belonged—it was as if that simple, ordinary act might have been a sign that investigators were giving up. Dionise refused to take that step. He would see the files sitting on the corner of the desk and say to himself— *Someday that one will be solved.* His heart told him that putting away the files was like filing away Rebecca Huismann's memory into a dark hole where it would never again be found. His head told him that he was crazy, but as long as tips came in, in his heart, he felt like he could reconcile keeping the case active.

"People would still call, and we would investigate every lead," Dionise said proudly.

But the best lead Lansing detectives got was from the Raleigh Police Department on a brisk fall day in October 2005. When Sergeant Clem Perry and Detective Joey Dionise finished talking, it was clear to both cops that Drew Planten may have killed Rebecca Huismann. *Six years, six long years.* Dionise almost couldn't believe it. But then Perry dropped the bombshell, the information that sealed the deal for Dionise.

"Well, we recovered a .45 caliber pistol," Perry told Dionise.

"Look, I think we're coming out there," Dionise said excitedly.

Dionise immediately hung up the phone and called one of his detectives with the news. He couldn't keep it to himself. Even though Dionise didn't have the evidence in his hands yet, he had always believed the gun would be the key to solving the case. His mind drifted back to the files on the corner of the desk. He had never given up on Rebecca Huismann, and with good reason. Despite what others may have thought, the case was solvable. He always believed that.

"It looks good," Dionise said to his detective on the phone after hanging up with Perry. "It looks real good. We're going to Raleigh."

## Rebecca Huismann

"The state police were waiting for me when I got home from school that day," Glenna Huismann, a teacher and Rebecca Huismann's mother, said as she remembered the day her daughter was killed—October 19, 1999. "What happened to her, us, only happens to other people you don't know. You never think it could happen to you."

Glenna said her daughter was a vivacious, outgoing young woman who dreamed about traveling the world and taking part in wild adventures. She wanted to bungee jump and see the pyramids in Egypt. Rebecca wanted to do it all. She had big plans for a big life. She was working to save money in order to go back to school at Lansing Community College to study acting. She had recently become engaged to her boyfriend, Ernie, and was planning to get married in 2000.

Rebecca was also very creative and talented. She loved

to sing, write, sew, take photographs, and paint. Glenna remembered her daughter making Halloween costumes, sewing Native American costumes for a friend, and designing a school sweatshirt. She also wrote poetry and created paintings that were so good she used them to barter for things like having work done on her car.

As far as dancing at the men's club, Glenna said, "it was not [Rebecca's] life's ambition," and Glenna always felt very sad that the media in Lansing could never get beyond this label in order to show the world who Rebecca really was. In her mind, her daughter was the sum of many wonderful things and being a dancer at a men's club barely registered on the Richter scale of Rebecca's life.

Glenna said her daughter was also someone who, not unlike Stephanie Bennett, was fiercely loyal to her family and friends. Also like Stephanie, Rebecca seemed to bring out the best in others and make any room she entered a brighter place.

"Rebecca was funny," Glenna said. "She could make you laugh and sometimes just shake your head. She laughed a lot, got crazy. [Rebecca] could be gutsy."

Throughout the six-year investigation, Glenna and Rebecca's father, Bernard, kept hoping there would be a break in the case, and an arrest would be made.

"We were discouraged sometimes, but we never lost hope. We prayed a lot," Glenna said.

## Full Circle

Agent Mark Boodee was asked to analyze some of the items investigators had taken out of Planten's apartment. There were two laundry baskets—one they believed belonged to Stephanie Bennett and one other—two used tampons, several pairs of women's underwear, multiple bras, and a pair of pantyhose.

Boodee reported back that Stephanie's DNA was found on the pair of pantyhose and on a pair of black cotton thong underwear taken from Planten's apartment. This concrete evidence was just more confirmation for him and the investigators that Planten had not only committed the crime, but had taken trophies as mementos of what he had done. Even though Planten's DNA was thought to be slam dunk evidence all by itself, every additional item that linked Planten to Stephanie made the case that much stronger. Again, like the laundry basket, there was no good reason for Planten to have Stephanie's underwear or her pantyhose in his apartment.

After analyzing the evidence collected from Planten's apartment, Boodee's work was done until it was time to prepare for trial. He would no doubt be called to testify in court about his DNA analysis throughout the investigation. He felt good about what he and the detectives had accomplished, even though it had taken more than three years to solve the case.

"It was a long and winding road. It started off with a bang," Boodee said, remembering the excitement of that initial weekend after the murder when he first created a DNA profile for the killer. Then it seemed to him as though the investigation ground to a screeching halt as the investigative team spun their wheels through hundreds of elimination samples. "And then it was the sprint to the finish in the end. It was a career case. It was one of those cases you look back and hang your hat on and say, this is all that I ever hoped for when I wanted to get into forensic DNA analysis."

## Shattered Beliefs

Joanne Reilly was having a hard time processing what had just happened to Drew Planten. Even with all of his bizarre behavior, Reilly had been so sure that Planten wasn't a killer. In the process of helping police, she had come to know and like Planten in a motherly way. She worried about his self-imposed isolation from others and his lack of eating. She saw him as an outsider, someone who simply needed some affirmation from others to blossom and spring out of his shell. Reilly had felt like she was just the right person to make this transformation happen. Every time Planten would do something strange, it would make her question his innocence, but she was still unconvinced of his guilt until the bitter end.

"I was so stupid, I didn't think he did it until the major called me and said that the DNA was a match, and that they had the building surrounded," Reilly said. "I thought I *knew* him, but I didn't. That just totally shook up my feelings of being able to assess people correctly."

At the same time, Reilly felt like she had helped achieve justice for Stephanie, and for that feeling, she was grateful.

In her last e-mail to the detectives on October 20, 2005, at 8:05 P.M., Reilly was still trying to sort out the shock of the whole ordeal:

Hi Ken, Jackie and Clem, I just wanted to say that I am in awe of you three and everyone else I met during the investigation. I applaud you highly. You should all receive promotions out of this.

Reilly went on to say that she would like to get together with the detectives again at some point to find out what her responsibilities would be as far as going to court and testifying in the case.

I also want to repeat what I told you yesterday Ken. I not only will testify, I want to testify against Drew if it will help your case. I keep seeing in the news that RPD is not revealing the source of the matching DNA.

Thank you, but I participated in this fully expecting to be "outed" at some point if the DNA was a match. Please let me know what you plan to do.

But even in her willingness to testify against Planten, there was still a part of Reilly, the mother in her, that worried about Planten's state of mind in prison. She had seen him strapped to the wheelchair on the television news in his first court appearance and heard the reporter say that he appeared to be catatonic and was refusing to eat. Reilly couldn't get the image of him being wheeled into the courtroom out of her mind. It was literally haunting her. To Reilly, in the video, Planten looked like "a monster," not like the quiet, gentle man with whom she had worked side by side with for months. Part of her couldn't help but feel that what had happened to him was all her fault, even if logically she knew it was the choices he made that put him there.

We are worried about Drew trying to starve himself to death. He is a very disciplined and focused man as you know and I'm sure he would have no problem doing just that.

Finally, Reilly asked the detectives to allow the fertilizer laboratory to re-open again. The lab itself was still surrounded with yellow police tape and being treated as a crime scene. Reilly felt like the employees needed to get back to work for practical purposes, but also for everyone's sanity, so that they could put the tragedy behind them. Reilly went on to say that her staff would make Planten's locker at the lab available to investigators, although there was a strong suspicion his backpack that he always kept with him would not be in there. Because it might have contained evidence, and Planten knew police were onto him. Detectives guessed that he'd thrown his backpack away in one of the many Dumpsters bound for the landfill on lab cleanup day.

Reilly finished her lengthy e-mail the same way she'd started—with the highest praise for the investigators.

> I am going to try to get some sleep tonight. I didn't sleep a wink last night. You all take care. We are all so proud of you.-Joanne

# CHAPTER THIRTEEN

# Connecting the Dots

## November 2005

It is better to know some of the questions than all of the
answers.

—JAMES THURBER

"Was that something else that I considered thinking about
this case, that it might be more than Stephanie Bennett?
Sure," prosecutor Susan Spurlin said. After she spoke with
investigators from Michigan about Planten's possible connection to the Rebecca Huismann case, she realized they
might just be dealing with the tip of the iceberg as far as
the number of victims went.

Lansing Detective Joey Dionise came to Raleigh to see
for himself what the North Carolina investigators had on
Drew Planten. He was shown what appeared to be stolen
mail from Rebecca's mailbox, a newspaper clipping about
her murder, and a video game box that also appeared to
have come from Rebecca's house in Michigan. Dionise
was wildly impressed that the Raleigh detectives had un-
covered these critical pieces of evidence hidden beneath
the overwhelming amount of junk in Planten's apartment.

During the search, Raleigh investigators had also found

two .45-caliber handguns in the apartment. One gun, a Glock, was quickly ruled out by the Michigan State Crime Lab. Based on what they already knew about the make and model of the weapon used to kill Rebecca Huismann, analysts said this was definitely not the murder weapon. However, the other gun looked like a more promising potential match. Dionise took the second gun back to Lansing with him and personally hand-delivered it to the analysts at the crime lab.

Agents with the North Carolina State Bureau of Investigation crime lab conferred with Michigan agents regarding the weapon. It was tested in North Carolina first, before being sent back with Dionise to Michigan for more testing. After ballistics testing, agents in both states very quickly determined after that, without a doubt, the handgun found in Planten's apartment in Raleigh was the gun that killed Rebecca Huismann in Lansing, Michigan, in 1999.

"That's the gun, the one that killed her," Sergeant Reinhart Pope of the Michigan crime lab told Dionise excitedly over the phone.

Suddenly, Dionise's cold case was hot again. He now had the murder weapon *and* a suspect. As a result, he wanted to learn everything he could about Planten's movements in Michigan. So, Dionise called the original homicide task force back together again and shared this new and compelling information about Rebecca's case. Between all of the agencies, Dionise figured they had enough resources to help him build a strong enough case to take to Ingham County District Attorney Stuart Dunnings.

Dionise also decided it was time to speak with Rebecca's parents again. He knew it was only a matter of time before the information got out, and the last thing he wanted was for these grieving parents to be blindsided. Dionise met with Glenna Huismann, and filled her in on the latest developments. He said the first question out of her mouth was the same thing she had wanted to know six years earlier, "Why?" Dionise cautioned her not to get her hopes up yet and to keep the information quiet until they were sure the district attorney would agree to charge Planten with Rebecca's murder.

"[Our] prayers were answered when Planten was arrested. Sometimes God puts his own stamps on things. Planten was arrested on the six year anniversary of Rebecca's death," Glenna said. But she heeded Dionise's warning not to get too excited until the charge in Michigan was imminent. "We were hopeful. Of course. Things happened fast after that. All the dots were connected."

Planten had no criminal record in Michigan to speak of except for a few minor traffic tickets. For most of the time he had lived there, he stayed with his mother in Charlotte. But he had attended Michigan State University in Lansing and, at one point, had lived briefly within a few miles of Rebecca's house.

While investigators determined that Planten wasn't a patron at the men's club where Rebecca Huismann worked as a dancer, a man matching his description had been seen walking his dog in her neighborhood early in the morning more than once in the weeks leading up to her murder. Further investigation showed that on one occasion an officer had approached the man and asked him what he was doing out so late and if he lived nearby. The "officer contact," as police referred to these reports, with the dog walker included his name and had been logged into the Lansing Police Department's system. *It was Drew Planten*. This was part of their routine procedure of keeping track of everyone who was approached by patrol officers for any reason. At the time, Planten didn't live in the area and told police he was just visiting friends in the neighborhood. This confirmed sighting of Planten in Rebecca's neighborhood around the time of her killing, along with the gun found in his apartment, was enough to convince Dionise they had the right guy.

"He was lying in wait, a stalker," said Dionise of the picture that was starting to develop in his head about Planten. "He still didn't stand out as a killer. But we knew he was the one. What made him go to this extreme?"

Motive in the Rebecca Huismann case was the thing that confounded Dionise more than anything. Unlike the Stephanie Bennett case, this attack involved no sexual assault. It was down and dirty, almost like a professional hit, but that didn't make any sense either. Investigators couldn't find anyone with any reason to want Rebecca dead. The only thing Dionise could come up with was that Planten may have become obsessed with the young woman.

"He wanted her. He knew she had a boyfriend. He knew he couldn't have her," Dionise said. "If he couldn't have her, *nobody* could have her."

Psychologist Michael Teague agreed with Detective Dionise that the killer was probably obsessed with Rebecca. What he couldn't get past was the fact that Planten had apparently shot her before he got a chance to abduct and rape her.

"I think when he shot the girl in Michigan, that was an aborted act of something," Teague said. "I don't think he meant to do it. I don't know if he was trying to kidnap her, but I don't think the shooting was in his plan."

When Dionise visited the detectives in Raleigh, he tried to make an appointment to speak with Drew Planten at Central Prison. He hoped that Planten would realize he was cooked and would simply confess to Rebecca's murder. Dionise's fantasy, however, was short-lived. Predictably, Planten sent word through his attorney that he refused to meet with or talk to the Michigan investigators.

When Dionise returned to Michigan from Raleigh, he sent detectives to Planten's mother's home in Charlotte to try to speak with her about her son. But they reported back to him that Sarah Chandler told the investigators in no uncertain terms to "leave us alone."

Even without talking to Planten or his family, Dionise

believed he had enough evidence with the gun and the other items found in Planten's apartment to make the case against him. Dionise felt like "it was a great circumstantial case." He was delighted when Stuart Dunnings agreed with him.

"He was going to be charged with murder for Rebecca's death," Dionise said confidently.

Wake County Assistant District Attorney Susan Spurlin was also talking to Dunnings. With Planten about to be charged with another count of first-degree murder, the question of who had primary jurisdiction had to be decided. In other words—who would try him first? Given the fact that Raleigh police had made their case first, Spurlin argued strongly that the first trial needed to be in North Carolina. There was also the additional issue that North Carolina had the death penalty, and Michigan did not. If Planten was convicted and received the death penalty in North Carolina, there would be no need for Michigan authorities to try him there.

Spurlin said she was determined to make sure Planten's fate would be decided by a Wake County jury.

## Indictment Day

On November 1, 2005, the news reporters lurked around the hallway in the Wake County Courthouse waiting for Detective Ken Copeland to finish testifying in front of the grand jury regarding Drew Planten. The Bennett case had come to the grand jury in record time—less than two weeks. But prosecutor Susan Spurlin said that the case was so solid, she saw no need to wait any longer.

"They've been phenomenally thorough," Spurlin said of the investigators. "There's no question about it. It is one of the best, most comprehensive, complete, well-run investigations that I've seen. They've done an *excellent* job."

On his way out of the grand jury room, Copeland ducked down the hallway and tried to sneak into the elevator unnoticed without talking to the media. Still, reporters spotted him and yelled out in his direction asking him for a comment. He said he was late for a meeting, thanked them for how well they had covered the case, and backed into an elevator with a little wave as the gray metal doors closed swiftly in front of him.

It was typical—before an arrest, the police needed the media to help them get leads and advance the case. But after an arrest, investigators said as little as possible leading up to the trial. Their biggest fear was revealing something that might compromise the integrity of the case in the courtroom.

Luckily, prosecutors were not bound by the same fears of the media as police. Spurlin had agreed to do an interview as soon as news broke that the grand jury had returned a true bill for first-degree murder against Planten. The fact that Planten had been indicted was no big surprise; what everyone really wanted to know was whether the state would seek the death penalty against him.

Prosecutors very rarely expressed their intentions to seek the death penalty outside of the courtroom, but as an indicator of how strong they felt the case was, Spurlin let the cat out of the bag.

"We'll have a hearing in superior court in a few weeks where the state will officially declare the case a capital murder case," Spurlin said without reservation.

Within minutes, every news website in Raleigh had the story posted. If convicted, Planten was now possibly facing what Stephanie Bennett had received—a death sentence.

## Serial Tendencies

The Rebecca Huismann case opened up a whole new set of possibilities for investigators who had suspected that Drew Planten may have killed other women, but had had nothing concrete to connect him to other crimes until now. The Michigan case prompted the Raleigh Police Department and other local law enforcement agencies to look even more closely at Planten when it came to other unsolved homicides in their areas.

"Any police department that is worth their salt on a case of this nature would be remiss if they did not look into other cases. So, yes we are examining other unsolved cases and looking at Mr. Planten to see if there is a possibility that he was involved in other crimes in our jurisdiction," Major Dennis Lane said outside the police department during an interview on November, 3, 2005. "We're certainly not at the end of our investigation. We certainly have more work to do, more leads to follow up on to tie our case together."

Michigan authorities also started to relook at their unsolved cases, specifically at the case of the woman found raped and strangled in East Lansing with a small velvet jewelry bag stuffed in her mouth. While it bore little resemblance to the Huismann case, it had strong similarities with the Bennett case. The woman had been raped, like Stephanie, and gagged, like Stephanie. Because investigators had now connected Drew Planten to both Stephanie Bennett and Rebecca Huismann, it only made sense for authorities to rethink Planten's possible connection to other cold cases in their areas.

The Raleigh police detectives also tried to follow up on every possible lead involving where Planten had been, and what he had been doing, since Stephanie's murder. It was their strong belief that killers did not tend to take a break for this long, but they needed cold hard evidence, not just speculation, if they were going to link Planten to any other crimes.

"We found evidence where he had rented a car for one day here and there and drove hundreds of miles roundtrip," Sergeant Clem Perry said. Considering that Planten was antisocial, investigators wondered where Planten could have possibly been going with the rental cars and what exactly he might have been doing.

Planten's father, Robert Planten, had died in a house fire on April 9, 1993, in Cheyenne, Wyoming, under somewhat suspicious circumstances. Raleigh investigators even looked closely at this case, especially after learning that Planten's estranged father had been abusive to his wife and his sons. But after talking to authorities in Wyoming, Detective Jackie Taylor said they could never get anyone to confirm the death was the result of anything other than an accidental stove fire.

What continued to trip up investigators was the fact that serial killers tend to do the same things over and over again. Yet, the two cases in which Planten was now a suspect, Rebecca Huismann's murder and Stephanie Bennett's murder, were so completely different. One victim was shot; the other victim was strangled. One woman was raped; one woman was not. Because detectives couldn't even determine a pattern with these two cases, they found it almost impossible to form a pattern they could track nationwide when it came to other cases in which Planten may have been involved.

Still, psychologist Teague was convinced that Planten, if not technically a serial killer (defined as someone who'd taken three or more lives) was well on his way to becoming one.

"There's probably a third body that we've not found out there that would qualify him as a serial killer," Teague said with confidence. Serial killers, he noted, are "just not human. They don't have any human qualities, obviously no empathy."

There were unsolved murders every day across the country where the information never got entered into a national crime database. There were women killed along the I-95 corridor who were never even reported as missing because they had no identification on them and were estranged from their families and friends.

Early on, investigators had presented the case to the Violent Criminal Apprehension Program, to the FBI, and at homicide conferences throughout the country. The thought was that another police department might be dealing with a similar case connected to the same suspect. But they had no luck in finding any case just like Stephanie Bennett's.

Detective Jackie Taylor agreed with Teague's theory that there were other unknown victims. "I don't think he went that long without killing," she said of Planten.

"I'm convinced he had done so too," Detective Copeland added.

Lieutenant Chris Morgan, on the other hand, was never convinced that Planten was connected to other murders besides Stephanie Bennett's and Rebecca Huismann's. Morgan believed Planten was reeling after what appeared to be his botched assault on Rebecca. He believed it was a murder Planten hadn't really intended to commit, and thought Planten then spent the next few years planning his attack on Stephanie. To Morgan's thinking, Planten was then afraid he could never top that one, and so he laid low looking for another similar opportunity, which never came his way.

"I think [she] was the perfect victim. The crime went perfectly; nothing went wrong in this crime for Drew Planten," Morgan said with disgust. "Everything about him was fantasy and ritual. I think Planten had this fear, 'If I try to do this again, it's not going to be the same. It won't be as good.'"

## Death Knell

"The state does officially declare in writing and in open court that we will be seeking the death penalty in this case," prosecutor Susan Spurlin said to the Superior Court judge Donald Stephens, as she stood in front of his bench.

Spurlin wore a red power suit to court on the day of the Rule 24 hearing. Seeking the death penalty wasn't a decision she entered into lightly, and even though she knew that law-and-order Stephens, given the nature of the crime, would most likely accept her request, she still had to go through the legal motions to make it official.

First, she laid out the details of the case to the judge to support her decision to seek the death penalty.

"What the evidence will show is that on May 21 of 2002, Stephanie Bennett was found nude, having been strangled and having been sexually assaulted in her apartment," Spurlin said in a professional, solemn tone. "There's also evidence that both her hands and her feet had been bound, Your Honor, and semen was recovered from the body of Stephanie Bennett."

Drew Planten was not required to be at the hearing, and therefore he was not, but his court-appointed attorney, Kirk Osborne, sat at the defense table and appeared to be listening intently to every word Spurlin uttered. Osborne was an accomplished defense lawyer from Chapel Hill who would, without a doubt, give Planten excellent representation. With his long gray hair and wire-framed glasses he had an artistic look about him, but in the courtroom, Spurlin knew he was a worthy adversary.

"They approached this defendant and requested his DNA. He refused to provide a sample, but officers were able to obtain a sample of Drew Planten's DNA," Spurlin said with an increasing level of intensity in her voice. "When that DNA was compared with the semen that was taken from Stephanie Bennett, it was found to be a positive match."

Spurlin paused for a moment after saying Planten's DNA was a match. It was almost as if she wanted to make sure that very important fact sunk in for everyone in the courtroom. Her subtext: *It was a match; does anyone have any question as to what that means?*

Spurlin went on to say that personal belongings taken from Stephanie Bennett's apartment had been found in Planten's apartment during a search by police. She also talked about how other items from that search led them to an unsolved murder case in Lansing, Michigan—that of Rebecca Huismann. The gun that had been used to kill Rebecca was also found in Planten's apartment, she told the judge.

"They found that the projectile that was used to kill Rebecca Huismann, and the spent shell casing that was recovered there at the scene, was a positive match from that weapon," Spurlin said.

Again she paused, letting the fact that the murder weapon used to kill a Michigan woman six years before Planten's arrest in Raleigh had been found in Planten's apartment. Spurlin's silence once again had a read-between-the-lines quality to it: *What else could this possibly mean other than the obvious?*

Under North Carolina law, to seek the death penalty the state must prove there are two or more aggravating factors that merit the sentence. Spurlin had no shortage of aggravating factors in the Bennett case. She laid them out to the court.

"The murder was committed during the commission of a rape, possibly during the commission of a robbery, and the crime was especially heinous, atrocious, and cruel," Spurlin said, letting the tiniest bit of emotion creep into her voice.

During the hearing the state also asked that they be

able to redact personal information about people interviewed during the investigation—addresses, phone numbers, Social Security numbers—before handing over the documents to Planten's attorney as required under the law, during what's known as the discovery process. Spurlin argued that hundreds of people were interviewed early on in the case that had absolutely nothing to do with the murder, and they should not be penalized for their cooperation by having their personal information made part of the public record.

Osborne, on the other hand, argued that he needed access to *all* of this information so he and his client could determine if it was relevant or not to the case. He said that without this information, he could not guarantee Planten would get a fair trial.

"We will want to run down everything. This is a very serious case and we believe that we're entitled to that material under the statute and request that none of this information be redacted from discovery," Osborne said in a booming voice that belied his mellow appearance.

Stephens struck down Osborne's objection and accepted the state's motion to redact the information. He also declared the case a capital case, which meant the state was free to seek the death penalty. The judge ordered the state to copy and deliver all of its documents to Osborne by the end of January. He also appointed another attorney for Planten who by law was entitled to two court-appointed attorneys in a death penalty case.

After the hearing, Spurlin and her partner, Assistant District Attorney Becky Holt, held an impromptu press conference in the courthouse hallway. They told the media that they had talked to Carmon Bennett about the decision to seek the death penalty in the case but declined to say what his opinion was. It was standard for prosecutors to discuss the issue with the victim's family in these types of cases and take their feelings into consideration. This didn't mean prosecutors always acquiesced to the family's wishes, but their thoughts did play a major role in making the decision.

The prosecutors also spoke about how they were consulting with Michigan authorities on which jurisdiction would try Planten for murder first, given the fact that he was now directly implicated in the Huismann case.

Recently released search warrants of Planten's apartment for the first time publicly revealed the role of Joanne Reilly, Planten's supervisor, in helping police get his DNA. Reporters were naturally curious about her connection to the case and how that might play out in court.

"We are thrilled that people, citizens that are out there, are willing to cooperate, and that's what she did," Spurlin said to the group of journalists assembled in the hallway outside the courtroom. "That's what makes the justice system work when citizens are involved as well. It's a *good thing,*" Holt stressed.

It appeared the case was moving along smoothly— exactly how Spurlin and Holt hoped it would. But experienced litigators know derailment is always possible even when the case appears to be chugging smoothly down the track with no obstacles in sight.

## Going North

WRAL reporter Melissa Buscher and photographer Ed Wilson traveled to Michigan to talk to investigators there about the Huismann case and to get some perspective from her family, as well as from Drew Planten's family.

"When we were in Michigan, everything just seemed to fit," Melissa said. At one time, Planten had lived in a house in Rebecca Huismann's neighborhood. Police in Lansing told Buscher that Planten was without a doubt the person they believed killed Rebecca. They also told her that they were even looking at him in connection with several other unsolved homicides of women in the area.

Buscher, being an experienced reporter, knew that it was always better to knock on someone's door than risk being rejected in a phone call. Face-to-face, journalists always have a better chance of getting someone to talk to them. So, she and Wilson traveled to Newaygo, Michigan, and knocked on Glenna and Bernard Huismann's door. They answered, and then invited the news crew into their home without a camera.

"We sat in their living room for about an hour, looked at pictures, and they shared stories with us about their daughter. They were overwhelmed that after so many years the painful memories about their daughter's death were resurfacing," Buscher remembered sadly. "They chose not to share their story in public [at that time], politely declining to go on-camera."

Wilson and Buscher also journeyed to visit Sarah Chandler, Drew Planten's mother, who lived about one hundred miles south of Newaygo in Charlotte, Michigan. Chandler met with the news crew at her law office, a charming old Victorian house that she had converted into her place of business. It was surprising that she agreed to do an interview on-camera.

"She was adamant that her son was *not* involved," Buscher recalled.

"Drew was always a very shy, I call it, reserved person," Chandler told Buscher. She said given her son's personality she could not imagine him doing something like the crimes he was accused of committing. She said she did not believe her son had ever even owned a gun, despite the fact that police said they found a gun on him when he was arrested.

Chandler told Buscher her son was an athlete, a good student, and someone who was loved and supported by his family.

"He always had loving family members around him," Chandler said. "Never did he feel like he was alone in the world or deserted."

Chandler, instead of dwelling on the accusations against her son, chose instead to show Buscher pictures of Planten during happier times—him playing sports and graduating from Michigan State University in 1995.

Buscher left Chandler's house that day not sure if she was dealing with a mother who was simply in desperate denial, or truly in the dark.


## Preparing for Battle

For Susan Spurlin, the case was starting to come together, but she had been sitting in the prosecutor's seat far too long to take anything for granted. Having the case declared capital meant that the jury selection process would be long and arduous. They had to choose jurors who were "death penalty qualified," meaning they would be willing to consider sentencing Planten to death if he was convicted. The major issue in qualifying jurors in these cases was that they often *said* they could consider the death penalty during the selection process, but when it came right down to it, they had a change of heart during the trial. To weed these people out, the selection process needed to be intense and in depth.

"It's a case where the jury has to make that ultimate decision, so you're very passionate about presenting everything so that the jury can in fact make *that* decision," Spurlin said.

With her many years of experience, Spurlin knew that a death penalty case was the toughest case to try. She was ready for the challenge, yet even with excellent evidence in the case, she knew there would still be many obstacles along the way.

"There is no such thing as a slam dunk," Spurlin said.

"You never know what the jury is going to do, or what they're going to respond to."

Spurlin was wading her way through the thousands of pages contained in the case file that investigators had been compiling for three and a half years. Not only did she need to bring herself up to speed on the case, but she needed to make sure she wasn't missing anything that might come back to bite her at trial.

"More than I've had in any other murder case," Spurlin said of the sheer number of pages she had to go through and read. "It was an enormous amount of material."

As part of the trial process known as "discovery," Spurlin's office was copying the voluminous case file and sending every single page to Drew Planten's attorney, Kirk Osborne. A great deal of the paperwork dealt with dead-end leads that had nothing to do with Planten, but Spurlin felt like she still had to familiarize herself with all of it. It was part of her strategy to be able to anticipate anything and everything the defense might bring up at trial as a red herring to distract the jury.

"In any capital murder you want to know as much about the defendant as you can possibly know. The jury might only know information about the size of a quarter, but I think a prosecutor needs to know information that would almost fill this room," Spurlin said, gesturing with both arms around her modest, square office with its gray walls and two-story-high ceilings.

Spurlin was getting into "the zone," as her husband liked to call it. She was intently buckling down and immersing herself in the Bennett case. During those times, she slept with a legal pad by her bed so that if something about the case came to her in the middle of the night, she could sit up and write it down immediately so that it would not be lost.

On Spurlin's wall in her courthouse office was a picture of Stephanie Bennett in happier times, joking around in a red sash and a big purple felt hat like the Cat in the Hat wore. In the photograph, Stephanie also wore a blue tank top and her now-familiar all-American-girl smile. Spurlin wanted a constant reminder of who she was really working for. Seeing Stephanie so joyful and full of life in the photograph gave her all the motivation she needed to continue pursuing the case day in and day out.

Carmon Bennett had given the picture to Spurlin when she'd traveled to Virginia to meet the family for the first time. Spurlin felt like it was a critical part of the process for the victim's family to meet her and to know she cared deeply about Stephanie and the case. Beneath her professional cool exterior, Spurlin always had a soft spot in her heart for victims' families and what they had gone through. She knew that she couldn't ever walk in their shoes, but, with their help, at least she might be able to understand a little bit of what they were experiencing.

"It was to say, 'Hello, I know that I'm walking into your life, and I'm taking on a very important role in the prosecution of the death of your daughter,'" said Spurlin of her trip to the Bennett home in Virginia. "This is who I am. I like to meet them. I like them to put a face with a name."

It was early December 2005 when Spurlin and her partner Rebecca Holt headed to Rocky Mount to meet with Stephanie's family. Holt was no stranger to high-profile murder cases herself. Her most recent case had involved Ann Miller, who'd ultimately pleaded guilty to poisoning her husband, Eric Miller, with arsenic. She had worked on the case with Lieutenant Chris Morgan. With the culmination of that case, Holt now had the time to fully assist Spurlin with the Bennett case, and there was no one else Spurlin would've rather had on her team.

Spurlin also took Morgan with her to the Bennetts'. She knew how close Morgan had become to the family in the first two years of the investigation and felt like the Bennetts might be more open to her introduction if it came through

Morgan. Spurlin wanted their relationship to start out on the right foot.

Morgan was glad to help Spurlin get to know Stephanie's family. He felt it was the least he could do; the fact that he hadn't been able to solve the case himself still gnawed at him almost daily, but he was able to put his pride aside for the sake of the justice he had been seeking all along.

Morgan recalled that Stephanie's father was more enthusiastic than Morgan had ever seen him before on that early December visit with Spurlin and Holt in Virginia. Morgan said Carmon was uncharacteristically raring to go, ready to do whatever he had to do to make sure that Drew Planten not only got convicted but also received the death penalty. It was very clear where Carmon stood on the topic of capital punishment, especially when it came to the man police said murdered his daughter.

"He was ready to go out and fight another battle," Morgan said about Carmon that day. Morgan figured his excitement was the result of three-plus years of holding all of his fury inside. Now he was like a champagne bottle whose cork had been popped, overflowing with renewed vigor and confidence in the justice system that had finally rewarded him for his patience. He was ready to slay the dragon.

After chatting for a while, prosecutors Spurlin and Holt asked Carmon and Jennifer if they could take a peek into Stephanie's bedroom in an effort to get to know the victim a little bit better. Anything personal they gleaned from seeing her room, even the tiniest detail, might help them paint a more personal picture of Stephanie for the jury. "That bedroom was very much like it had been in 2002. It was us wanting to get to know Stephanie," said Spurlin solemnly. "It was important for me to somehow connect with the victim."

The blue and white flowery room with its teddy bears, smiling photographs, and proudly displayed diplomas told

Spurlin quite a lot. What Spurlin learned about Stephanie that day was that she was the kind of girl almost anybody would want as a daughter, sister, or friend. Spurlin knew it would be up to her to relay to the jury what a tremendous loss this death was to so many people, but she had to do it in the calm, measured tone the courtroom required of her.

"If I had any emotion that I felt about her, any tears that I might have cried about Carmon's loss, the loss of so many people with her death, were emotions that I would experience and I would have to set aside," said Spurlin. "I can't take those kinds of emotions into the courtroom because it would definitely interfere with my effectiveness."

At this point in the investigation Spurlin had not yet looked at the crime scene pictures or the autopsy photographs of Stephanie's body. The joke around the office was that Spurlin "didn't do pictures." She usually waited until she was close to trial to finally pull out the pictures because they were so difficult for her to look at no matter how many cases she had prosecuted.

Spurlin didn't need the photographs in front of her to prepare her case. She needed instead to get inside the victim's head and try to understand what happened on May 21, 2002. After poring over all of the evidence, there was one chilling detail that stood out in her mind—a detail she needed to relay to the jury above everything else. Surely, at some point during the attack, it had to have become very clear to Stephanie that this man was not about to let her go. No matter what she did to keep calm and acquiesce to his demands, she was not going to walk away from this alive. *Stephanie Bennett knew she was going to die.*

"Just imagine that," Spurlin said.

# CHAPTER FOURTEEN

# Bittersweet Justice

### January 2, 2006

It is unwise to be too sure of one's own wisdom. It is healthy to be reminded that the strongest might weaken and the wisest might err.

—GANDHI

The Christmas season had always been Stephanie Bennett's favorite time of year. While her loss was always felt more intensely by her family and friends as the holidays neared, 2005 was the first time since her murder that anyone who loved Stephanie had come close to finding some kind of peace. The single electric candle in the window in her father's Virginia home seemed to shine a little brighter this year. While the trial and its difficult details loomed in the distance, the knowledge that Stephanie's suspected killer was behind bars let everyone breathe a little bit easier. Smiles had returned even to Carmon Bennett's face. Joy had become a rare thing in the Bennett house since Stephanie's death.

The investigators were now concentrating on new murder cases, but their victory in solving a three-plus-year-old unsolved case was the best Christmas present anyone in police work could have imagined. They knew they couldn't rest on their laurels forever, but even if they knew the glory would be fleeting, for the time being it was nice to bask in their accomplishment.

For a brief moment, all was right with the world in Raleigh, North Carolina. A feeling of safety had returned to the community and there was an overwhelming sense that justice might be more than a vague concept bantered around in a law school classroom, a tangible phenomenon within reach.

## In Control

"An officer who was doing routine rounds at Central Prison noticed inmate Planten in his cell, unresponsive, entered the cell and it appeared he was in the process of a suicide attempt," said Keith Acree, the spokesman for the North Carolina Department of Correction. "He was taken quickly to the emergency room here at Central Prison Hospital where the medical staff attempted to resuscitate him. They were not able to. He was pronounced dead at 2:37."

On Monday, January 2, 2006, Drew Planten was found hanging in his cell from a bedsheet with a plastic bag over his head. After years of investigation, the case had come to a final, screeching halt. Planten had been kept in an isolated prison cell where he spent twenty-three hours a day confined in the state's maximum security prison, yet it seemed as though, even there, he'd still been running the show. He had managed to take charge of his destiny from the bowels of one of the most secure correctional institutions in the state.

Acree stood just outside the entrance of Central Prison that bitter winter night, the darkness behind him illuminated only by the lights from the television cameras, and spoke to reporters. He said that Planten had been allowed out of his cell for one hour of recreation a day. Citing privacy issues, Acree refused to comment directly on Planten's mental health status or his treatment, but said he had improved tremendously compared to the seemingly catatonic man who had been sent to them from the Wake County Jail on October 20, 2005.

"He had been cooperative and responsive with our staff. When he first arrived here in October, he was silent and would not speak to staff and was uncooperative, but that only lasted a few days, and he had been very cooperative in recent months," Acree said. "If an inmate is desperate to kill himself it's very difficult to keep him from doing that despite any extraordinary measures we might take."

Acree went on to say the State Bureau of Investigation was called in to investigate the suicide. Its agents would make a final report as to whether or not the prison was negligent in any way when it came to Planten's ability to take his own life.

## Derailment

Morgan got the call at home from Sergeant Perry that afternoon. He was sitting in his worn leather recliner in his den—his man cave—a room that had been added onto the side of his modest ranch home and that both housed his stuff and gave him a place to hide from his family and watch sports on one of the many television sets crammed into the tiny room.

Perry got right to the point. "I need Susan Spurlin's home number," he told Morgan. "Planten just hung himself in Central Prison."

Morgan gave Perry the number and asked him if he had called Carmon Bennett yet. Perry had not. Out of deference to their long-standing relationship, Morgan agreed to take the heat off of Perry and call Carmon himself. It was the least he could do to be the one to break the news to

Carmon that his daughter's accused killer would never be brought to justice. It was yet another step in the healing process for Morgan, who wanted to continue trying to do whatever he could for the Bennett family.

As soon as he got off of the phone with Perry, Morgan decided to call Carmon right away. He didn't want him to hear about Planten's suicide from some other source. Morgan knew it was only a matter of hours before the news traveled to Rocky Mount either via the Internet, or through a phone call from someone in Raleigh who saw it on the news.

"I knew he was going to be upset," Morgan said. And he was right.

"What does this mean?" Carmon asked Morgan after he told him what had happened.

"It means he's guilty, and he killed himself," Morgan replied with his honest opinion.

"You mean there's not going to be a trial?" Carmon asked.

"No, Carmon, it's the end," Morgan said regretfully.

## The End of the Line

Perry called prosecutor Spurlin at home. For state employees, Monday, January 2, 2006, was considered a holiday since New Year's Day had fallen on a Sunday. He hated to bother her at home, but Perry knew it was only a matter of time before the story hit the news, and she needed to hear it from him, not from television or the web.

"I was shocked, but not so surprised that that would have been Drew Planten's choice," Spurlin said, acknowledging she had suspected he was suicidal after he was arrested and found to have a loaded weapon in his pants. "But I was very surprised that it had happened, that he had been able to end it that way. And I think he truly wanted to end it on his terms," she added bitterly.

When Spurlin hung up the phone with Perry, she sat for a few minutes, shell-shocked and unable to process what she had just learned. She decided to call her boss, District Attorney Colon Willoughby, and vent about the situation. She knew that he, of all people, would understand her deep frustration over what had happened.

"My feelings were so mixed about what [Planten's death] meant. On the one hand, that outcome is what the state would be seeking following a trial," said Spurlin, referring to her belief that Planten would have received the death penalty if convicted. "This way, the victim's family didn't go through the pain of having to relive the death of Stephanie Bennett. But at the same time, I felt like I'd really been robbed."

Spurlin told Willoughby over the phone about her anger and about the fact that not having a trial meant neither she nor the investigators nor the family would ever have the answers they longed for in this case. Spurlin had desperately wanted just one crack at Planten on the witness stand in a courtroom.

"I always kind of dreamed that I might have the opportunity to cross-examine him," Spurlin said, even though she knew it was highly unlikely Planten's attorneys would have ever let him take the stand.

Even if that opportunity had not presented itself, surely Planten's mental health would have come into question at some point in the trial preparation. Experts from both sides would have tested and interviewed Planten and submitted reports to the court regarding his mental health status. This in itself might have helped provide clues to the lingering question of why. It was so rare for investigators to get a glimpse into the mind of a killer who preyed on strangers. The chance to study a person like this would have been a once in a lifetime opportunity.

The detectives who had worked so hard to make the case

were just as upset as Spurlin by the news. Perry was the one who called them and filled them in on the situation.

"We felt robbed," Detective Jackie Taylor said of Planten's suicide. "You worked *so hard,* and you can't describe it."

Both Taylor and Detective Ken Copeland had hoped they would learn more about Planten through the trial process, about whether he had been involved in other crimes and, if so, what his motivations had been. Many people told the detectives that Planten's suicide was a good outcome; the taxpayers would not have to pay for a long, drawn-out trial, and the victim's family would in turn not have to go through the painful process of hearing all of the gruesome details of Stephanie's death. But Taylor and Copeland both rejected this twisted idea of justice.

"That's not how we felt at all," Taylor said, remembering the resentment she felt after realizing Planten was still calling the shots even from a prison cell.

Copeland believed the suicide was Planten's ultimate and final act of control. "Drew's biggest fear, his biggest punishment, was people sitting there and staring at him, people looking at him," Copeland said. And now he would never have to deal with that again, Copeland thought. Planten had escaped as triumphantly as if he had scaled the prison walls.

That first night, the night of Planten's arrest, he had closed his eyes at the police station and refused to speak. Copeland felt like that was the beginning of Planten's complete withdrawal from the world, a foreshadowing of what was to come. He wanted to block everything and everyone out for good.

"I think his whole thing was, 'If I close my eyes this will go away,'" Copeland said, trying to imagine what Planten was thinking that night.

"I don't think he was catatonic. I don't think he was having a mental breakdown. He was withdrawing into himself, which was his security," Taylor said.

Raleigh detectives knew they also had to tell Lansing police about what had happened. Perry volunteered to call Detective Joey Dionise. Dionise remembered getting that "dreary call" from Perry just as everything seemed to finally be coming together with the Huismann case.

"Over in a minute," Dionise said heatedly. "I just said to myself, 'Oh shit, you're never going to know why he killed her because he's dead.' "

Dionise in turn knew he had to tell Rebecca's parents, Glenna and Bernard Huismann. They actually took the news better than he expected they would.

"I was relieved there would be no trial," Glenna said. "Planten had refused to talk to anyone. I guess the answer is he was a very sick man."

While the cops were feeling cheated about Planten's suicide, Joanne Reilly, Planten's former supervisor, who had helped police get his DNA, was deeply saddened by the news. It was still hard for her to reconcile what Planten had been accused of doing with the young man she had come to know and like. Her motherly instincts had always been to protect Planten—they were hard to turn off even after she found out he was the prime suspect in Stephanie's murder.

"I grieved the person I knew," Reilly said, breaking into tears. "I wanted to write to his mom, but I never did. I just would tell her that I was so sorry that her son had died and that he was a nice person to me and always did a good job."

## End of Story

Planten would never be convicted by a jury, or sentenced by a judge to life in prison, or the death penalty. Instead, he died as the man *accused* of killing Stephanie Bennett, although to this day investigators still say the perfect DNA match cast him in their minds beyond a shadow of a doubt as the man who took Stephanie's life.

"There were some questions that could have been answered, but now they never will be," Carmon Bennett said in a phone interview with WRAL after Planten's suicide. "There's one thing about this—the hands that took my daughter's life took his life. Maybe there's some consolation there."

But for Carmon, there was no real consolation in the way things had ended. It had been a long, painful journey, and one that ended without even Planten's explanations as a reward.

Michael Teague and Chris Morgan were interviewed while their reactions were still raw and before they had time to fully process what had happened.

Teague spoke about how he had sensed the first night in the interview room at the Raleigh Police Department that Planten had suicidal tendencies. He said the fact that Planten *appeared* to be doing better at Central Prison was probably part ruse and part relief. Teague believed Planten's improved demeanor came partially from the fact that he had made peace with his decision to end his life and was just waiting for the right time to do it.

"I think he really realized that everything was going to come out, and this was going to be really bad for him, bad for his family. And he thinks just right then, he probably decided that he was going to commit suicide, and it probably took him this long to work up all the ability to do that," Teague said.

Morgan's angst over the suicide was less about the fact that it had happened and more about the fact that Planten could have potentially helped investigators understand the criminal mind like no other suspect ever had.

"I'll always wonder if Planten could have told us why

people do these things," Morgan said. "Would he have ever told us? I don't know, but now it's not a possibility."

Probably the most frustrating thing for Morgan was that after playing cat and mouse with investigators for three and a half years, this man was still in charge of his fate even from a prison cell where he seemingly had no freedom.

"There's nobody to try. There's nobody to answer the questions. The disturbing thing about it is he's had this control over everything the whole time. He controlled his own destiny," Morgan said shaking his head.

## Game Over

"I remember being sort of conflicted," Angela Smith, the woman police believed Planten had stalked after Stephanie's murder, said upon hearing of his suicide. "You never want to be happy that someone has died, let alone committed suicide. But at the same time it was a relief—not just that I would not have to face him in a courtroom—but that I was never going to have to worry about him getting out on bail. I would never have to worry about him escaping from prison," she said frankly. "It was over, and that was it. And that felt really good."

In the days after Planten's suicide, police contacted everyone involved in the case and let them know they would not be needed to testify. There would be no trial. Planten had chosen his own version of the death penalty.

Privately, the investigators, prosecutors, and family members stewed, but publicly, they all put on their game faces and tried to spin the ending as a blessing, something southerners are especially good at.

"It's over," prosecutor Susan Spurlin said, looking weary behind her desk in her bleak courthouse office that she thankfully spent little time in. "The outcome is probably a good outcome. The Bennetts don't have to go through a trial," she said, sounding unconvinced of her own words.

While most prosecutors say little about a suspect's guilt before he is convicted, Spurlin had had no compunction about condemning the man whose DNA was found all over Stephanie Bennett, and whose gun had killed Rebecca Huismann.

"We know beyond any doubt that he's killed two people. They are looking at him as a suspect in other homicides. But yes, the world is a safer place," Spurlin said with confidence.

Perry held a press conference outside the Raleigh Police Department to talk about where the investigation would go from there.

"There are a lot of mixed emotions. We would very much have liked to have brought Mr. Planten into a courtroom. We would have loved to have heard him explain why he did this, but unfortunately, we're not going to get that opportunity," Perry said with unabashed resentment in his voice.

The unusually large crowd of reporters and photographers pressed Perry for more details about the case, but he stood his ground and gave little new information, saying the case was not closed—*not yet.*

"The fact that he has ended his life has not ended our investigation," Perry said definitively.

Perry told the press their investigators would continue to look at any murder cases that might have a link to Planten to see if they could close other unsolved homicide cases.

Like Spurlin, Perry had no problem saying a trial was not needed to prove Planten's guilt.

"I can say without any hesitation or reservation that Drew Planten killed Stephanie Bennett," said Perry. "I think it's very safe to say that Drew Planten was a very dangerous man and I think he was probably capable of doing just about anything."

Michigan District Attorney Stuart Dunnings spoke to WRAL's Melissa Buscher by phone about Planten's suicide. It was clear by his tone of voice that this outcome was not the ending he had expected. Dunnings was still reveling in the fact that his department had finally solved a six-year-old case when he got the news that Planten was dead.

Before they were contacted by Raleigh police detectives, Dunnings admitted his investigators had been "up a tree" with no real leads in Rebecca's murder. When he got the word Raleigh authorities might have a suspect with a connection to their case, he had approached it cautiously at first.

"You sort of have a hopeful trepidation because a lot of times you think you have a lead and it doesn't pan out," Dunnings said as he recalled what he thought at that time.

But once Michigan's crime laboratory was able to confirm the gun found in Planten's apartment was the gun that killed Rebecca, Dunnings's trepidation turned from healthy skepticism into cautious optimism. That along with the circumstantial evidence that Planten had been seen in Rebecca Huismann's neighborhood was enough to convince investigators and Dunnings that they finally had their suspect.

"I'm convinced in my mind that Mr. Planten was responsible for Miss Huismann's murder," Dunnings said. "Had yesterday not happened, we would have been issuing charges against Mr. Planten."

## A Mother's Desperate Stand

Sarah Chandler, Drew Planten's mother, also spoke with Buscher by telephone in a recorded interview that same week. Chandler said she learned about her son's suicide from his lawyer, Kirk Osborne.

"My mind was just devastated. I couldn't believe that

they could allow this to happen when he was being held supposedly in a psychiatric ward where they would be mindful of his demeanor and mood. Of course I'm devastated. It's tragic," Chandler said, sounding like she was still in shock.

Chandler told Buscher the last time she saw her son at Central Prison, he had said some things that made her worry about his state of mind.

"The last time I visited him he was very depressed," Chandler said. "He sounded like he had lost hope of ever getting out of there."

Chandler said she was thinking about what she could do to "rectify the situation," which coming from a lawyer implied she was already thinking about filing a lawsuit against the prison for negligence.

"I'm very concerned because they're supposed to keep him safe until trial, and that's what they're supposed to try and do, and I don't know that they tried very hard," Chandler said with quiet desperation in her voice.

She said in her heart she still felt like her son was innocent and thought maybe that's why he took his own life—because he saw no other way out of an impossible situation.

But like everyone else connected to the case, Chandler could only speculate. Only two people really knew what happened at the Bridgeport Apartments on May 21, 2002, and they were both dead. The truth was that Drew Planten took more than his own life the day he died; he took to his grave the knowledge of why Stephanie and Rebecca died. Because of this, even in death, Planten's power over the people who loved Stephanie remained intact. Yet with every passing day, his grip on their lives would lessen, pushed back by the power of the loving memories Stephanie left behind.

## Lasting Impressions

"Over the years that I worked on that case, I got to know, in a sense, *know* her. She made an impression on me that I'll never forget," Chris Morgan said, echoing the sentiments of so many people who had worked on the case.

Stephanie Bennett was not a young woman anyone involved in the case was ever going to forget. And the case itself—a once in a career case for a cop—was not something any of the detectives who worked on it would ever forget either.

"This case would not have been solved if it were not for Ken Copeland and Jackie Taylor. There's no doubt in my mind," Sergeant Perry said. "We were bouncing theories, after theories, after theories, and Ken cut right through the theories and went right to what made sense to him, and *that's* what cleared this case."

Prosecutor Susan Spurlin agreed that having Taylor and Copeland on the case made all the difference.

"They're both methodical. They're both thorough. They went back and started looking at everything with fresh eyes," said Spurlin. "It's inspirational that they solved the case. With hard work *anything* is possible."

"Don't get away from the facts," Copeland said regarding how he solved the Bennett case, and now, how he approaches other cases. "I don't have a theory. The minute I have a theory, then I've set my mind on something, and I'm afraid I'll close out something else."

Copeland said his sense of justice comes from bringing some sense of peace to Stephanie's family, especially to her father, Carmon Bennett.

"I didn't make him a promise, but he looked at me for help, and I said, 'I'll do the best that I can,'" Copeland said. "I like to think that Jackie and I helped that family get the resolution that they needed."

Copeland said the investigation into Stephanie's murder was the most emotionally draining case in which he had ever been involved. It wasn't the kind of case you could just leave at the office. It almost consumed him as he methodically went back and shuffled through all of the evidence that had been gathered in the case looking for that needle in the haystack.

"I would think about it on the way home. I would think about it when I got home. The next morning I'd get up—I'd think about it on the way back to work," Copeland said, shaking his head as he remembered his borderline obsession with the investigation.

But that perseverance paid off, even though the detectives were never quite sure that it would.

"When we started this investigation I don't know that either one of us ever thought in the backs of our minds that we would solve it," Taylor said. "We were going to try our best, and felt like we had a good shot at it. But when you actually end up solving it, it's unbelievable."

Michigan Detective Joey Dionise has had many high-profile murder cases since this one—several involving serial killers. But for some reason, the Huismann case was the one he has never been able to shake. Maybe it's the fact that it didn't end the way he had hoped it would—with a trial and a conviction. But when he is pushed to reflect on the outcome, he can't help but come to the conclusion that at least the case files are finally back in the file cabinet now where they belong and not sitting homeless and dusty on some detective's desk waiting for a tip to come in.

"We solved the case—six years later," Dionise said with pride. "I hope we gave the family some peace."

At any given time, State Bureau of Investigation Agent Mark Boodee had been working on fifty cases with a backlog of nine hundred DNA samples waiting on the shelves to be analyzed by him. But he personally agreed to fast-track the Stephanie Bennett case for reasons that to this day he has a hard time putting into words. It was just one of those cases from which he couldn't turn away.

"I volunteered to take this case on a rush basis. At the time I had a daughter that was very close in age to her, and it could have been anyone's daughter," Boodee said.

Because he never wants to forget her, a picture of Stephanie Bennett smiling in a pink dress with a dainty gold necklace around her neck still sits on Boodee's desk. It is nestled warmly among pictures of Boodee's wife and children as if they were protecting her, surrounding her with their own family's love.

"You see in her someone that you know from your own life. You can picture something like this happening to someone in your own life, and you don't want that to happen," said Boodee. "You're trying to work for justice. You're trying to make sure the process works the way it is supposed to."

It may have been bittersweet justice, but to those who worked on Stephanie's behalf and to those who loved Stephanie, a type of justice *was* achieved. No more innocent women would die at the hands of Stephanie's killer, and that alone made the world feel like a safer place.

# Epilogue

*The only cure for grief is action.*
—G. H. LEWES

I took my last trip to visit Stephanie Bennett's parents in Virginia on January 4, 2006. In many ways, this was the trip I had been dreading the most. My other journeys to see Carmon Bennett and Mollie Hodges had been when the case was still unsolved. The weight of their grief and their growing frustration permeated our earlier meetings, but they were still working toward something, a goal, *an arrest*.

Now, with Drew Planten's suicide, it was clear to everyone, despite what the police said about the investigation continuing, that the case was truly over. There was nothing for Stephanie's parents to work toward anymore. There would be no further arrests, no trial. In my heart, I was worried about how they were going to approach this new phase of their lives.

My last meeting with Carmon was in his sunroom at the back of his house, a spot where we had sat and chatted on many other occasions. The room hadn't changed a bit, but Carmon had. Like many murder victims' parents I had seen, Carmon had visibly aged every day that passed without his precious daughter. He had always spoken to me through a clenched jaw. I saw him as a man trying to take control of his emotions during what had to be the most gut-wrenching period in his life. But on this day, his jaw was a little more relaxed or maybe just more resigned to the truth of how the tragedy had finally played out.

"It took a few minutes for it to sink in. I'm happy in a way, and sad in a way," Carmon said honestly of his re-action to Planten's death. "We were actively seeking the death penalty, and it just got carried out in a way other than it should have."

Once again, as a parent, I tried to wrap my head around how Carmon Bennett could go on with his life after experiencing such an unimaginable loss. It was something that was almost impossible for me to grasp, something I continued to grapple with no matter how many times I had spoken to him. In my eyes, the parents of murdered children were among the most heroic people I had never known. They had survived the absolute worst tragedy. Yet they were able, by virtue of their steely resolves, to somehow do ordinary things like breathe, eat, walk, talk, and even occasionally smile. And all of this when one's natural instinct would to be to curl up in a fetal position and block out the world.

After I left Carmon's house, I traveled across town where Stephanie's mother, Mollie Hodges, met me on a bench in a small tranquil park near her home. She described what she thought when she first got the call from a Raleigh detective that Planten was dead.

"It was a surprise, sort of shocking too, [a] disappoint-ment; we were hoping to get some answers. We'll never get the answers we need," Mollie said with weariness in her voice.

Mollie said she was sorry for Planten's mother, Sarah

Chandler, because she knew what it was like to lose a child. But she did not feel any sadness for Planten.

"I hope he suffered. I hope he suffered these last days he had. I hope he suffered from day one that they arrested him and put him in jail. I hope it just ached his heart. I hope he was just in bitter pain the whole time," Mollie said through pursed lips without a hint of remorse in her voice.

Mollie had never been one to hide her emotions in front of the camera. On this day, they seemed as raw as they had ever been, close to the surface and intense. It was as if Planten's death suddenly brought back the intense anger she had experienced just after Stephanie was murdered.

Mollie said there was some consolation in not having to live through a trial, but that had to be weighed against what they might have learned if Planten had faced a jury.

"That's one good thing we don't have to face, the fact of going through the trial, the details of what happened to her, seeing the gruesome pictures. In a way it's a good ending," Mollie said, her voice trailing off into the cool January breeze.

But for Mollie and Carmon there would never truly be a good ending to this horrendous story. Mollie said her faith in God was what sustained her. She was sure Stephanie was in heaven and that gave her a small amount of peace in what had become a life that was for the most part devoid of peace.

"I know where Stephanie's at, and I know where he's at," Mollie's words trailed off in the wind. It was up to me to fill in the blanks.

## Someone to Blame

In May 2008, Drew Planten's mother, Sarah Chandler, did file a lawsuit against the state of North Carolina for failing to protect her son from himself. Even though the State

Bureau of Investigation had ruled there was no foul play or negligence involved in Planten's suicide, Chandler's lawsuit alleged her son was taken off suicide watch prematurely after his mental health appeared to be improving and was then not given proper counseling or oversight.

Chandler said her son had been diagnosed with "acute stress reaction," yet he was put in solitary confinement where he was permitted outside his cell just one hour a day. She maintained this type of isolation only made his condition worse. During that period of time, Chandler's lawsuit alleged that Planten got no psychological counseling whatsoever.

"His condition severely deteriorated. He became withdrawn and unresponsive again," the lawsuit stated. "His declining mental status culminated in Drew's death when he hung himself."

Chandler's lawsuit against the state and Carmon Bennett's lawsuit against the Bridgeport Apartments are both still pending in the North Carolina court system.

## Riding Off into the Sunset

Stephanie's picture remained tacked up on Susan Spurlin's wall above her desk in the courthouse. It reflected Stephanie's humorous side in happier times. In the photograph, Stephanie was wearing a big purple felt hat, a red satin sash, and a mischievous grin. Of all the pictures Carmon offered Spurlin on her trip to Virginia, this was the one she took. It was the one she wanted. Spurlin wanted to remember Stephanie as a young woman full of life, not a young woman whose life had been tragically cut short.

Spurlin kept the picture as a symbol of Stephanie's murder case and of the all murder cases she has prosecuted before and after Stephanie.

"It reminds you that there are no guarantees for anyone

tomorrow," Spurlin said. "There are no guarantees in this world for any of us."

Several years after Planten's suicide, Spurlin called Carmon Bennett one day out of the blue. She had been asked to do an interview for a network television program about the case, and she wanted to make sure it was okay with him. As they talked, Carmon told the prosecutor that he was on his way to the local high school to present a scholarship in Stephanie's name, a program he had created to honor his daughter's memory. Spurlin looked down at the calendar on her desk and suddenly realized it was May 21, 2008, the sixth anniversary of Stephanie's murder—of all days, something had made her choose that one to make that phone call.

In the time that she had known Stephanie's father, Spurlin had shared her love of horseback riding with Carmon. It was something safe they could talk about besides Stephanie. Being someone who owned land and lived in the country, Spurlin always felt like Carmon might enjoy owning horses. After their conversations, she said he became so intrigued by the idea, he decided to get some horses to roam the rolling hills of his rural Virginia property.

On this day, May 21, 2008, the anniversary of Stephanie's murder, as Susan Spurlin talked to Carmon Bennett about horses, she was again reminded of why she loved to ride.

"It's my serenity where the wind blows in one ear and out the other. It helps me maintain perspective and sanity because I can really get away from it all," Spurlin said with a broad smile. And in her job there was a lot to get away from.

And maybe that's the day the idea started to ferment in her head—*there are no guarantees*—that it was time to ride off into the sunset. So, on April 1, 2009, after twenty-six years as a prosecutor, Spurlin finally loaded all her personal belongings from her office into a box, including her picture of Stephanie Bennett, and said good-bye to the Wake County District Attorney's Office.

She went home, mounted her horse, and said hello to the rest of her life.

## Journalists Have Feelings Too

"I remember how angry I was at the suspect, and that he stayed under the radar for so long," former WRAL reporter Len Besthoff said. "It bothered me that this kind young lady, brave enough to leave the comfortable confines of the Blue Ridge Mountain area, and just getting started on her own, had such an awful end to her life. It infuriated me."

For everyone at WRAL-TV who covered the case, it is etched in his or her memory forever. First, because it was a random crime involving an innocent young woman. Second, because it took so long to solve the case. And third, because it ended in a way that left everyone, including the journalists who covered it, feeling like they had been cheated out of answers.

"They left behind loving families who are forced to go on with their life and always wonder what would have become of their lovely daughters. As a parent myself, that was the most difficult part of this case," said former WRAL reporter Melissa Buscher.

"I think the biggest heartbreak for me, aside from the murder, is for Stephanie's family not to have the answers they were so desperately seeking," said photographer Chad Flowers.

For me, the case is a constant reminder that tragedy can happen to the most undeserving person, that justice is not always served, and that grief does not always lessen with time. As with everyone who was involved in the case, I lived with Stephanie's image in my mind throughout the investigation. But it wasn't until I began writing this book that her essence truly took up residence in my heart. Unfortunately, Stephanie Bennett is now one of several victims I have come to know in death that I would have liked to have known in life. May she rest in peace.

**Penguin Group (USA) Online**

*What will you be reading tomorrow?*

Patricia Cornwell, Nora Roberts, Catherine Coulter,
Ken Follett, John Sandford, Clive Cussler,
Tom Clancy, Laurell K. Hamilton, Charlaine Harris,
J. R. Ward, W.E.B. Griffin, William Gibson,
Robin Cook, Brian Jacques, Stephen King,
Dean Koontz, Eric Jerome Dickey, Terry McMillan,
Sue Monk Kidd, Amy Tan, Jayne Ann Krentz,
Daniel Silva, Kate Jacobs...

You'll find them all at
**penguin.com**

*Read excerpts and newsletters,
find tour schedules and reading group guides,
and enter contests.*

Subscribe to Penguin Group (USA) newsletters
and get an exclusive inside look
at exciting new titles and the authors you love
long before everyone else does.

PENGUIN GROUP (USA)
penguin.com